History: A Journey Through the Ages/Themes in Indian History

History: A Journey Through the Ages/Themes in Indian History

R.N. Dhar

2008

CYBER TECH PUBLICATIONS
4264/3, Ansari Road, Daryaganj, New Delhi-110002 (India)
Ph.: 011-23244078. Fax: 011-23280028
E-Mail: cyberpublicationsdelhi@yahoo.com

HISTORY: A JOURNEY THROUGH THE AGES/THEMES IN INDIAN HISTORY

R.N. Dhar

First Edition 2008

Published by :

G.S. Rawat for **Cyber Tech Publications**
4264/3, Ansari Road, Daryaganj, New Delhi-110002 (India)
Ph.: 011-23244078. Fax: 011-23280028
E-Mail: cyberpublicationsdelhi@yahoo.com

Printed at : **Amit Enterprises**, Maujpur, Delhi, (9810878184)

Preface

The book is primarily meant as a reference book for these who are keen to know their past. The book covers the history of ancient India from prehistoric times to about the eighth century. An effort has been made in this book to highlight the forces and factors behind the rise, growth and spread of civilization and culture in ancient India rather than present details of dynastic history. The growth and diffusion of various aspects of civilization, the peculiar form of social system that developed in India and state formation have been treated clearly.

In medieval India it covers from about eight century to about the early eighteenth century. Effort has been made in this book to highlight the forces and factors which moulded India society and culture in medieval times. The book points out the significant changes that took place in the medieval period of our history.

In modern period of Indian history it lays emphasis on forces, movements and institutions rather than on details of military and diplomatic events, and on the biographical details of individual administrators and leaders. The development in Indian society, economy and polity in the eighteenth century have been discussed in order to indicate the historical conditions which enabled a company of foreign merchants to conquer this vast country.

Latest works of reputed historians have been consulted in preparation of the book and their disagreements as well as consensus have been brought out. The matter has been so compiled and arranged that the book contains all the useful study material contained in about fifteen standard works published in this field.

The language of the book is precise and simple. The aim is that the students should get the maximum useful material in a handy book and in a language which they can easily understand.

I believe that the book in its present form will be useful for the readers.

—*Author*

Contents

1

An Introduction to India

India is a land of ancient civilization, with cities and villages, cultivated fields, and great works of art dating back 4,000 years. India's high population density and variety of social, economic, and cultural configurations are the products of a long process of regional expansion. In the last decade of the twentieth century, such expansion has led to the rapid erosion of India's forest and wilderness areas in the face of ever increasing demands for resources and gigantic population pressures—India's population is projected to exceed 1 billion by the twenty-first century.

Such problems are a relatively recent phenomenon. Rhinoceros inhabited the North Indian plains as late as the sixteenth century. Historical records and literature of earlier periods reveal the motif of the forest everywhere. Stories of merchant caravans typically included travel through long stretches of jungle inhabited by wild beasts and strange people; royal adventures usually included a hunting expedition and meetings with unusual beings. In the Mahabharata and the Ramayana, early epics that reflect life in India before 1000 B.C. and 500 B.C., respectively, the forest begins at the edge of the city, and the heroes regularly spend periods of exile wandering far from civilization before returning to rid the world of evil. The formulaic rituals of the Vedas also reflect attempts to create a regulated, geometric space from the raw products of nature.

The country's past serves as a reminder that India today, with its overcrowding and scramble for material gain, its poverty and outstanding intellectual accomplishments, is a society in constant change. Human beings, mostly humble folk, have within a period of 200 generations turned the wilderness into one of the most complicated societies in the world. The process began in the northwest in the third millennium B.C., with the Indus Valley, or Harappan, civilization, when an agricultural economy gave rise to extensive urbanization and long-distance trade. The second stage occurred during the first millennium B.C., when the Ganga-Yamuna river basin and several southern river deltas experienced extensive agricultural expansion and population growth, leading to the rebirth of cities, trade, and a sophisticated urban culture.

By the seventh century A.D., a dozen core regions based on access to irrigation-supported kingdoms became tied to a pan-Indian cultural tradition and participated in increasing cross-cultural ties with other parts of Asia and the Middle East. India's inclusion within a global trading economy after the thirteenth century culminated in the arrival of Portuguese explorers, traders, and missionaries, beginning in 1498. Although there were ebbs and flows in the pattern, the overall tendency was for peasant cultivators and their overlords to expand agriculture and animal husbandry into new ecological zones, and to push hunting and gathering societies farther into the hills.

By the twentieth century, most such tribal groups, although constituting a substantial minority within India, lived in restricted areas under severe pressure from the caste-based agricultural and trading societies pressing from the plains. Because this evolution took place over more than forty centuries and encompassed a wide range of ecological niches and peoples, the resulting social pattern is extremely complicated and alters constantly.

India had its share of conquerors who moved in from the northwest and overran the north or central parts of the country. These migrations began with the Aryan peoples of the second millennium B.C. and culminated in the unification of the entire country for the first time in the seventeenth century under the Mughals. Mostly these conquerors were nomadic or seminomadic people who adopted or expanded the agricultural economy and contributed new cultural forms or religions, such as Islam.

The Europeans, primarily the English, arrived in force in the early seventeenth century and by the eighteenth century had made a profound impact on India. India was forced, for the first time, into a subordinate role within a world system based on industrial production rather than agriculture. Many of the dynamic craft or cottage industries that had long attracted foreigners to India suffered extensively under competition with new modes of mass production fostered by the British. Modern institutions, such as universities, and technologies, such as railroads and mass communication, broke with Indian intellectual traditions and served British, rather than Indian, economic interests. A country that in the eighteenth century was a magnet for trade was, by the twentieth century, an underdeveloped and overpopulated land groaning under alien domination. Even at the end of the twentieth century, with the period of colonialism well in the past, Indians remain sensitive to foreign domination and are determined to prevent the country from coming under such domination again.

Through India's long history, religion has been the carrier and preserver of culture. One distinctive aspect of the evolution of civilization in India has been the importance of hereditary priesthoods, often Brahmans, who have functioned as intellectual elites. The heritage preserved by these groups had its origin in the Vedas and allied bodies of literature in the Sanskrit language, which evolved in North India during the second millennium B.C. This tradition always accepted a wide range of paths to ultimate truth, and thus encompassed numerous rituals and forms of divinity within a polytheistic system. Generally, Brahmans supported the phenomenon known as Sanskritization, or the inclusion of local or regional traditions within Sanskrit literary models and pan-Indian cultural motifs. In this way, there has been a steady spread of North Indian cultural and linguistic forms throughout the country. This process has not gone unopposed. Siddhartha Gautama (the Buddha) and Mahavira (founder of Jainism) in the fifth century B.C. represented alternative methods for truth-seekers; they renounced the importance of priesthoods in favor of monastic orders without reference to birth. The largest challenge came from Islam, which rests on Arabic rather than Sanskritic cultural traditions, and has served, especially since the eleventh century, as an important alternative religious path. The interaction of Brahmanical religious forms with local variations and with separate religions creates another level of complexity in Indian social life.

Closely allied with religious belief, and deeply rooted in history, caste remains an important feature of Indian society. Caste in many Indian languages is jati, or birth—a system of classifying and separating people from birth within thousands of different groups labeled by occupation, ritual status, social etiquette, and language. Scholars have long debated the origins of this system, and have suggested as the origin religious concepts of reincarnation, the incorporation of many ethnic groups within agricultural systems over the millennia, or occupational stratification within emerging class societies. What is certain is that nineteenth-century British administrators, in their drive to classify and regulate the many social groups they encountered in everyday administration, established lists or schedules of different caste groups. At that time, it seemed that the rules against intermarriage and interdining that defined caste boundaries tended to freeze these groups within unchanging little societies, a view that fit well with imperialistic models imposed on India as a whole. Experience during the twentieth century has demonstrated that the caste system is capable of radical change and adaptation.

Modernization and urbanization have led to a decline in the outward display of caste exclusiveness, so that issues of caste may never emerge directly on public transit or in the workplace. Entire castes have changed their status, claiming higher positions as they shed their traditional occupations or accumulate money and power. In many villages, however, the segregation of castes by neighborhood and through daily behavior still exists at the end of the twentieth century. In the cities, segregation takes more subtle forms, emerging directly at times of marriage but existing more often as an undercurrent of discrimination in educational opportunities, hiring, and promotion. The British schedules of different castes, especially those of very low or Untouchable (Dalit) groups, later became the basis for affirmative-action programs in independent India that allowed some members of the most oppressed caste groups access to good education and high-paying jobs. The reservation of positions for Backward Classes has remained a sore point with higher-ranked groups and has contributed to numerous political confrontations. Meanwhile, attempts by low-ranking (and desperately poor) castes to organize and agitate against discrimination have been met with violence in most Indian states and territories. Caste, therefore, is a very live issue.

Religious, caste, and regional diversity exist in India against a background of poverty. At independence in 1947, the British left India in terrible condition. The country emerged from World War II with a rudimentary scientific and industrial base and a rapidly expanding population that lived primarily in villages and was divided by gross inequalities in status and wealth. Under the leadership of Jawaharlal Nehru, India's first prime minister (1947-64), India addressed its economic crisis through a combination of socialist planning and free enterprise. During the 1950s and 1960s, large government investments made India as a whole into one of the most industrialized nations in the world. Considerable expenditure on irrigation facilities and fertilizer plants, combined with the introduction of high-yield variety seeds in the 1960s, allowed the Green Revolution to banish famine. The abolition of princely states and large land holdings, combined with (mostly ineffective) land redistribution schemes, also eliminated some of the most glaring inequalities in the countryside and in some areas, such as Punjab, stimulated the growth of middle-sized entrepreneurial farms. Building on the education system bequeathed by the British, India established an infrastructure of universities, basic research institutes, and applied research facilities that trained one of the world's largest scientific and technical establishments.

The socialist model of development remained dominant in India through the 1970s, under the leadership of Prime Minister Indira Gandhi, Nehru's daughter. Government-owned firms controlled iron and steel, mining, electronics, cement, chemicals, and other major industries. Telecommunications media, railroads, and eventually the banking industry were nationalized. Import-substitution policies, designed to encourage Indian firms and push out multinational corporations, included strict and time-consuming procedures for obtaining licenses and laws that prohibited firms from operating in India without majority ownership by Indian citizens or corporations. These rules were instrumental, for example, in driving IBM from India in the 1970s, leading to the growth of an indigenous Indian computer industry. By the late 1980s, however, after Mrs. Gandhi's 1984 assassination, the disadvantages of the centrally planned economy began to outweigh its benefits. Inefficiency in public-sector firms, lack of entrepreneurial innovation, excessive bureaucracy, and the inability of the Indian scientific and technical apparatus to transfer technology to marketable goods kept many Indian firms from being competitive in international markets.

Under Prime Minister Rajiv Gandhi and his successors, the national and state-level (states, union territories, and the national capital territory) governments liberalized licensing requirements and eventually rescinded rules on foreign ownership, while taking steps to scale down government market share in a number of high-technology markets. Multinational firms began to reenter India in the late 1980s and the early 1990s, as the government encouraged private enterprise and international sales in its search for foreign exchange. India began to open its economy to the world.

Indian-style socialism was probably necessary in the years after independence to protect the nation from foreign economic domination, but its biggest problem was that it did not eliminate poverty. The vast majority of India's population continued to live in small agricultural villages with few public amenities. A significant minority of the population in the 1990s live below the Indian definition of the poverty line, surviving at subsistence level, unemployed or underemployed, with little education or opportunity for training, and suffering from a variety of curable health problems. There are also some 200 million people who live above the official poverty line, but whose lives remain precariously balanced on the border of destitution. The per capita income of India as a whole remains among the lowest in the world. One of the biggest issues facing India as its economy has changed direction is that free-market capitalism offers little help for this large mass of people, who lack the skills or opportunity to participate in the new economy.

The big social story of India in the 1980s and the 1990s is the emergence of the middle class. This group includes members of prosperous farming families, as well as the primarily urban-based professional, administrative, and business elites who benefited from forty years of government protection and training. By the mid-1990s, the drive toward modernization had transformed 26.1 percent of the country into urban areas, where, amid masses of impoverished citizens, a sizable class of consumers has arisen. The members of this increasingly vocal middle class chafe under the older, regulated economy and demand a loosening of economic controls to make consumer goods available on the free market. They want education for their children that prepare them for technical and professional careers, increasingly in the private sector instead of the traditional sinecures in government offices. They build their well-appointed brick houses in exclusive suburban neighborhoods or surround their lots with high walls amid urban squalor, driving their scooters or automobiles to work while their children attend private schools.

The result of these processes over the course of fifty years is a dynamic, modernizing India with major class cleavages. The upper 1 or 2 percent of the population includes some of the wealthiest people in the world, who can be seen at the racetrack in the latest fashions from Paris or Tokyo, who travel extensively outside India for business, pleasure, or advanced medical care, and whose children attend the most exclusive English-language schools within India and abroad. For the middle class, which makes up between 15 and 25 percent of the population, the end of the twentieth century is a time of relative prosperity: incomes generally keep pace with inflation and jobs may still be obtained through family connections. The increase in consumer goods, such as washing machines and electric kitchen appliances, makes life easier and reduces dependence on lower-class (and low-caste) servants. For the industrial working class, the 1990s are a period of transition as dynamic new industries grow, mostly in the private sector, while many large government-sponsored plants are in jeopardy. The trade union movement, closely connected in some states with communist parties, finds itself under considerable pressure during a period of structural change in the economy. For large numbers of peasants and dwellers in urban slums, a way out of poverty remains as elusive as it had seemed for their grandparents at independence.

The political system responsible for these gigantic successes and failures has been democratic; India has called itself "the world's largest democracy." Paradoxically, it was the autocratic rule of the British that gave birth to the rule of the people. Democratization started when a group of concerned British citizens in India and well-to-do Indian professionals gathered in Bombay in 1885 to form a political debating society, the Indian National Congress. Originally conceived as a lobbying group, the Congress after 1900 became radicalized and took the forefront in a drive for home rule that encompassed elected assemblies and parliamentary procedure. In the face of British intransigence, the Congress soon became the leading organization within a broad-based freedom struggle that finally forced the British out in 1947. Mohandas Karamchand Gandhi (the Mahatma or Great Soul) was a central figure in this struggle because he was able to turn the Congress from an elite pressure group into a mass movement that mobilized hundreds of millions of people against the immorality of a foreign, nondemocratic system.

Gandhi perfected nonviolent techniques for general strikes and civil disobedience, and coordinated demonstrations with mass publicity; the techniques that he popularized have played a part in later Indian and world politics (including the United States civil rights movement). He evolved a philosophy of political involvement as sacrifice for the good of the world and played the role of a holy man who was also a cagey politician—an image that remained important for Indian political figures after independence.

In a move to undercut British industrial superiority, Gandhi encouraged a return to a communal, rustic life and village handicrafts as the most humane way of life. Finally, he railed against the segregation of the caste system and religious bigotry that reduced large minorities within India to second-class citizenship. Gandhi was thus able to unite European humanistic and democratic ideas with Indian concepts of an interdependent, responsible community to create a unique political philosophy complete with action plan. In the last years before his assassination in 1948, Gandhi's idiosyncratic program fell out of step with the modernization paradigm of Nehru and the leadership of an independent India, and his ideas became a background theme within Indian political economy. On a regular basis, however, Indian leaders continue to hearken back to his message and employ his organizational and media tactics on the independent Indian political scene.

The Congress remained the most important political organization in India after independence. Except for brief periods in the late 1970s and late 1980s and until the mid-1990s, the Congress always controlled Parliament and chose the prime minister. The political dynasty of Jawaharlal Nehru (1947-64), his daughter Indira Gandhi (1965-77, 1980-84), and her son Rajiv Gandhi (1984-89) was crucial in keeping the Congress in power and also providing continuity in leadership for the country. The party was able to appeal to a wide segment of the poor (including low castes and Muslims) through its ideology of social equality and welfare programs, while appealing to the more prosperous voters—usually from upper castes—by preserving private property and supporting village community leadership. Because it stayed in power so long, the Congress was able to dispense government benefits to a wide range of constituencies, which prompted charges of corruption and led to Congress reversals in the late 1980s. Because it affected a type of socialist policy, the Congress diffused or incorporated left-wing political rhetoric and prevented the growth of a communist-led insurrection that might have been expected under the difficult social conditions existing in India.

Although a vibrant communist movement remains a force in Indian politics, it manifests itself at the state level of government rather than in national political power or large-scale revolutionary turmoil. Challenges from the right were small as well until the early 1990s, when the Bharatiya Janata Party (BJP—Indian People's Party) emerged as a serious contender for national leadership. The BJP advocated a blend of Hindu nationalism that inserted religious issues into the heart of national political debates, unlike the secular ideology that officially dominated Indian political thought after independence. In the early 1990s, however, the Congress, after having entered its second century of dominance over the Indian political landscape, continued to hold on to power with a middle-of-the-road message and smaller majorities.

The federal structure of India, embodied in the constitution of 1951, attempts to strike a balance between a strong central government and the autonomous governments of the nation-sized states, each with a distinct culture and deep historical roots, that make up the union. A formidable array of powers at the center makes it possible for the central government to intervene in state issues; these powers include control over the military, the presence of an appointed governor to monitor affairs within each state, and the ability of the president to suspend state-level legislatures in times of internal disorder and declare direct President's Rule. In theory, these powers should come into play rarely because the regular administration of the states resides with elected assemblies and chief ministers appointed through parliamentary procedures. State governments have extensive powers over almost all of their internal affairs. The framers of the national constitution constructed a series of checks and balances among the legislative, executive, and judicial branches at the center, and between the center and the states, designed to provide national security while allowing a maximum of state autonomy within the diversified union.

The Indian political system has proven to be flexible and durable, but major internal conflicts have threatened the constitution. In practice, the elected office of the nation's president has gravitated toward the formal and ritual aspects of executive power, while the office of the prime minister, backed up by a majority in Parliament, the cabinet, national security forces, and the bureaucracy of the Indian Administrative Service, has wielded the actual power. The national Parliament has not developed an independent committee structure and critical tradition that could stand against the force of the executive branch. The judiciary, while remaining independent and at times crucial in determining national policy, has stayed in the background and is subject to future change through constitutional amendments. The constitution itself has been subject to numerous amendments since its adoption in 1950.

By August 1996, the constitution had been amended eighty times.

National politics have become contests to set up the appointment of the prime minister, who then has considerable power to interfere directly or through a cooperative president in all aspects of national life. The most drastic example of this power occurred in 1975, when Indira Gandhi implemented the constitutional provision for a declaration of Emergency, suspending civil rights for eighteen months, using Parliament as a tool for eliminating opposition, and ruling with the aid of a small circle of advisers. The more common form of executive interference has been the suspension of state legislatures under a variety of pretexts and the implementation of President's Rule. This typically has occurred when opposition parties have captured state legislatures and set in motion policies unfavorable to the prime minister's party. After Indira Gandhi's assassination in 1984, her successors engaged in such overt acts of interference less often.

The main opposition to the national executive comes from the states, in a variety of legal and extralegal struggles for regional autonomy. Most of the states have developed specific political identities based on forms of ethnicity that claim a long historical past. The most common identifying characteristic is language. Agitation in what became the state of Andhra Pradesh led the way in the 1950s, resulting in the reorganization of state boundaries along linguistic lines. Agitations in the state of Tamil Nadu in the 1960s resulted in domination of the state by parties dedicated officially to Tamil nationalism.

In the northeast, regional struggles have coalesced around tribal identities, leading to the formation of a number of small states based on dominant tribal groupings. Farther south, in Kerala and West Bengal, communist parties have upheld the banner of regionalism by capturing state assemblies and implementing radical socialist programs against the wishes of the central government.

The regional movements most threatening to national integration have occurred in the northwest. The Indian government divided the state of Punjab twice after independence—Haryana and Himachal Pradesh were sliced off—before it achieved a Sikh majority population in what remained of Punjab. That majority allowed the Sikh-led Akali Dal (Eternal Party) to capture the state assembly in the early 1980s. By then radical separatist elements were determined to fight for an independent Sikh Punjab. The result was an army attack on Sikh militants occupying the Golden Temple in Amritsar, Indira Gandhi's assassination by her Sikh bodyguards, both in 1984, and a ten-year internal security struggle that has killed thousands. In India's state of Jammu and Kashmir (often referred to as Kashmir), where Muslims constitute the majority of the population, regional struggle takes a different religious form and has created intense security problems that keep bilateral relations with Pakistan, which also lays claim to Kashmir, in a tense mode.

The central government usually has been able to defuse regional agitations by agreeing to redefinition of state boundaries or by guaranteeing differing degrees of regional autonomy, including acquiescence in the control of the state government by regional political parties. This strategy defused the original linguistic agitations through the 1970s, and led to the resolution of the destructive political and ethnic crises in Assam in the mid-1980s. When national security interests came into play, however, as in Punjab and Jammu and Kashmir, the central government did not hesitate to use force.

In the mid-1990s, India remains a strong unified nation, with a long history of constitutional government and democracy, but at any moment there are half a dozen regional political agitations underway and a dozen guerrilla movements in different parts of the country advocating various types of official recognition or outright independence based on ethnic affiliation. These movements have never seriously threatened the unity of the country as a whole. Because the benefits of union within India have outweighed the advantages of independence for most people within each state, there have always been moderate elements within the states willing to make deals with the central government, and security forces have proven capable of repressing any armed struggle at the regional level. In addition, state-level opposition, whether in the legislatures or in the streets, has been an effective means of preventing massive interference from New Delhi in the day-to-day lives of citizens, and thus has provided a crucial check that has preserved the democratic system and the constitution.

One of the most serious challenges to India's internal security and democratic traditions has come from so-called communal disorders, or riots, based on ethnic cleavages. The most typical form is a religious riot, mostly between Hindus and Muslims, although some of these disturbances also occur between different castes or linguistic groups. Most of these struggles start with neighborhood squabbles of little significance, but rapidly escalate into mob looting and burning, street fighting, and violent intervention by the police or paramilitary forces.

RELIGIOUS IDEOLOGY

Religious ideology has played only a small part in these events. Instead, the pressures of urban life in overcrowded, poorer neighborhoods, combined with competition for limited economic opportunities, create an environment in which ethnic differences become convenient labels for defining enemies, and criminal behavior becomes commonplace. Whether ignited by a street accident or a major political event, passions in these areas may be directed into mob action. However, after the catastrophe of independence (when hundreds of thousands in North India died during the partition of India and Pakistan and at least 12 million became refugees), and because the pattern of rioting has continued annually in various cities, a culture of distrust has grown up among a sizable minority of Hindus and Muslims. This distrust has manifested itself in the nationwide agitations fomented by elements of the BJP and communal Hindu parties in the early 1990s. It reached a peak in December 1992 with the dramatic destruction of the Babri Masjid, a mosque in Ayodhya (in Uttar Pradesh), and communal riots and bombings in major cities throughout India in early 1993. In this manner, the frictions of daily life in an overcrowded, poor nation have had a major impact on the national political agenda.

The internal conflict between Hindus and Muslims has received some of its stimulus since 1947 from the international conflict between India and Pakistan. One of the great tragedies of the freedom struggle was the relentless polarization of opinion between the Congress, which came to represent mostly Hindus, and the All-India Muslim League, which eventually stood behind a demand for a separate homeland for a Muslim majority. This division, encouraged under British rule by provisions for separate electorates for Muslims, led to the partition of Pakistan from India and the outbreak of hostilities over Kashmir. Warfare between India and Pakistan occurred in 1947, 1965, and 1971; the last conflict led to the independence of Bangladesh (formerly East Pakistan) and a major strategic victory by India.

The perception of Pakistan as an enemy nation has overshadowed all other Indian foreign policy considerations because neither country has relinquished claims over Kashmir, nor a series of border irritations continue to bedevil attempts at rapprochement. In the late 1980s, tensions over large-scale military maneuvers almost led to war, and regular fighting over glacial wastelands in Kashmir continues to keep the pressure high. An added dimension emerged in 1987 when Pakistan publicly admitted that it possessed nuclear weapons capability, matching Indian nuclear capabilities demonstrated in 1974. In the mid-1990s, both nations continue to devote a large percentage of their military budgets to developing or to purchasing advanced weaponry, which is mostly aimed at each other—a serious drain of resources needed for economic growth.

India is a complex geographic, historical, religious, social, economic, and political entity. India is one of the oldest human civilizations and yet displays no cultural features common to all its members. It is one of the richest nations in history, but most of its people are among the poorest in the world. Its ideology rests on some of the most sublime concepts of humanism and nonviolence, but deep-seated discrimination and violent responses are daily news. It has one of the world's most stable political structures, but that structure is constantly in crisis. The nation is seeking a type of great power status, but no one is sure what that involves. India, in the end, defies easy analysis.

KINGDOMS AND EMPIRES

From their original settlements in the Punjab region, the Aryans gradually began to penetrate eastward, clearing dense forests and establishing "tribal" settlements along the Ganga and Yamuna (Jamuna) plains between 1500 and ca. 800 B.C. By around 500 B.C., most of northern India was inhabited and had been brought under cultivation, facilitating the increasing knowledge of the use of iron implements, including ox-drawn plows, and spurred by the growing population that provided voluntary and forced labor. As riverine and inland trade flourished, many towns along the Ganga became centers of trade, culture, and luxurious living. Increasing population and surplus production provided the bases for the emergence of independent states with fluid territorial boundaries over which disputes frequently arose.

The rudimentary administrative system headed by tribal chieftains was transformed by a number of regional republics or hereditary monarchies that devised ways to appropriate revenue and to conscript labor for expanding the areas of settlement and agriculture farther east and south, beyond the Narmada River. These emergent states collected revenue through officials, maintained armies, and built new cities and highways. By 600 B.C., sixteen such territorial powers—including the Magadha, Kosala, Kuru, and Gandhara—stretched across the North India plains from modern-day Afghanistan to Bangladesh. The right of a king to his throne, no matter how it was gained, was usually legitimized through elaborate sacrifice rituals and genealogies concocted by priests who ascribed to the king divine or superhuman origins.

The victory of good over evil is epitomized in the epic Ramayana (The Travels of Rama, or Ram in the preferred modern form), while another epic, Mahabharata (Great Battle of the Descendants of Bharata), spells out the concept of dharma and duty. More than 2,500 years later, Mohandas Karamchand (Mahatma) Gandhi, the father of modern India, used these concepts in the fight for independence. The Mahabharata records the feud between Aryan cousins that culminated in an epic battle in which both gods and mortals from many lands allegedly fought to the death, and the Ramayana recounts the kidnapping of Sita, Rama's wife, by Ravana, a demonic king of Lanka (Sri Lanka), her rescue by her husband (aided by his animal allies), and Rama's coronation, leading to a period of prosperity and justice. In the late twentieth century, these epics remain dear to the hearts of Hindus and are commonly read and enacted in many settings. In the 1980s and 1990s, Ram's story has been exploited by Hindu militants and politicians to gain power, and the much disputed Ramjanmabhumi, the birth site of Ram, has become an extremely sensitive communal issue, potentially pitting Hindu majority against Muslim minority.

THE MAURYAN EMPIRE

By the end of the sixth century B.C., India's northwest was integrated into the Persian Achaemenid Empire and became one of its satrapies. This integration marked the beginning of administrative contacts between Central Asia and India.

Although Indian accounts to a large extent ignored Alexander the Great's Indus campaign in 326 B.C., Greek writers recorded their impressions of the general conditions prevailing in South Asia during this period. Thus, the year 326 B.C. provides the first clear and historically verifiable date in Indian history. A two-way cultural fusion between several Indo-Greek elements—especially in art, architecture, and coinage—occurred in the next several hundred years. North India's political landscape was transformed by the emergence of Magadha in the eastern Indo-Gangetic Plain. In 322 B.C., Magadha, under the rule of Chandragupta Maurya, began to assert its hegemony over neighboring areas. Chandragupta, who ruled from 324 to 301 B.C., was the architect of the first Indian imperial power—the Mauryan Empire (326-184 B.C.)—whose capital was Pataliputra, near modern-day Patna, in Bihar.

Situated on rich alluvial soil and near mineral deposits, especially iron, Magadha was at the center of bustling commerce and trade. The capital was a city of magnificent palaces, temples, a university, a library, gardens, and parks, as reported by Megasthenes, the third-century B.C. Greek historian and ambassador to the Mauryan court. Legend states that Chandragupta's success was due in large measure to his adviser Kautilya, the Brahman author of the Arthashastra (Science of Material Gain), a textbook that outlined governmental administration and political strategy. There was a highly centralized and hierarchical government with a large staff, which regulated tax collection, trade and commerce, industrial arts, mining, vital statistics, welfare of foreigners, maintenance of public places including markets and temples, and prostitutes. A large standing army and a well-developed espionage system were maintained. The empire was divided into provinces, districts, and villages governed by a host of centrally appointed local officials, who replicated the functions of the central administration.

Ashoka, grandson of Chandragupta, ruled from 269 to 232 B.C. and was one of India's most illustrious rulers. Ashoka's inscriptions chiseled on rocks and stone pillars located at strategic locations throughout his empire—such as Lampaka (Laghman in modern Afghanistan), Mahastan (in modern Bangladesh), and Brahmagiri (in Karnataka)—constitute the second set of datable historical records. According to some of the inscriptions, in the aftermath of the carnage resulting from his campaign against the powerful kingdom of Kalinga (modern Orissa), Ashoka renounced bloodshed and pursued a policy of nonviolence or ahimsa, espousing a theory of rule by righteousness. His toleration for different religious beliefs and languages reflected the realities of India's regional pluralism although he personally seems to have followed Buddhism. Early Buddhist stories assert that he convened a Buddhist council at his capital, regularly undertook tours within his realm, and sent Buddhist missionary ambassadors to Sri Lanka.

Contacts established with the Hellenistic world during the reign of Ashoka's predecessors served him well. He sent diplomatic-cum-religious missions to the rulers of Syria, Macedonia, and Epirus, who learned about India's religious traditions, especially Buddhism. India's northwest retained many Persian cultural elements, which might explain Ashoka's rock inscriptions—such inscriptions were commonly associated with Persian rulers. Ashoka's Greek and Aramaic inscriptions found in Kandahar in Afghanistan may also reveal his desire to maintain ties with people outside of India.

After the disintegration of the Mauryan Empire in the second century B.C., South Asia became a collage of regional powers with overlapping boundaries. India's unguarded northwestern border again attracted a series of invaders between

200 B.C. and A.D. 300. As the Aryans had done, the invaders became "Indianized" in the process of their conquest and settlement. Also, this period witnessed remarkable intellectual and artistic achievements inspired by cultural diffusion and syncretism. The Indo-Greeks, or the Bactrians, of the northwest contributed to the development of numismatics; they were followed by another group, the Shakas (or Scythians), from the steppes of Central Asia, who settled in western India. Still other nomadic people, the Yuezhi, who were forced out of the Inner Asian steppes of Mongolia, drove the Shakas out of northwestern India and established the Kushana Kingdom (first century B.C.-third century A.D.). The Kushana Kingdom controlled parts of Afghanistan and Iran, and in India the realm stretched from Purushapura (modern Peshawar, Pakistan) in the northwest, to Varanasi (Uttar Pradesh) in the east, and to Sanchi (Madhya Pradesh) in the south. For a short period, the kingdom reached still farther east, to Pataliputra. The Kushana Kingdom was the crucible of trade among the Indian, Persian, Chinese, and Roman empires and controlled a critical part of the legendary Silk Road. Kanishka, who reigned for two decades starting around A.D. 78, was the most noteworthy Kushana ruler. He converted to Buddhism and convened a great Buddhist council in Kashmir. The Kushanas were patrons of Gandharan art, a synthesis between Greek and Indian styles, and Sanskrit literature. They initiated a new era called Shaka in A.D. 78, and their calendar, which was formally recognized by India for civil purposes starting on March 22, 1957, is still in use.

DECCAN AND THE SOUTH

During the Kushana Dynasty, an indigenous power, the Satavahana Kingdom (first century B.C.-third century A.D.), rose in the Deccan in southern India. The Satavahana, or Andhra, Kingdom was considerably influenced by the Mauryan political model, although power was decentralized in the hands of local chieftains, who used the symbols of Vedic religion and upheld the varnashramadharma. The rulers, however, were eclectic and patronized Buddhist monuments, such as those in Ellora (Maharashtra) and Amaravati (Andhra Pradesh). Thus, the Deccan served as a bridge through which politics, trade, and religious ideas could spread from the north to the south. Farther south were three ancient Tamil kingdoms—Chera (on the west), Chola (on the east), and Pandya (in the south)—frequently involved in internecine warfare to gain regional supremacy. They are mentioned in Greek and Ashokan sources as lying at the fringes of the Mauryan Empire. A corpus of ancient Tamil literature, known as Sangam (academy) works, including Tolkappiam, a manual of Tamil grammar by Tolkappiyar, provides much useful information about their social life from 300 B.C. to A.D. 200. There is clear evidence of encroachment by Aryan traditions from the north into a predominantly indigenous Dravidian culture in transition.

Dravidian social order was based on different ecoregions rather than on the Aryan varna paradigm, although the Brahmans had a high status at a very early stage. Segments of society were characterized by matriarchy and matrilineal succession—which survived well into the nineteenth century—cross-cousin marriage, and strong regional identity. Tribal chieftains emerged as "kings" just as people moved from pastoralism toward agriculture, sustained by irrigation based on rivers, small-scale tanks (as man-made ponds are called in India) and wells, and brisk maritime trade with Rome and Southeast Asia.

Discoveries of Roman gold coins in various sites attest to extensive South Indian links with the outside world. As with Pataliputra in the northeast and Taxila in the northwest (in modern Pakistan), the city of Madurai, the Pandyan capital (in modern Tamil Nadu), was the center of intellectual and literary activities. Poets and bards assembled there under royal patronage at successive concourses and composed anthologies of poems, most of which have been lost. By the end of the first century B.C., South Asia was crisscrossed by overland trade routes, which facilitated the movements of Buddhist and Jain missionaries and other travelers and opened the area to a synthesis of many cultures.

INDIA GUPTA AND HARSHA

The Classical Age refers to the period when most of North India was reunited under the Gupta Empire (ca. A.D. 320-550).

Because of the relative peace, law and order, and extensive cultural achievements during this period, it has been described as a "golden age" that crystallized the elements of what is generally known as Hindu culture with all its variety, contradiction, and synthesis. The golden age was confined to the north, and the classical patterns began to spread south only after the Gupta Empire had vanished from the historical scene. The military exploits of the first three rulers—Chandragupta I (ca. 319-335), Samudragupta (ca. 335-376), and Chandragupta II (ca. 376-415)—brought all of North India under their leadership. From Pataliputra, their capital, they sought to retain political preeminence as much by pragmatism and judicious marriage alliances as by military strength. Despite their self-conferred titles, their overlordship was threatened and by 500 ultimately ruined by the Hunas (a branch of the White Huns emanating from Central Asia), who were yet another group in the long succession of ethnically and culturally different outsiders drawn into India and then woven into the hybrid Indian fabric.

Under Harsha Vardhana (or Harsha, r. 606-47), North India was reunited briefly, but neither the Guptas nor Harsha controlled a centralized state, and their administrative styles rested on the collaboration of regional and local officials for administering their rule rather than on centrally appointed personnel. The Gupta period marked a watershed of Indian culture: the Guptas performed Vedic sacrifices to legitimize their rule, but they also patronized Buddhism, which continued to provide an alternative to Brahmanical orthodoxy.

The most significant achievements of this period, however, were in religion, education, mathematics, art, and Sanskrit literature and drama. The religion that later developed into modern Hinduism witnessed a crystallization of its components: major sectarian deities, image worship, devotionalism, and the importance of the temple. Education included grammar, composition, logic, metaphysics, mathematics, medicine, and astronomy. These subjects became highly specialized and reached an advanced level. The Indian numeral system—sometimes erroneously attributed to the Arabs, who took it from India to Europe where it replaced the Roman system—and the decimal system are Indian inventions of this period.

Aryabhatta's expositions on astronomy in 499, moreover, gave calculations of the solar year and the shape and movement of astral bodies with remarkable accuracy. In medicine, Charaka and Sushruta wrote about a fully evolved system, resembling those of Hippocrates and Galen in Greece. Although progress in physiology and biology was hindered by religious injunctions against contact with dead bodies, which discouraged dissection and anatomy, Indian physicians excelled in pharmacopoeia, caesarean section, bone setting, and skin grafting.

THE SOUTHERN RIVALS

When Gupta disintegration was complete, the classical patterns of civilization continued to thrive not only in the middle Ganga Valley and the kingdoms that emerged on the heels of Gupta demise but also in the Deccan and in South India, which acquired a more prominent place in history. In fact, from the mid-seventh to the mid-thirteenth centuries, regionalism was the dominant theme of political or dynastic history of South Asia. Three features, as political scientist Radha Champakalakshmi has noted, commonly characterize the sociopolitical realities of this period. First, the spread of Brahmanical religions was a two-way process of Sanskritization of local cults and localization of Brahmanical social order. Second was the ascendancy of the Brahman priestly and landowning groups that later dominated regional institutions and political developments. Third, because of the seesawing of numerous dynasties that had a remarkable ability to survive perennial military attacks, regional kingdoms faced frequent defeats but seldom total annihilation.

Peninsular India was involved in an eighth-century tripartite power struggle among the Chalukyas (556-757) of Vatapi, the Pallavas (300-888) of Kanchipuram, and the Pandyas (seventh through the tenth centuries) of Madurai. The Chalukya rulers were overthrown by their subordinates, the Rashtrakutas, who ruled from 753 to 973. Although both the Pallava and Pandya kingdoms were enemies, the real struggle for political domination was between the Pallava and Chalukya realms.

Despite interregional conflicts, local autonomy was preserved to a far greater degree in the south where it had prevailed for centuries. The absence of a highly centralized government was associated with a corresponding local autonomy in the administration of villages and districts. Extensive and well-documented overland and maritime trade flourished with the Arabs on the west coast and with Southeast Asia. Trade facilitated cultural diffusion in Southeast Asia, where local elites selectively but willingly adopted Indian art, architecture, literature, and social customs.

The interdynastic rivalry and seasonal raids into each other's territory notwithstanding, the rulers in the Deccan and South India patronized all three religions—Buddhism, Hinduism, and Jainism.

The religions vied with each other for royal favor, expressed in land grants but more importantly in the creation of monumental temples, which remain architectural wonders. The cave temples of Elephanta Island (near Bombay, or Mumbai in Marathi), Ajanta, and Ellora (in Maharashtra), and structural temples of Kanchipuram (in Tamil Nadu) are enduring legacies of otherwise warring regional rulers. By the mid-seventh century, Buddhism and Jainism began to decline as sectarian Hindu devotional cults of Shiva and Vishnu vigorously competed for popular support.

Although Sanskrit was the language of learning and theology in South India, as it was in the north, the growth of the bhakti (devotional) movements enhanced the crystallization of vernacular literature in all four major Dravidian languages: Tamil, Telugu, Malayalam, and Kannada; they often borrowed themes and vocabulary from Sanskrit but preserved much local cultural lore.

Examples of Tamil literature include two major poems, Cilappatikaram (The Jewelled Anklet) and Manimekalai (The Jewelled Belt); the body of devotional literature of Shaivism and Vaishnavism—Hindu devotional movements; and the reworking of the Ramayana by Kamban in the twelfth century. A nationwide cultural synthesis had taken place with a minimum of common characteristics in the various regions of South Asia, but the process of cultural infusion and assimilation would continue to shape and influence India's history through the centuries.

DELHI SULTANATE

Islam was propagated by the Prophet Muhammad during the early seventh century in the deserts of Arabia. Less than a century after its inception, Islam's presence was felt throughout the Middle East, North Africa, Spain, Iran, and Central Asia. Arab military forces conquered the Indus Delta region in Sindh in 711 and established an Indo-Muslim state there. Sindh became an Islamic outpost where Arabs established trade links with the Middle East and were later joined by teachers or sufis, but Arab influence was hardly felt in the rest of South Asia. By the end of the tenth century, dramatic changes took place when the Central Asian Turkic tribes accepted both the message and mission of Islam. These warlike people first began to move into Afghanistan and Iran and later into India through the northwest. Mahmud of Ghazni (971-1030), who was also known as the "Sword of Islam," mounted seventeen plundering expeditions between 997 and 1027 into North India, annexing Punjab as his eastern province. The invaders' effective use of the crossbow while at a gallop gave them a decisive advantage over their Indian opponents, the Rajputs. Mahmud's conquest of Punjab foretold ominous consequences for the rest of India, but the Rajputs appear to have been both unprepared and unwilling to change their military tactics, which ultimately collapsed in the face of the swift and punitive cavalry of the Afghans and Turkic peoples.

In the thirteenth century, Shams-ud-Din Iletmish (or Iltutmish; r. 1211-36), a former slave-warrior, established a Turkic kingdom in Delhi, which enabled future sultans to push in every direction; within the next 100 years, the Delhi Sultanate extended its sway east to Bengal and south to the Deccan, while the sultanate itself experienced repeated threats from the northwest and internal revolts from displeased, independent-minded nobles. The sultanate was in constant flux as five dynasties rose and fell: Mamluk or Slave (1206-90), Khalji (1290-1320), Tughluq (1320-1413), Sayyid (1414-51), and Lodi (1451-1526). The Khalji Dynasty under Ala-ud-Din (r. 1296-1315) succeeded in bringing most of South India under its control for a time, although conquered areas broke away quickly. Power in Delhi was often gained by violence—nineteen of the thirty-five sultans were assassinated—and was legitimized by reward for tribal loyalty. Factional rivalries and court intrigues were as numerous as they were treacherous; territories controlled by the sultan expanded and shrank depending on his personality and fortunes.

Both the Quran and sharia (Islamic law) provided the basis for enforcing Islamic administration over the independent Hindu rulers, but the sultanate made only fitful progress in the beginning, when many campaigns were undertaken for plunder and temporary reduction of fortresses. The effective rule of a sultan depended largely on his ability to control the strategic places that dominated the military highways and trade routes, extract the annual land tax, and maintain personal authority over military and provincial governors. Sultan Ala-ud-Din made an attempt to reassess, systematize, and unify land revenues and urban taxes and to institute a highly centralized system of administration over his realm, but his efforts were abortive. Although agriculture in North India improved as a result of new canal construction and irrigation methods, including what came to be known as the Persian wheel, prolonged political instability and parasitic methods of tax collection brutalized the peasantry. Yet trade and a market economy, encouraged by the free-spending habits of the aristocracy, acquired new impetus both inland and overseas. Experts in metalwork, stonework, and textile manufacture responded to the new patronage with enthusiasm.

SOUTHERN DYNASTIES

The sultans' failure to hold securely the Deccan and South India resulted in the rise of competing southern dynasties: the Muslim Bahmani Sultanate (1347-1527) and the Hindu Vijayanagar Empire (1336-1565). Zafar Khan, a former provincial governor under the Tughluqs, revolted against his Turkic overlord and proclaimed himself sultan, taking the title Ala-ud-Din Bahman Shah in 1347. The Bahmani Sultanate, located in the northern Deccan, lasted for almost two centuries, until it fragmented into five smaller states in 1527. The Bahmani Sultanate adopted the patterns established by the Delhi overlords in tax collection and administration, but its downfall was caused in large measure by the competition and hatred between deccani (domiciled Muslim immigrants and local converts) and paradesi (foreigners or officials in temporary service). The Bahmani Sultanate initiated a process of cultural synthesis visible in Hyderabad, where cultural flowering is still expressed in vigorous schools of deccani architecture and painting.

Founded in 1336, the empire of Vijayanagar (named for its capital Vijayanagar, "City of Victory," in present-day Karnataka) expanded rapidly toward Madurai in the south and Goa in the west and exerted intermittent control over the east coast and the extreme southwest. Vijayanagar rulers closely followed Chola precedents, especially in collecting agricultural and trade revenues, in giving encouragement to commercial guilds, and in honoring temples with lavish endowments. Added revenue needed for waging war against the Bahmani sultans was raised by introducing a set of taxes on commercial enterprises, professions, and industries. Political rivalry between the Bahmani and the Vijayanagar rulers involved control over the Krishna-Tunghabadhra river basin, which shifted hands depending on whose military was superior at any given time. The Vijayanagar rulers' capacity for gaining victory over their enemies was contingent on ensuring a constant supply of horses—initially through Arab traders but later through the Portuguese—and maintaining internal roads and communication networks. Merchant guilds enjoyed a wide sphere of operation and were able to offset the power of landlords and Brahmans in court politics. Commerce and shipping eventually passed largely into the hands of foreigners, and the ruler provided special facilities and tax concessions for them. Arabs and Portuguese competed for influence and control of west coast ports, and, in 1510, Goa passed into Portuguese possession.

The city of Vijayanagar itself contained numerous temples with rich ornamentation, especially the gateways, and a cluster of shrines for the deities. Most prominent among the temples was the one dedicated to Virupaksha, a manifestation of Shiva, the patron-deity of the Vijayanagar rulers. Temples continued to be the nuclei of diverse cultural and intellectual activities, but these activities were based more on tradition than on contemporary political realities. (However, the first Vijayanagar ruler—Harihara I—was a Hindu who converted to Islam and then reconverted to Hinduism for political expediency.) The temples sponsored no intellectual exchange with Islamic theologians because Muslims were generally assigned to an "impure" status and were thus excluded from entering temples. When the five rulers of what was once the Bahmani Sultanate combined their forces and attacked Vijayanagar in 1565, the empire crumbled at the Battle of Talikot.

THE MUGHAL ERA

In the early sixteenth century, descendants of the Mongol, Turkish, Iranian, and Afghan invaders of South Asia—the Mughals—invaded India under the leadership of Zahir-ud-Din Babur. Babur was the great-grandson of Timur Lenk (Timur the Lame, from which the Western name Tamerlane is derived), who had invaded India and plundered Delhi in 1398 and then led a short-lived empire based in Samarkand (in modern-day Uzbekistan) that united Persian-based Mongols (Babur's maternal ancestors) and other West Asian peoples. Babur was driven from Samarkand and initially established his rule in Kabul in 1504; he later became the first Mughal ruler (1526-30). His determination was to expand eastward into Punjab, where he had made a number of forays. Then an invitation from an opportunistic Afghan chief in Punjab brought him to the very heart of the Delhi Sultanate, ruled by Ibrahim Lodi (1517-26). Babur, a seasoned military commander, entered India in 1526 with his well-trained veteran army of 12,000 to meet the sultan's huge but unwieldy and disunited force of more than 100,000 men. Babur defeated the Lodi sultan decisively at Panipat (in modern-day Haryana, about ninety kilometers north of Delhi). Employing gun carts, moveable artillery, and superior cavalry tactics, Babur achieved a resounding victory. A year later, he decisively defeated a Rajput confederacy led by Rana Sangha. In 1529 Babur routed the joint forces of Afghans and the sultan of Bengal but died in 1530 before he could consolidate his military gains. He left behind as legacies his memoirs (Babur Namah), several beautiful gardens in Kabul, Lahore, and Agra, and descendants who would fulfill his dream of establishing an empire in Hindustan.

When Babur died, his son Humayun (1530-56), also a soldier, inherited a difficult task. He was pressed from all sides by a reassertion of Afghan claims to the Delhi throne, by disputes over his own succession, and by the Afghan-Rajput march into Delhi in 1540. He fled to Persia, where he spent nearly ten years as an embarrassed guest at the Safavid court. In 1545 he gained a foothold in Kabul, reasserted his Indian claim, defeated Sher Khan Sur, the most powerful Afghan ruler, and took control of Delhi in 1555.

Humayun's untimely death in 1556 left the task of further imperial conquest and consolidation to his thirteen-year-old son, Jalal-ud-Din Akbar (r. 1556-1605). Following a decisive military victory at the Second Battle of Panipat in 1556, the regent Bayram Khan pursued a vigorous policy of expansion on Akbar's behalf. As soon as Akbar came of age, he began to free himself from the influences of overbearing ministers, court factions, and harem intrigues, and demonstrated his own capacity for judgment and leadership. A "workaholic" who seldom slept more than three hours a night, he personally oversaw the implementation of his administrative policies, which were to form the backbone of the Mughal Empire for more than 200 years. He continued to conquer, annex, and consolidate a far-flung territory bounded by Kabul in the northwest, Kashmir in the north, Bengal in the east, and beyond the Narmada River in the south—an area comparable in size to the Mauryan territory some 1,800 years earlier.

Akbar built a walled capital called Fatehpur Sikri (Fatehpur means Fortress of Victory) near Agra, starting in 1571. Palaces for each of Akbar's senior queens, a huge artificial lake, and sumptuous water-filled courtyards were built there. The city, however, proved short-lived, perhaps because the water supply was insufficient or of poor quality, or, as some historians believe, Akbar had to attend to the northwest areas of his empire and simply moved his capital for political reasons. Whatever the reason, in 1585 the capital was relocated to Lahore and in 1599 to Agra.

Akbar adopted two distinct but effective approaches in administering a large territory and incorporating various ethnic groups into the service of his realm. In 1580 he obtained local revenue statistics for the previous decade in order to understand details of productivity and price fluctuation of different crops. Aided by Todar Mal, a Rajput king, Akbar issued a revenue schedule that the peasantry could tolerate while providing maximum profit for the state. Revenue demands, fixed according to local conventions of cultivation and quality of soil, ranged from one-third to one-half of the crop and were paid in cash. Akbar relied heavily on land-holding zamindars. They used their considerable local knowledge and influence to collect revenue and to transfer it to the treasury, keeping a portion in return for services rendered. Within his administrative system, the warrior aristocracy (mansabdars) held ranks (mansabs) expressed in numbers of troops, and indicating pay, armed contingents, and obligations. The warrior aristocracy was generally paid from revenues of nonhereditary and transferrable jagirs (revenue villages).

An astute ruler who genuinely appreciated the challenges of administering so vast an empire, Akbar introduced a policy of reconciliation and assimilation of Hindus (including Maryam al-Zamani, the Hindu Rajput mother of his son and heir, Jahangir), who represented the majority of the population. He recruited and rewarded Hindu chiefs with the highest ranks in government; encouraged intermarriages between Mughal and Rajput aristocracy; allowed new temples to be built; personally participated in celebrating Hindu festivals such as Dipavali, or Diwali, the festival of lights; and abolished the jizya (poll tax) imposed on non-Muslims. Akbar came up with his own theory of "rulership as a divine illumination," enshrined in his new religion Din-i-Ilahi (Divine Faith), incorporating the principle of acceptance of all religions and sects. He encouraged widow marriage, discouraged child marriage, outlawed the practice of sati, and persuaded Delhi merchants to set up special market days for women, who otherwise were secluded at home. By the end of Akbar's reign, the Mughal Empire extended throughout most of India north of the Godavari River. The exceptions were Gondwana in central India, which paid tribute to the Mughals, and Assam, in the northeast.

Mughal rule under Jahangir (1605-27) and Shah Jahan (1628-58) was noted for political stability, brisk economic activity, beautiful paintings, and monumental buildings. Jahangir married the Persian princess whom he renamed Nur Jahan (Light of the World), who emerged as the most powerful individual in the court besides the emperor. As a result, Persian poets, artists, scholars, and officers—including her own family members—lured by the Mughal court's brilliance and luxury, found asylum in India. The number of unproductive, time-serving officers mushroomed, as did corruption, while the excessive Persian representation upset the delicate balance of impartiality at the court. Jahangir liked Hindu festivals but promoted mass conversion to Islam; he persecuted the followers of Jainism and even executed Guru Arjun Das, the fifth saint-teacher of the Sikhs. Nur Jahan's abortive schemes to secure the throne for the prince of her choice led Shah Jahan to rebel in 1622. In that same year, the Persians took over Kandahar in southern Afghanistan, an event that struck a serious blow to Mughal prestige.

Between 1636 and 1646, Shah Jahan sent Mughal armies to conquer the Deccan and the northwest beyond the Khyber Pass. Even though they demonstrated Mughal military strength, these campaigns consumed the imperial treasury. As the state became a huge military machine, whose nobles and their contingents multiplied almost fourfold, so did its demands for more revenue from the peasantry. Political unification and maintenance of law and order over wide areas encouraged the emergence of large centers of commerce and crafts—such as Lahore, Delhi, Agra, and Ahmadabad—linked by roads and waterways to distant places and ports. The world-famous Taj Mahal was built in Agra during Shah Jahan's reign as a tomb for his beloved wife, Mumtaz Mahal. It symbolizes both Mughal artistic achievement and excessive financial expenditures when resources were shrinking. The economic position of peasants and artisans did not improve because the administration failed to produce any lasting change in the existing social structure. There was no incentive for the revenue officials, whose concerns primarily were personal or familial gain, to generate resources independent of dominant Hindu zamindars and village leaders, whose self-interest and local dominance prevented them from handing over the full amount of revenue to the imperial treasury. In their ever-greater dependence on land revenue, the Mughals unwittingly nurtured forces that eventually led to the break-up of their empire. The last of the great Mughals was Aurangzeb (r. 1658-1707), who seized the throne by killing all his brothers and imprisoning his own father. During his fifty-year reign, the empire reached its utmost physical limit but also witnessed the unmistakable symptoms of decline. The bureaucracy had grown bloated and excessively corrupt, and the huge and unwieldy army demonstrated outdated weaponry and tactics. Aurangzeb was not the ruler to restore the dynasty's declining fortunes or glory. Awe-inspiring but lacking in the charisma needed to attract outstanding lieutenants, he was driven to extend Mughal rule over most of South Asia and to reestablish Islamic orthodoxy by adopting a reactionary attitude toward those Muslims whom he had suspected of compromising their faith.

Aurangzeb was involved in a series of protracted wars—against the Pathans in Afghanistan, the sultans of Bijapur and Golkonda in the Deccan, and the Marathas in Maharashtra. Peasant uprisings and revolts by local leaders became all too common, as did the conniving of the nobles to preserve their own status at the expense of a steadily weakening empire. The increasing association of his government with Islam further drove a wedge between the ruler and his Hindu subjects. Aurangzeb forbade the building of new temples, destroyed a number of them, and reimposed the jizya. A puritan and a censor of morals, he banned music at court, abolished ceremonies, and persecuted the Sikhs in Punjab. These measures alienated so many that even before he died challenges for power had already begun to escalate. Contenders for the Mughal throne fought each other, and the short-lived reigns of Aurangzeb's successors were strife-filled. The Mughal Empire experienced dramatic reverses as regional governors broke away and founded independent kingdoms. The Mughals had to make peace with Maratha rebels, and Persian and Afghan armies invaded Delhi, carrying away many treasures, including the Peacock Throne in 1739.

THE MARATHAS

The tale of the Marathas' rise to power and their eventual fall contains all the elements of a thriller: adventure, intrigue, and romanticism. Maratha chieftains were originally in the service of Bijapur sultans in the western Deccan, which was under siege by the Mughals. Shivaji Bhonsle (1627-80), a tenacious and fierce fighter recognized as the "father of the Maratha nation," took advantage of this conflict and carved out his own principality near Pune, which later became the Maratha capital. Adopting guerrilla tactics, he waylaid caravans in order to sustain and expand his army, which soon had money, arms, and horses. Shivaji led a series of successful assaults in the 1660s against Mughal strongholds, including the major port of Surat. In 1674 he assumed the title of "Lord of the Universe" at his elaborate coronation, which signaled his determination to challenge the Mughal forces as well as to reestablish a Hindu kingdom in Maharashtra, the land of his origin. Shivaji's battle cries were swaraj (translated variously as freedom, self-rule, independence), swadharma (religious freedom), and goraksha (cow protection). Aurangzeb relentlessly pursued Shivaji's successors between 1681 and 1705 but eventually retreated to the north as his treasury became depleted and as thousands of lives had been lost either on the battlefield or to natural calamities. In 1717 a Mughal emissary signed a treaty with the Marathas confirming their claims to rule in the Deccan in return for acknowledging the fictional Mughal suzerainty and remission of annual taxes. Yet the Marathas soon captured Malwa from Mughal control and later moved east into Orrisa and Bengal; southern India also came under their domain. Recognition of their political power finally came when the Mughal emperor invited them to act as auxiliaries in the internal affairs of the empire and still later to help the emperor in driving the Afghans out of Punjab.

The Marathas, despite their military prowess and leadership, were not equipped to administer the state or to undertake socioeconomic reform. Pursuing a policy characterized by plunder and indiscriminate raids, they antagonized the peasants. They were primarily suited for stirring the Maharashtrian regional pride rather than for attracting loyalty to an all-India confederacy. They were left virtually alone before the invading Afghan forces, headed by Ahmad Shah Abdali (later called Ahmad Shah Durrani), who routed them on the blood-drenched battlefield at Panipat in 1761. The shock of defeat hastened the break-up of their loosely knit confederacy into five independent states and extinguished the hope of Maratha dominance in India.

THE SIKHS

The Afghan defeat of the Maratha armies accelerated the breakaway of Punjab from Delhi and helped the founding of Sikh overlordship in the northwest. Rooted in the bhakti movements that developed in the second century B.C. but swept across North India during the fifteenth and sixteenth centuries, the Sikh religion appealed to the hard-working peasants. The Sikh khalsa (army of the pure) rose up against the economic and political repressions in Punjab toward the end of Aurangzeb's rule. Guerrilla fighters took advantage of the political instability created by the Persian and Afghan onslaught against Delhi, enriching themselves and expanding territorial control. By the 1770s, Sikh hegemony extended from the Indus in the west to the Yamuna in the east, from Multan in the south to Jammu in the north. But the Sikhs, like the Marathas, were a loose, disunited, and quarrelsome conglomerate of twelve kin-groups. It took Ranjit Singh (1780-1839), an individual with modernizing vision and leadership, to achieve supremacy over the other kin-groups and establish his kingdom in which Sikhs, Hindus, and Muslims lived together in comparative equality and increasing prosperity. Ranjit Singh employed European officers and introduced strict military discipline into his army before expanding into Afghanistan, Kashmir, and Ladakh.

ADVENT OF EUROPEANS

The quest for wealth and power brought Europeans to Indian shores in 1498 when Vasco da Gama, the Portuguese voyager, arrived in Calicut (modern Kozhikode, Kerala) on the west coast. In their search for spices and Christian converts, the Portuguese challenged Arab supremacy in the Indian Ocean, and, with their galleons fitted with powerful cannons, set up a network of strategic trading posts along the Arabian Sea and the Persian Gulf. In 1510 the Portuguese took over the enclave of Goa, which became the center of their commercial and political power in India and which they controlled for nearly four and a half centuries.

Economic competition among the European nations led to the founding of commercial companies in England (the East India Company, founded in 1600) and in the Netherlands (Verenigde Oost-Indische Compagnie—the United East India Company, founded in 1602), whose primary aim was to capture the spice trade by breaking the Portuguese monopoly in Asia. Although the Dutch, with a large supply of capital and support from their government, preempted and ultimately excluded the British from the heartland of spices in the East Indies (modern-day Indonesia), both companies managed to establish trading "factories" (actually warehouses) along the Indian coast. The Dutch, for example, used various ports on the Coromandel Coast in South India, especially Pulicat (about twenty kilometers north of Madras), as major sources for slaves for their plantations in the East Indies and for cotton cloth as early as 1609. (The English, however, established their first factory at what today is known as Madras only in 1639.) Indian rulers enthusiastically accommodated the newcomers in hopes of pitting them against the Portuguese. In 1619 Jahangir granted them permission to trade in his territories at Surat (in Gujarat) on the west coast and Hughli (in West Bengal) in the east. These and other locations on the peninsula became centers of international trade in spices, cotton, sugar, raw silk, saltpeter, calico, and indigo.

English company agents became familiar with Indian customs and languages, including Persian, the unifying official language under the Mughals. In many ways, the English agents of that period lived like Indians, intermarried willingly, and a large number of them never returned to their home country. The knowledge of India thus acquired and the mutual ties forged with Indian trading groups gave the English a competitive edge over other Europeans. The French commercial interest—Compagnie des Indes Orientales (East India Company, founded in 1664)—came late, but the French also established themselves in India, emulating the precedents set by their competitors as they founded their enclave at Pondicherry (Puduchcheri) on the Coramandel Coast.

In 1717 the Mughal emperor, Farrukh-siyar (r. 1713-19), gave the British—who by then had already established themselves in the south and the west—a grant of thirty-eight villages near Calcutta, acknowledging their importance to the continuity of international trade in the Bengal economy. As did the Dutch and the French, the British brought silver bullion and copper to pay for transactions, helping the smooth functioning of the Mughal revenue system and increasing the benefits to local artisans and traders. The fortified warehouses of the British brought extraterritorial status, which enabled them to administer their own civil and criminal laws and offered numerous employment opportunities as well as asylum to foreigners and Indians. The British factories successfully competed with their rivals as their size and population grew. The original clusters of fishing villages (Madras and Calcutta) or series of islands (Bombay) became headquarters of the British administrative zones, or presidencies as they generally came to be known. The factories and their immediate environs, known as the White-town, represented the actual and symbolic preeminence of the British—in terms of their political power—as well as their cultural values and social practices; meanwhile, their Indian collaborators lived in the Black-town, separated from the factories by several kilometers.

The British company employed sepoys—European-trained and European-led Indian soldiers—to protect its trade, but local rulers sought their services to settle scores in regional power struggles. South India witnessed the first open confrontation between the British and the French, whose forces were led by Robert Clive and François Dupleix, respectively. Both companies desired to place their own candidate as the nawab, or ruler, of Arcot, the area around Madras. At the end of a protracted struggle between 1744 and 1763, when the Peace of Paris was signed, the British gained an upper hand over the French and installed their man in power, supporting him further with arms and lending large sums as well. The French and the British also backed different factions in the succession struggle for Mughal viceroyalty in Bengal, but Clive intervened successfully and defeated Nawab Siraj-ud-daula in the Battle of Plassey (Palashi, about 150 kilometers north of Calcutta) in 1757. Clive found help from a combination of vested interests that opposed the existing nawab: disgruntled soldiers, landholders, and influential merchants whose commercial profits were closely linked to British fortunes.

Later, Clive defeated the Mughal forces at Buxar (Baksar, west of Patna in Bihar) in 1765, and the Mughal emperor (Shah Alam, r. 1759-1806) conferred on the company administrative rights over Bengal, Bihar, and Orissa, a region of roughly 25 million people with an annual revenue of 40 million rupees. The imperial grant virtually established the company as a sovereign power, and Clive became the first British governor of Bengal.

Besides the presence of the Portuguese, Dutch, British, and French, there were two lesser but noteworthy colonial groups. Danish entrepreneurs established themselves at several ports on the Malabar and Coromandel coasts, in the vicinity of Calcutta and inland at Patna between 1695 and 1740. Austrian enterprises were set up in the 1720s on the vicinity of Surat in modern-day southeastern Gujarat. As with the other non-British enterprises, the Danish and Austrian enclaves were taken over by the British between 1765 and 1815.

BRITISH RULE IN INDIA

A multiplicity of motives underlay the British penetration into India: commerce, security, and a purported moral uplift of the people. The "expansive force" of private and company trade eventually led to the conquest or annexation of territories in which spices, cotton, and opium were produced. British investors ventured into the unfamiliar interior landscape in search of opportunities that promised substantial profits. British economic penetration was aided by Indian collaborators, such as the bankers and merchants who controlled intricate credit networks. British rule in India would have been a frustrated or half-realized dream had not Indian counterparts provided connections between rural and urban centers. External threats, both real and imagined, such as the Napoleonic Wars (1796-1815) and Russian expansion toward Afghanistan (in the 1830s), as well as the desire for internal stability, led to the annexation of more territory in India. Political analysts in Britain wavered initially as they were uncertain of the costs or the advantages in undertaking wars in India, but by the 1810s, as the territorial aggrandizement eventually paid off, opinion in London welcomed the absorption of new areas. Occasionally the British Parliament witnessed heated debates against expansion, but arguments justifying military operations for security reasons always won over even the most vehement critics.

The British soon forgot their own rivalry with the Portuguese and the French and permitted them to stay in their coastal enclaves, which they kept even after independence in 1947. The British, however, continued to expand vigorously well into the 1850s. A number of aggressive governors-general undertook relentless campaigns against several Hindu and Muslim rulers. Among them were Richard Colley Wellesley (1798-1805), William Pitt Amherst (1823-28), George Eden (1836-42), Edward Law (1842-44), and James Andrew Brown Ramsay (1848-56; also known as the Marquess of Dalhousie). Despite desperate efforts at salvaging their tottering power and keeping the British at bay, many Hindu and Muslim rulers lost their territories: Mysore (1799, but later restored), the Maratha Confederacy (1818), and Punjab (1849). The British success in large measure was the result not only of their superiority in tactics and weapons but also of their ingenious relations with Indian rulers through the "subsidiary alliance" system, introduced in the early nineteenth century. Many rulers bartered away their real responsibilities by agreeing to uphold British paramountcy in India, while they retained a fictional sovereignty under the rubric of Pax Britannica. Later, Dalhousie espoused the "doctrine of lapse" and annexed outright the estates of deceased princes of Satara (1848), Udaipur (1852), Jhansi (1853), Tanjore (1853), Nagpur (1854), and Oudh (1856).

European perceptions of India, and those of the British especially, shifted from unequivocal appreciation to sweeping condemnation of India's past achievements and customs. Imbued with an ethnocentric sense of superiority, British intellectuals, including Christian missionaries, spearheaded a movement that sought to bring Western intellectual and technological innovations to Indians. Interpretations of the causes of India's cultural and spiritual "backwardness" varied, as did the solutions. Many argued that it was Europe's mission to civilize India and hold it as a trust until Indians proved themselves competent for self-rule. The immediate consequence of this sense of superiority was to open India to more aggressive missionary activity. The contributions of three missionaries based in Serampore (a Danish enclave in Bengal)—William Carey, Joshua Marshman, and William Ward—remained unequaled and have provided inspiration for future generations of their successors. The missionaries translated the Bible into the vernaculars, taught company officials local languages, and, after 1813, gained permission to proselytize in the company's territories. Although the actual number of converts remained negligible, except in rare instances when entire groups embraced Christianity, such as the Nayars in the south or the Nagas in the northeast, the missionary impact on India through publishing, schools, orphanages, vocational institutions, dispensaries, and hospitals was unmistakable.

The British Parliament enacted a series of laws, among which the Regulating Act of 1773 stood first, to curb the company traders' unrestrained commercial activities and to bring about some order in territories under company control. Limiting the company charter to periods of twenty years, subject to review upon renewal, the 1773 act gave the British government supervisory rights over the Bengal, Bombay, and Madras presidencies. Bengal was given preeminence over the rest because of its enormous commercial vitality and because it was the seat of British power in India (at Calcutta), whose governor was elevated to the new position of governor-general. Warren Hastings was the first incumbent (1773-85). The India Act of 1784, sometimes described as the "half-loaf system," as it sought to mediate between Parliament and the company directors, enhanced Parliament's control by establishing the Board of Control, whose members were selected from the cabinet. The Charter Act of 1813 recognized British moral responsibility by introducing just and humane laws in India, foreshadowing future social legislation, and outlawing a number of traditional practices such as sati and thagi (or thugee, robbery coupled with ritual murder).

As governor-general from 1786 to 1793, Charles Cornwallis (the Marquis of Cornwallis), professionalized, bureaucratized, and Europeanized the company's administration. He also outlawed private trade by company employees, separated the commercial and administrative functions, and remunerated company servants with generous graduated salaries. Because revenue collection became the company's most essential administrative function, Cornwallis made a compact with Bengali zamindars, who were perceived as the Indian counterparts to the British landed gentry. The Permanent Settlement system, also known as the zamindari system, fixed taxes in perpetuity in return for ownership of large estates; but the state was excluded from agricultural expansion, which came under the purview of the zamindars. In Madras and Bombay, however, the ryotwari (peasant) settlement system was set in motion, in which peasant cultivators had to pay annual taxes directly to the government.

Neither the zamindari nor the ryotwari systems proved effective in the long run because India was integrated into an international economic and pricing system over which it had no control, while increasing numbers of people subsisted on agriculture for lack of other employment. Millions of people involved in the heavily taxed Indian textile industry also lost their markets, as they were unable to compete successfully with cheaper textiles produced in Lancashire's mills from Indian raw materials.

Beginning with the Mayor's Court, established in 1727 for civil litigation in Bombay, Calcutta, and Madras, justice in the interior came under the company's jurisdiction. In 1772 an elaborate judicial system, known as adalat, established civil and criminal jurisdictions along with a complex set of codes or rules of procedure and evidence. Both Hindu pandits and Muslim qazis (sharia court judges) were recruited to aid the presiding judges in interpreting their customary laws, but in other instances, British common and statutory laws became applicable. In extraordinary situations where none of these systems was applicable, the judges were enjoined to adjudicate on the basis of "justice, equity, and good conscience." The legal profession provided numerous opportunities for educated and talented Indians who were unable to secure positions in the company, and, as a result, Indian lawyers later dominated nationalist politics and reform movements.

Education for the most part was left to the charge of Indians or to private agents who imparted instruction in the vernaculars. But in 1813, the British became convinced of their "duty" to awaken the Indians from intellectual slumber by exposing them to British literary traditions, earmarking a paltry sum for the cause. Controversy between two groups of Europeans—the "Orientalists" and "Anglicists"—over how the money was to be spent prevented them from formulating any consistent policy until 1835 when William Cavendish Bentinck, the governor-general from 1828 to 1835, finally broke the impasse by resolving to introduce the English language as the medium of instruction. English replaced Persian in public administration and education.

The company's education policies in the 1830s tended to reinforce existing lines of socioeconomic division in society rather than bringing general liberation from ignorance and superstition. Whereas the Hindu English-educated minority spearheaded many social and religious reforms either in direct response to government policies or in reaction to them, Muslims as a group initially failed to do so, a position they endeavored to reverse. Western-educated Hindu elites sought to rid Hinduism of its much criticized social evils: idolatry, the caste system, child marriage, and sati. Religious and social activist Ram Mohan Roy (1772-1833), who founded the Brahmo Samaj (Society of Brahma) in 1828, displayed a readiness to synthesize themes taken from Christianity, Deism, and Indian monism, while other individuals in Bombay and Madras initiated literary and debating societies that gave them a forum for open discourse. The exemplary educational attainments and skillful use of the press by these early reformers enhanced the possibility of effecting broad reforms without compromising societal values or religious practices.

The 1850s witnessed the introduction of the three "engines of social improvement" that heightened the British illusion of permanence in India. They were the railroads, the telegraph, and the uniform postal service, inaugurated during the tenure of Dalhousie as governor-general. The first railroad lines were built in 1850 from Howrah (Haora, across the Hughli River from Calcutta) inland to the coalfields at Raniganj, Bihar, a distance of 240 kilometers. In 1851 the first electric telegraph line was laid in Bengal and soon linked Agra, Bombay, Calcutta, Lahore, Varanasi, and other cities. The three different presidency or regional postal systems merged in 1854 to facilitate uniform methods of communication at an all-India level. With uniform postal rates for letters and newspapers—one-half anna and one anna, respectively (sixteen annas equalled one rupee)—communication between the rural and the metropolitan areas became easier and faster. The increased ease of communication and the opening of highways and waterways accelerated the movement of troops, the transportation of raw materials and goods to and from the interior, and the exchange of commercial information.

The railroads did not break down the social or cultural distances between various groups but tended to create new categories in travel. Separate compartments in the trains were reserved exclusively for the ruling class, separating the educated and wealthy from ordinary people. Similarly, when the Sepoy Rebellion was quelled in 1858, a British official exclaimed that "the telegraph saved India." He envisaged, of course, that British interests in India would continue indefinitely.

INDIA IN 1858-1947

On May 10, 1857, Indian soldiers of the British Indian Army, drawn mostly from Muslim units from Bengal, mutinied in Meerut, a cantonment eighty kilometers northeast of Delhi. The rebels marched to Delhi to offer their services to the Mughal emperor, and soon much of north and central India was plunged into a year-long insurrection against the British.

The uprising, which seriously threatened British rule in India, has been called many names by historians, including the Sepoy Rebellion, the Great Mutiny, and the Revolt of 1857; many people in South Asia, however, prefer to call it India's first war of independence. Undoubtedly, it was the culmination of mounting Indian resentment toward British economic and social policies over many decades. Until the rebellion, the British had succeeded in suppressing numerous riots and "tribal" wars or in accommodating them through concessions, but two events triggered the violent explosion of wrath in 1857. First, was the annexation in 1856 of Oudh, a wealthy princely state that generated huge revenue and represented a vestige of Mughal authority. The second was the British blunder in using cartridges for the Lee-Enfield rifle that were allegedly greased with animal fat, which was offensive to the religious beliefs of Muslim and Hindu sepoys. The rebellion soon engulfed much of North India, including Oudh and various areas once under the control of Maratha princes. Isolated mutinies also occurred at military posts in the center of the subcontinent. Initially, the rebels, although divided and uncoordinated, gained the upper hand, while the unprepared British were terrified, and even paralyzed, without replacements for the casualties. The civil war inflicted havoc on both Indians and British as each vented its fury on the other; each community suffered humiliation and triumph in battle as well, although the final outcome was victory for the British. The last major sepoy rebels surrendered on June 21, 1858, at Gwalior (Madhya Pradesh), one of the principal centers of the revolt. A final battle was fought at Sirwa Pass on May 21, 1859, and the defeated rebels fled into Nepal.

The spontaneous and widespread rebellion later fired the imagination of the nationalists who would debate the most effective method of protest against British rule. For them, the rebellion represented the first Indian attempt at gaining independence. This interpretation, however, is open to serious question.

POST-REBELLION DEVELOPMENTS

The civil war was a major turning point in the history of modern India. In May 1858, the British exiled Emperor Bahadur Shah II (r. 1837-57) to Burma, thus formally liquidating the Mughal Empire. At the same time, they abolished the British East India Company and replaced it with direct rule under the British crown. In proclaiming the new direct-rule policy to "the Princes, Chiefs, and Peoples of India," Queen Victoria (who was given the title Empress of India in 1877) promised equal treatment under British law, but Indian mistrust of British rule had become a legacy of the 1857 rebellion. Many existing economic and revenue policies remained virtually unchanged in the post-1857 period, but several administrative modifications were introduced, beginning with the creation in London of a cabinet post, the secretary of state for India. The governor-general (called viceroy when acting as the direct representative of the British crown), headquartered in Calcutta, ran the administration in India, assisted by executive and legislative councils. Beneath the governor-general were the provincial governors, who held power over the district officials, who formed the lower rungs of the Indian Civil Service. For decades the Indian Civil Service was the exclusive preserve of the British-born, as were the superior ranks in such other professions as law and medicine. The British administrators were imbued with a sense of duty in ruling India and were rewarded with good salaries, high status, and opportunities for promotion. Not until the 1910s did the British reluctantly permit a few Indians into their cadre as the number of English-educated Indians rose steadily.

The viceroy announced in 1858 that the government would honor former treaties with princely states and renounced the "doctrine of lapse," whereby the East India Company had annexed territories of rulers who died without male heirs. About 40 percent of Indian territory and between 20 and 25 percent of the population remained under the control of 562 princes notable for their religious (Islamic, Sikh, Hindu, and other) and ethnic diversity. Their propensity for pomp and ceremony became proverbial, while their domains, varying in size and wealth, lagged behind sociopolitical transformations that took place elsewhere in British-controlled India.

A more thorough reorganization was effected in the constitution of army and government finances. Shocked by the extent of solidarity among Indian soldiers during the rebellion, the government separated the army into the three presidencies.

British attitudes toward Indians shifted from relative openness to insularity and xenophobia, even against those with comparable background and achievement as well as loyalty. British families and their servants lived in cantonments at a distance from Indian settlements. Private clubs where the British gathered for social interaction became symbols of exclusivity and snobbery that refused to disappear decades after the British had left India. In 1883 the government of India attempted to remove race barriers in criminal jurisdictions by introducing a bill empowering Indian judges to adjudicate offenses committed by Europeans. Public protests and editorials in the British press, however, forced the viceroy, George Robinson, Marquis of Ripon (who served from 1880 to 1884), to capitulate and modify the bill drastically. The Bengali Hindu intelligentsia learned a valuable political lesson from this "white mutiny": the effectiveness of well-orchestrated agitation through demonstrations in the streets and publicity in the media when seeking redress for real and imagined grievances.

INDIA INDEPENDENCE MOVEMENT

The decades following the Sepoy Rebellion were a period of growing political awareness, manifestation of Indian public opinion, and emergence of Indian leadership at national and provincial levels. Ominous economic uncertainties created by British colonial rule and the limited opportunities that awaited the ever-expanding number of Western-educated graduates began to dominate the rhetoric of leaders who had begun to think of themselves as a "nation," despite fissures along the lines of region, religion, language, and caste. Inspired by the suggestion made by A.O. Hume, a retired British civil servant, seventy-three Indian delegates met in Bombay in 1885 and founded the Indian National Congress. They were mostly members of the upwardly mobile and successful Western-educated provincial elites, engaged in professions such as law, teaching, and journalism. They had acquired political experience from regional competition in the professions and from their aspirations in securing nomination to various positions in legislative councils, universities, and special commissions.

At its inception, the Congress had no well-defined ideology and commanded few of the resources essential to a political organization. It functioned more as a debating society that met annually to express its loyalty to the Raj and passed numerous resolutions on less controversial issues such as civil rights or opportunities in government, especially the civil service. These resolutions were submitted to the viceroy's government and, occasionally, to the British Parliament, but the Congress's early gains were meager. Despite its claim to represent all India, the Congress voiced the interests of urban elites; the number of participants from other economic backgrounds remained negligible.

By 1900, although the Congress had emerged as an all-India political organization, its achievement was undermined by its singular failure to attract Muslims, who had by then begun to realize their inadequate education and under-representation in government service. Muslim leaders saw that their community had fallen behind the Hindus. Attacks by Hindu reformers against religious conversion, cow killing, and the preservation of Urdu in Arabic script deepened their fears of minority status and denial of their rights if the Congress alone were to represent the people of India. For many Muslims, loyalty to the British crown seemed preferable to cooperation with Congress leaders. Sir Sayyid Ahmad Khan (1817-98) launched a movement for Muslim regeneration that culminated in the founding in 1875 of the Muhammadan Anglo-Oriental College at Aligarh, Uttar Pradesh (renamed Aligarh Muslim University in 1921). Its objective was to educate wealthy students by emphasizing the compatibility of Islam with modern Western knowledge. The diversity among India's Muslims, however, made it impossible to bring about uniform cultural and intellectual regeneration.

Sir George Curzon, the governor-general (1899-1905), ordered the partition of Bengal in 1905. He wanted to improve administrative efficiency in that huge and populous region, where the Bengali Hindu intelligentsia exerted considerable influence on local and national politics. The partition created two provinces: Eastern Bengal and Assam, with its capital at Dhaka (then spelled Dacca), and West Bengal, with its capital at Calcutta (which also served as the capital of British India). An ill-conceived and hastily implemented action, the partition outraged Bengalis. Not only had the government failed to consult Indian public opinion but the action appeared to reflect the British resolve to "divide and rule." Widespread agitation ensued in the streets and in the press, and the Congress advocated boycotting British products under the banner of swadeshi.

The Congress-led boycott of British goods was so successful that it unleashed anti-British forces to an extent unknown since the Sepoy Rebellion. A cycle of violence, terrorism, and repression ensued in some parts of the country. The British tried to mitigate the situation by announcing a series of constitutional reforms in 1909 and by appointing a few moderates to the imperial and provincial councils. In 1906 a Muslim deputation met with the viceroy, Gilbert John Elliot (1905-10), seeking concessions from the impending constitutional reforms, including special considerations in government service and electorates. The All-India Muslim League was founded the same year to promote loyalty to the British and to advance Muslim political rights, which the British recognized by increasing the number of elective offices reserved for Muslims in the India Councils Act of 1909. The Muslim League insisted on its separateness from the Hindu-dominated Congress, as the voice of a "nation within a nation."

In what the British saw as an additional goodwill gesture, in 1911 King-Emperor George V (r. 1910-36) visited India for a durbar (a traditional court held for subjects to express fealty to their ruler), during which he announced the reversal of the partition of Bengal and the transfer of the capital from Calcutta to a newly planned city to be built immediately south of Delhi, which became New Delhi.

WAR, REFORMS AND AGITATION

World War I began with an unprecedented outpouring of loyalty and goodwill toward the British, contrary to initial British fears of an Indian revolt. India contributed generously to the British war effort, by providing men and resources. About 1.3 million Indian soldiers and laborers served in Europe, Africa, and the Middle East, while both the Indian government and the princes sent large supplies of food, money, and ammunition. But disillusionment set in early. High casualty rates, soaring inflation compounded by heavy taxation, a widespread influenza epidemic, and the disruption of trade during the war escalated human suffering in India. The prewar nationalist movement revived as moderate and extremist groups within the Congress submerged their differences in order to stand as a unified front. The Congress even succeeded in forging a temporary alliance with the Muslim League—the Lucknow Pact, or Congress-League Scheme of Reforms—in 1916, over the issues of devolution of political power and the future of Islam in the Middle East.

The British themselves adopted a "carrot and stick" approach in recognition of India's support during the war and in response to renewed nationalist demands. In August 1917, Edwin Montagu, the secretary of state for India, made the historic announcement in Parliament that the British policy for India was "increasing association of Indians in every branch of the administration and the gradual development of self-governing institutions with a view to the progressive realization of responsible government in India as an integral part of the British Empire." The means of achieving the proposed measure were later enshrined in the Government of India Act of 1919, which introduced the principle of a dual mode of administration, or dyarchy, in which both elected Indian legislators and appointed British officials shared power. The act also expanded the central and provincial legislatures and widened the franchise considerably. Dyarchy set in motion certain real changes at the provincial level: a number of noncontroversial or "transferred" portfolios—such as agriculture, local government, health, education, and public works—were handed over to Indians, while more sensitive matters such as finance, taxation, and maintaining law and order were retained by the provincial British administrators.

The positive impact of reform was seriously undermined in 1919 by the Rowlatt Acts, named after the recommendations made the previous year to the Imperial Legislative Council by the Rowlatt Commission, which had been appointed to investigate "seditious conspiracy." The Rowlatt Acts, also known as the Black Acts, vested the viceroy's government with extraordinary powers to quell sedition by silencing the press, detaining political activists without trial, and arresting any suspected individuals without a warrant. No sooner had the acts come into force in March 1919—despite opposition by Indian members on the Imperial Legislative Council—than a nationwide cessation of work (hartal) was called by Mohandas Karamchand Gandhi (1869-1948). Others took up his call, marking the beginning of widespread—although not nationwide—popular discontent. The agitation unleashed by the acts culminated on April 13, 1919, in Amritsar, Punjab. The British military commander, Brigadier Reginald E.H. Dyer, ordered his soldiers to fire at point-blank range into an unarmed and unsuspecting crowd of some 10,000 men, women, and children. They had assembled at Jallianwala Bagh, a walled garden, to celebrate a Hindu festival without prior knowledge of the imposition of martial law. A total of 1,650 rounds were fired, killing 379 persons and wounding 1,137 in the episode, which dispelled wartime hopes and goodwill in a frenzy of postwar reaction.

GANDHIAN ERA

That India opted for an entirely original path to solving this crisis and obtaining swaraj (independence) was due largely to Gandhi, commonly known as "Mahatma" (or Great Soul) or, as he himself preferred, "Gandhiji" (an honorific term for Gandhi). A native of Gujarat who had been educated in Britain, he was an obscure and unsuccessful provincial lawyer. Gandhi had accepted an invitation in 1893 to represent indentured Indian laborers in South Africa, where he stayed on for more than twenty years, emerging ultimately as the voice and conscience of thousands who had been subjected to blatant racial discrimination. He returned to India in 1915, virtually a stranger to public life but "fired with a religious vision of a new India, whose swaraj... would [be] a moral reformation of a whole people which would either convert the British also or render their Raj impossible by Indian withdrawal of support for it and its modern values," according to historian Judith M. Brown.

Gandhi's ideas and strategies of nonviolent civil disobedience, first applied during his South Africa days, initially appeared impractical to many educated Indians. In Gandhi's own words, "Civil disobedience is civil breach of unmoral statutory enactments," but as he viewed it, it had to be carried out nonviolently by withdrawing cooperation with the corrupt state. Observers realized Gandhi's political potential when he used the satyagraha during the anti-Rowlatt Acts protests in Punjab. In 1920, under Gandhi's leadership, the Congress was reorganized and given a new constitution, whose goal was swaraj. Membership in the party was opened to anyone prepared to pay a token fee, and a hierarchy of committees—from district, to province, to all-India—was established and made responsible for discipline and control over a hitherto amorphous and diffuse movement. During his first nationwide satyagraha, Gandhi urged the people to boycott British education institutions, law courts, and products (in favor of swadeshi); to resign from government employment; to refuse to pay taxes; and to forsake British titles and honors. The party was transformed from an elite organization to one of mass national appeal.

Although Gandhi's first nationwide satyagraha was too late to influence the framing of the new Government of India Act of 1919, the magnitude of disorder resulting from the movement was unparalleled and presented a new challenge to foreign rule. Gandhi was forced to call off the campaign in 1922 because of atrocities committed against police. However, the abortive campaign marked a milestone in India's political development. For his efforts, Gandhi was imprisoned until 1924. On his release from prison, he set up an ashram (a rural commune), established a newspaper, and inaugurated a series of reforms aimed at the socially disadvantaged within Hindu society, the rural poor, and the Untouchables. His popularity soared in Indian politics as he reached the hearts and minds of ordinary people, winning support for his causes as no one else had ever done before. By his personal and eclectic piety, his asceticism, his vegetarianism, his espousal of Hindu-Muslim unity, and his firm belief in ahimsa, Gandhi appealed to the loftier Hindu ideals. For Gandhi, moral regeneration, social progress, and national freedom were inseparable.

Emerging leaders within the Congress—Jawaharlal Nehru, Vallabhbhai Patel, Rajendra Prasad, C. Rajagopalachari, Maulana Abdul Kalam Azad, Subhas Chandra Bose, and Jayaprakash (J.P.) Narayan—accepted Gandhi's leadership in articulating nationalist aspirations but disagreed on strategies for wresting more concessions from the British. The Indian political spectrum was further broadened in the mid-1920s by the emergence of both moderate and militant parties, such as the Swaraj Party (sometimes referred to as the Swarajist Party), the Mahasabha Party (literally, great council; an orthodox Hindu communal party), the Unionist Party, the Communist Party of

India, and the Socialist Independence for India League. Regional political organizations also continued to represent the interests of non-Brahmans in Madras, Mahars in Maharashtra, and Sikhs in Punjab.

The Congress, however, kept itself aloof from competing in elections. As voices inside and outside the Congress became more strident, the British appointed a commission in 1927, under Sir John Simon, to recommend further measures in the constitutional devolution of power. The British failure to appoint an Indian member to the commission outraged the Congress and others, and, as a result, they boycotted it throughout India, carrying placards inscribed "Simon, Go Back." In 1929 the Congress responded by drafting its own constitution under the guidance of Motilal Nehru (Jawaharlal's father) demanding full independence (purna swaraj) by 1930; the Congress went so far as to observe January 26, 1930, as the first anniversary of the first year of independence.

Gandhi reemerged from his long seclusion by undertaking his most inspired campaign, a march of about 400 kilometers from his commune in Ahmadabad to Dandi, on the coast of Gujarat between March 12 and April 6, 1930. At Dandi, in protest against extortionate British taxes on salt, he and thousands of followers illegally but symbolically made their own salt from sea water. Their defiance reflected India's determination to be free, despite the imprisonment of thousands of protesters. For the next five years, the Congress and government were locked in conflict and negotiations until what became the Government of India Act of 1935 could be hammered out. But by then, the rift between the Congress and the Muslim League had become unbridgeable as each pointed the finger at the other acrimoniously. The Muslim League disputed the claim by the Congress to represent all people of India, while the Congress disputed the Muslim League's claim to voice the aspirations of all Muslims.

The 1935 act, the voluminous and final constitutional effort at governing British India, articulated three major goals: establishing a loose federal structure, achieving provincial autonomy, and safeguarding minority interests through separate electorates. The federal provisions, intended to unite princely states and British India at the center, were not implemented because of ambiguities in safeguarding the existing privileges of princes. In February 1937, however, provincial autonomy became a reality when elections were held; the Congress emerged as the dominant party with a clear majority in five provinces and held an upper hand in two, while the Muslim League performed poorly.

INDEPENDENT INDIA

The Congress neither acknowledged the Muslim League's performance, albeit poor, in the elections nor deigned to form a coalition government with the League, a situation that led to the collapse of negotiations and mutual trust between the leaders. Mohammad Ali Jinnah, a Western-educated Muslim lawyer, took over the presidency of the moribund Muslim League and galvanized it into a national force under the battle cry of "Islam in danger." Jinnah doubted the motives of Gandhi and Nehru and accused them of practicing Hindu chauvinism. He relentlessly attacked the Congress-led ministries, accusing them of casteism, corruption, and nepotism. Skillfully, he succeeded in unifying various regional Islamic organizations and factions in Punjab and Bengal under the umbrella of the Muslim League.

Electoral gains by the Congress in 1937 were rendered ephemeral as its leaders ordered provincial ministries to resign in November 1939, when the viceroy (Victor Alexander John Hope, Marquis of Linlithgow—1936-43) declared India's entrance into World War II without consulting Indian leaders. Jinnah and the Muslim League welcomed the Congress withdrawal from government as a timely opportunity and observed a day of thanksgiving on December 22, 1939. Jinnah persuaded the participants at the annual Muslim League session in Lahore in 1940 to adopt what later came to be known as the Pakistan Resolution, demanding the division of India into two separate sovereign states, one Muslim, the other Hindu. Although the idea of Pakistan had been introduced as early as 1930 at Allahabad, very few had responded to it. However, the volatile political climate, the personal hostilities between the leaders, and the opportunism of Jinnah transformed the idea of Pakistan into a popular demand.

Between 1940 and 1942, the Congress launched two abortive agitations against the British, and 60,000 Congress members were arrested, including Gandhi and Nehru. Unlike the uncooperative and belligerent Congress, the Muslim League supported the British during World War II. Belated but perhaps sincere British attempts to accommodate the demands of the two rival parties, while preserving the unitary state in India, seemed unacceptable to both as they alternately rejected whatever proposal was put forward during the war years. As a result, a three-way impasse settled in: the Congress and the Muslim League doubted British motives in handing over power to Indians, while the British struggled to retain some hold on India while offering to give greater autonomy.

The Congress wasted precious time denouncing the British rather than allaying Muslim fears during the highly charged election campaign of 1946. Even the more mature Congress leaders, especially Gandhi and Nehru, failed to see how genuinely afraid the Muslims were and how exhausted and weak the British had become in the aftermath of the war. When it appeared that the Congress had no desire to share power with the Muslim League at the center, Jinnah declared August 16, 1946, Direct Action Day, which brought communal rioting and massacre in many places in the north. Partition seemed preferable to civil war. On June 3, 1947, Viscount Louis Mountbatten, the viceroy (1947) and governor-general (1947-48), announced plans for partition of the British Indian Empire into the nations of India and Pakistan, which itself was divided into east and west wings on either side of India. At midnight, on August 15, 1947, India strode to freedom amidst ecstatic shouting of "Jai Hind" (roughly, Long Live India), when Nehru delivered a memorable and moving speech on India's "tryst with destiny."

NATIONAL INTEGRATION

The euphoria of independence was short-lived as partition brought disastrous consequences for India in the wake of communal conflict. Partition unleashed untold misery and loss of lives and property as millions of Hindu and Muslim refugees fled either Pakistan or India. Both nations were also caught up in a number of conflicts involving the allocation of assets, demarcation of boundaries, equitable sharing of water resources, and control over Kashmir. At the same time, Indian leaders were faced with the stupendous task of national integration and economic development.

When the British relinquished their claims to paramountcy, the 562 independent princely states were given the option to join either of the two nations. A few princely states readily joined Pakistan, but the rest—except Hyderabad (the largest of the princely states with 132,000 square kilometers and a population of more than 14 million), Jammu and Kashmir (with 3 million inhabitants), and Junagadh (with a population of 545,000)—merged with India. India successfully annexed Hyderabad and Junagadh after "police actions" and promises of privileges to the rulers. The Hindu maharajah of predominantly Muslim Jammu and Kashmir remained uncommitted until armed tribesmen and regular troops from Pakistan infiltrated his domain, inducing him to sign the Instrument of Accession to India on October 27, 1947. Pakistan refused to accept the legality of the accession, and, as a result, war broke out. Kashmir remains a source of friction between the neighbors. The assassination of Mahatma Gandhi on January 30, 1948, in New Delhi, by a Hindu extremist opposed to Gandhi's openness to Muslims ended the tenuous celebration of independence and deepened the hatred and mutual suspicion in Hindu-Muslim relations.

Linguistic regionalism eventually reached a crisis stage and undermined the Congress' attempts at nation building. Whereas in the early 1920s, the Congress had deemed that the use of regional vernaculars in education and administration would facilitate the governance of the country, partition made the leaders, especially Nehru, realize how quickly such provincial or subnational interests would dismantle India's fragile unity. However, in the face of widespread agitation for linguistic separation of states, beginning with the Telangana Movement in 1953, in 1956 Nehru reluctantly accepted the recommendations of the States Reorganisation Commission, and the number of states grew by reorganization along linguistic lines. The states became the loci for democratization of political processes at district levels, for expression of regional culture and popular demands against a national culture and unity, for economic development at strategic localities in the rural areas, and for proliferation of opposition parties that ended the possibility of a pan-Indian two-party system.

NEHRU'S LEGACY

Jawaharlal Nehru (1889-1964), India's first prime minister, was the chief architect of domestic and foreign policies between 1947 and 1964. Born into a wealthy Kashmiri Brahman family and educated at Oxford, Nehru embodied a synthesis of ideals: politically an ardent nationalist, ideologically a pragmatic socialist, and secular in religious outlook, Nehru possessed a rare combination of intellect, breadth of vision, and personal charisma that attracted support throughout India. Nehru's appreciation for parliamentary democracy coupled with concerns for the poor and underprivileged enabled him to formulate policies that often reflected his socialist leanings. Both as prime minister and as Congress president, Nehru pushed through the Indian Parliament, dominated by members of his own party, a series of legal reforms intended to emancipate Hindu women and bring equality. These reforms included raising the minimum marriageable age from twelve to fifteen, empowering women to divorce their husbands and inherit property, and declaring illegal the ruinous dowry system.

The threat of escalating violence and the potential for "red revolution" across the country seemed daunting in the face of the country's growing population, unemployment, and economic inequality. Nehru induced Parliament to pass a number of laws abolishing absentee landlordism and conferring titles to land on the actual cultivators who could document their right to occupancy. Under his direction, the central Planning Commission allocated resources to heavy industries, such as steel plants and hydroelectric projects, and to revitalizing cottage industries. Whether producing sophisticated defense matériel or manufacturing everyday consumer goods, industrial complexes emerged across the country, accompanied by the expansion of scientific research and teaching at universities, institutes of technology, and research centers.

2

Economic History of India

Economic history of India, in the sense of the meaning of the term economic in its current sense, is at least 5000 years old.

INDUS VALLEY CIVILIZATION

The Indus Valley civilization, the first known permanent and predominantly urban settlement that flourished between 2800 BC to 1800 BC boasted of an advanced and thriving economic system. Its citizens practiced agriculture, domesticated animals, made sharp tools and weapons from copper, bronze and tin and traded with other cities. Evidence of well laid streets, layouts, drainage system and water supply in the valley's major cities, Harappa, Mohenjo-daro and Rakhigarhi reveals their knowledge of urban planning.

ANCIENT AND MEDIEVAL CHARACTERISTICS

Though ancient India had a significant urban population, much of India's population resided in villages, whose economy was largely isolated and self-sustaining. Agriculture was the predominant occupation of the populace and satisfied a village's food requirements besides providing raw materials for hand based industries like textile, food processing and crafts. Besides farmers, other classes of people were barbers, carpenters, doctors (Ayurvedic practitioners), goldsmiths, weavers, etc.

Religion

Religion, especially Hinduism, played an influential role in shaping economic activities. The system of castes and sub-castes, despite its social fallbacks, functioned much like medieval European guilds, ensuring division of labour and provided for training of apprentices. The caste system restricted people from changing one's occupation and aspiring to an upper caste's lifestyle. Thus, a barber could not become a goldsmith and even a highly skilled carpenter could not aspire to the lifestyle or privileges enjoyed by a Kshatriya (person of a warrior class). This barrier to mobility on labour restricted economic prosperity to a few castes.

Pilgrimage towns like Allahabad, Benares, Nasik, Puri, etc., mostly centred around rivers, developed into centres of trade and commerce. Religious functions, festivals and the practice of taking a pilgrimage resulted in a flourishing pilgrimage economy.

Family Business

In the joint family system, members of a family pooled their resources to maintain the family and invest in business ventures. The system ensured younger members were trained and employed in the family business and the older and disabled persons would be supported by the family. The system, by preventing the agricultural land from being split ensured higher yield because of the benefits of scale. The system curbed members from taking initiative because of the support system and family or work discords intertwined, leading to sub-division and fragmentation of land which lead to lower yield and productivity.

Organizational Entities

Along with the family-run business and individually owned business enterprises, ancient India possessed a number of other forms of engaging in business or collective activity, including the gana, pani, puga, vrata, sangha, nigama and sreni. Nigama, pani and sreni refer most often to economic organizations of merchants, craftspeople and artisans, and perhaps even para-military entities. In particular, the sreni was a complex organizational entity that shares many similarities with modern corporations, which were being used in India from around the 8th century BC until around the 10th century AD. The use of such entities in ancient India was widespread including virtually every kind of business, political and municipal activity.

The sreni was a separate legal entity which had the ability to hold property separately from its owners, construct its own rules for governing the behavior of its members, and for it to contract, sue and be sued in its own name. Some ancient sources have rules for lawsuits between two or more sreni and some sources make reference to a government official (Bhandagarika) who worked as an arbitrator for disputes amongst sreni from at least the 6th century BC onwards.

There were between 18 to 150 sreni at various times in ancient India covering both trading and craft activities. This level of specialization of occupations is indicative of a developed economy in which the sreni played a critical role. Some sreni could have over 1000 members as there were apparently no upper limits on the number of members.

The sreni had a considerable degree of centralized management. The headman of the sreni represented the interests of the sreni in the king's court and in many official business matters. The headman could also bind the sreni in contracts, set the conditions of work within the sreni, often received a higher salary, and was the administrative authority within the sreni. The headman was often selected via an election by the members of the sreni, who could also be removed from power by the general assembly. The headman often ran the enterprise with two to five executive officers, who were also elected by the assembly.

Coinage

Punch marked Silver Ingots, in circulation around 5th century BC and the first metallic coins were minted around 6th century BC by the Mahajanapadas of the Gangetic plains were the earliest traces of coinage in India. While India's many kingdoms and rulers issued coins, barter was still widely prevalent. Villages paid a portion of their agricultural produce as revenue while its craftsmen received a stipend out of the crops at harvest time for their services. Each village, as an economic unit was mostly self-sufficient.

MAURYA EMPIRE

During the Maurya Empire (c. 321-185 BC), there were a number of important changes and developments to the Indian economy. It was the first time most of India was unified under one ruler. With an empire in place, the trade routes throughout India became more secure thereby reducing the risk associated with the transportation of goods. The empire spent considerable resources building roads and maintaining them throughout India. The improved infrastructure combined with increased security, greater uniformity in measurements, and increasing usage of coins as currency enhanced trade. During this time, the Arthasastra ("science of state") was written by the Maurya prime minister and Takshashila University professor Chanakya. The Arthasastra is one of the most important ancient texts on economics, politics and administration. It was a treatise on how to maintain and expand power, obtain material gain, and administer an empire. It covers both theory and implementation and contains many clear and detailed rules regarding the governing of an empire.

The economic situation in the Maurya Empire is comparable to the Roman Empire several centuries later, which both had extensive trade connections and both had organizations similar to corporations. While Rome had organizational entities which were largely used for public state-driven projects, Maurya India had numerous private commercial entities which existed purely for private commerce. This was due to the Mauryas having to contend with pre-existing sreni hence they were more concerned about keeping the support of these pre-existing private commercial entities, while the Romans did not have such pre-existing entities to contend with hence they were able to prevent such entities from developing.

Exports

Surplus of Indian manufactures, like the muslin of Dacca, calicos of Bengal, shawls of Kashmir, other textiles and handicrafts, agricultural products like pepper, cinnamon, opium and indigo were exported to Europe, Middle East and South East Asia in return for gold and silver. Superstitions about sea faring may have existed among some Hindu groups, which meant that part of India's foreign trade may have been carried out by foreigners.

GDP Estimates

According to economic historian Angus Maddison in his book The World Economy: A Millennial Perspective, India had the world's largest economy in the 1st century and 11th century, with a 32.9% share of world GDP in the 1st century and 28.9% in 1000 CE. However, it must be noted that Maddison in his work was comparing geographic regions before 1500 and the comparisons between India and China were between geographic locations that included those countries. In 1700, when most of India was ruled by the Mughal Empire, it had a 24.4% share of world GDP, the largest at the time, which fell drastically to 3.8% by 1952. Another estimate of India's pre-colonial economy puts the revenue of Akbar's Mughal empire in 1600 at £17.5 million, in contrast to the entire treasury of Great Britain in 1800, which totalled £16 million.

BRITISH RULE

The British colonial rule created an institutional environment that did stabilize the law and order situation to a large extent. The British stifled the trade with rest of the world. They concentrated on exploiting the resources of India to their advantage. They created a well developed system of railways,telegraphs and a modern legal system. The infrastructure the British created was mainly geared towards the exploitation of resources of India. The British focus on their own interests created a situation in which India could not benefit from major changes in the world economy-industrialisation, growth in trade and production, and new thinking on economic policies followed by states. By the end of the colonial rule India inherited an economy that was one of the poorest in the world and totally stagnant, with industrial development stalled, agriculture unable to feed a rapidly accelerating population, who were subject to frequent famines, had one of the world's lowest life expectancy, suffered from pervasive malnutrition and was largely illiterate. The British rule ruined India economically.

Military History of India

India has a long military history dating back several millennia. The first reference of armies is found in the Vedas. The epics Ramayana and Mahabaratha contains information on standing armies and warfare techniques like the Chakravyuha used in the Kurukshetra War. The epics contains information on the usage of chariots, war elephants and even flying machines used in wars. There were many dynasties in India like the Magadha empire, Shishunaga dynasty, Nanda dynasty, Maurya Dynasty, Satavahana dynasty, Kushan empire, Gupta dynasty, Harsha's empire, Pandiyan and Chola empire, Chera dynasty, Pratiharas, Palas, Rashtrakutas, Rajputs, Vijayanagar empire, Chalukyas and Pallavas, Mughal Empire etc.

The Army of India were raised under British Raj in the 19th century and fought in both the World Wars. During World War II, the Army of India played a crucial role in checking the advance of Imperial Japan and also fought several battles against Axis forces in northern Africa and Italy.

Indian troops made up a substantial part of the British forces fighting the Japanese in Asia during World War II. Many of the troops that surrendered at Singapore to Japanese General Tomoyuki Yamashita, known as the "Tiger of the Orient" on February 15, 1942, were Indians. Some of these, approached as prisoners, chose to take up arms against the British with Subhash Chandra Bose, the leader of the Indian National Army fighting for Indian independence. Bose received training military training from Nazi Germany and substantial support from Imperial Japan.

Indian troops fighting for the British Army made a significant impact in the CBI (China, Burma, India) theater. They were among the troops pushed out of Burma in 1942 and made up a large portion of the troops who fought their way back into Burma (1943-45).

In 1944, the Imperial Japanese Army launched an invasion from Burma into India. On the one hand, the Japanese goal was to establish a presence in India with thoughts that the populace would rise up and help kick the British out. The other thought, based on Allied attacks from India into Burma, was to deny the British a base from which to launch further attacks. The Japanese invasion was stopped in bloody fighting and, some might say, the IJA used up much of its energy in the effort leading to its increased inability to stop the next Allied push into Burma.

The Indian armed forces succeeded the Military of British India following India's independence in 1947. The Indian armed forces fought in all three wars against Pakistan and a war with the People's Republic of China. India also fought in the Kargil War with Pakistan in 1999, the highest altitude mountain warfare in history. The Indian Armed Forces have participated in several United Nations peacekeeping operations and are presently the second largest contributor of troops to the peacekeeping force.

INDUS VALLEY CIVILISATION

The amazing uniformity of measurement systems across a number of sites suggests that the Indus Valley Civilisation was a single state. However, it seems that the large cities were controlled by small groups of merchants, landowners and priests. Therefore, no standing armies were involved.

The artifacts and texts from contemporaneous Egypt and Mesopotamia clearly depict battles. But the excavations at Harappan sites have not revealed a single artifact that depicts military, battles, prisoners or a human killing another human. Very few bronze weapons have been found. Fortified cities have been excavated which seems to indicate some defensive capability. Excavations do not indicate a well developed martial culture, which may be a reason for the eventual decline of the civilisation.

EARLY INDO-ARYANS

The Rigvedic tribes of Indo-Aryans were led by their tribal chieftain (raja) and engaged in wars with each other as well as other tribes. They used bronze weapons and had horse-drawn spoke-wheeled chariots described prominently in the Rigveda. The main share from the booty obtained during the cattle raids and battles went to the chief of the tribe. The warriors belonged to the Kshatriya varna. Earlier, most archaeologists believed that Aryan armies invaded peaceful Harappan cities and destroyed them. However, since none of the excavations indicate battle damage to the cities, the arrival of the Aryans is now more often dated to Late Harappan (Cemetery H) times. The earliest allusions to a specific battle are those to the Battle of the Ten Kings in Mandala 7 of the Rigveda.

THE MAHAJANAPADAS

During the post-Rigvedic (Iron Age) Vedic period (ca. 1100-500 BC), the Vedas and other associated texts contain references to warfare. The world's first military application of war elephants dates from around 1100 BC in ancient India and is mentioned in several Vedic Sanskrit hymns. The military art and science of Ancient India has been described in Dhanurveda.

The two great epics of India, the Ramayana and the Mahabharata, are centered around conflicts between the emerging Mahajanapadas and refer to military formations, theories of warfare and esoteric weaponry. Valmiki's Ramayana describes Ayodhya's military as defensive rather than aggressive. The city, it says, was strongly fortified and was surrounded by a deep moat. Ramayana describes Ayodhya in following words: "The city abounded in warriors undefeated in battle, fearless and skilled in the use of arms, resembling lions guarding their mountain caves". Mahabharata describes various military techniques like Chakravyuha used in the Kurukshetra War.

THE MAGADHA EMPIRE

Shishunaga Dynasty

King Bimbisara was an expansionist and conquered Anga in what is now West Bengal. He strengthened the military of Magadh's capital, Rajagriha. Ajatashatru built a new fort at Pataliputra, Magadh's new capital to launch an attack on Licchavis, across the Ganga River. Jain texts tell that he used two new weapons-a catapult and a covered chariot with swinging mace that has been compared to modern tanks.

Nanda Dynasty

The powerful Mahapadma Nanda defeated Ikshvakus, Panchalas, Kasis, Harhayas, Kalingas, Asmakas, Kurus, Maithilas, Surasenas and Vitihotras and assumed the title "the destroyer of the kshathriyas". At the time of Dhana Nanda, the Nandas had an army consisting of 80,000 cavalry, 200,000 infantry, 8,000 armed chariots, and 6,000 war elephants.Many historians hold the view that Alexander confined himself to the plains of Punjab for fear of the mighty Nandas.

Maurya Dynasty

According to Megasthenes, Chandragupta Maurya built an army consisting of 30,000 cavalry, 9,000 war elephants, and 600,000 infantry. Some modern historians feel that this is an exaggeration on the part of Megasthenes, who was serving as an ambassador from the Seleucid Empire. Chandragupta conquered all of northern India, establishing an empire from the Arabian Sea to the Bay of Bengal. He then conquered the regions to the east of the Indus river after defeating the Macedonians and Seleucus Nicator, and then moved southwards, taking over much of what is now Central India. The entire army was administrated by six chairs, one for each of the four arms of the army (infantry, cavalry, elephants, and chariots), one chair for the navy, and one for logistics and supply.

Infantry at this time was most commonly armed with a longbow made of bamboo, and a double-handed broadsword. Other foot soldiers could be armed with a large tower shield and a spear or javelins. The cavalry is not noted especially, but Megasthenese does mention that they were armed with a few spears, of which we can assume most were meant for hurling. Elephants were mounted, either bareback or with a howdah, with archers or javelineers, and with a mahout around the animal's neck. Chariots by this time were in definite decline, but still managed to stay an arm of the army by sheer virtue of their prestige.

In 185 BC, the last Mauryan king was assassinated by Pushyamitra Shunga, the Commander-in-Chief of the Mauryan armed forces.

EARLY MIDDLE KINGDOMS

Satavahana Dynasty

Simuka, the founder of the Satavahana dynasty, conquered Maharashtra, Malwa and part of Madhya Pradesh. His successor and brother Kanha (or Krishna) further extended his kingdom to the west and the south. He was succeeded by Satakarni I, who defeated the Sunga dynasty of North India. Gautamiputra Satakarni defeated the Western Kshatrapas ruler Nahapana. His brother Vashishtiputra Satakarni, was defeated by his Western Kshatrapa father-in-law in a battle.

Kushan Empire

Vima Takto, using the name "Soter Megas" (Great Saviour), conquered Gandhara and northern India in 68 AD. The Kushan warriors were assimilated into Indian society as Kshatriyas. Following Yuezhi's style, most of the Kushan nobles fought from horse back, supported by the heavier parts of the army, cataphracts. The coins of Kujula, Vima Takto, Vima Kadphises and Kanishka show the king usually unarmored, lightly armored than the later Kushan kings.

In many coins Kanishka appears to have a bow, but this interpretation is debatable. Some Buddhist texts indicate the use of Indian influences like elephants leading the attacks and the use of chariots. The elephants first appeared on the coins of Vima Kadphises and probably went on to become the mount of the kings.

The elephants are depicted with towers and a covering. It is not clear whether these were armor or just padding. Buddhist texts mention that the infantry were used to support these elephants. The historian Nikonorov suggests that the elephants used were provided by the Satraps. However, the main strength of the Kushan army came from its unarmored horses. The use of heavy cavalry increased later. Apart from the original Kushans and Indians, the Greeks, various mountain tribes, Sacas from northern India and Iranian mercenaries were also added to Kushan army. The Kidarites and Sassanids predominantly used cavalry. The Satraps provided them with additional India forces including elephants.

Gupta Dynasty

Siva-Dhanur-veda, considered a contemporary military classic gives information about the military system of the Guptas. They utilized war elephants, supplemented by additional armor. The use of horses, if any, was very limited. The use of chariots had heavily declined by the time of the Guptas, as they had not proved very useful against the Ancient Macedonians, Scythians, and other invaders. Guptas utilised heavy cavalry clad in mail armor and equipped with maces and lances, who would have used shock action to break the enemy line. They also heavily relied on infantry archers, and the bow was one of the dominant weapons of their army. Their longbow was composed of metal, or more typically bamboo, and fired a long bamboo cane arrow with a metal head. Iron shafts were used against armored elephants, and fire arrows were also part of the bowmen's arsenal. Archers were frequently protected by infantry equipped with shields, javelins, and longswords. Guptas also maintained a navy, allowing them to control regional waters.

Samudragupta seized the kingdoms of Shichchhatra and Padmavati early in his reign. Later, he took the Kingdom of Kota and attacked the tribes in Malvas, the Yaudheyas, the Arjunayanas, the Maduras and the Abhiras. By his death in 380, he had conquered over twenty kingdoms. Chandragupta II defeated the Saka Western Kshatrapas of Malwa, Gujarat and Saurashtra in a campaign lasting till 409. He had defeated his main opponent Rudrasimha III by 395. He also crushed the Bengal (Vanga) chiefdoms. Skandagupta defeated Pushyamitra. He repulsed the attack of Hephthalites or "White Huns", c. 455, but the expense of the wars drained the empire's resources and contributed to its decline.

LATE MIDDLE KINGDOMS

Harsha's Empire

Emperor Harshavardhana (606-648) ruled northern India for over forty years. His father, a king of Thanesar had gained prominence by successful wars against the Huns. Harsha had plans to conquer the whole of India, and carried on wars for thirty years with considerable success. By 612 he had built up a vast army with which he conquered nearly all North India up to the Narmada river. But, in 620 Harsha lost to Pulakesin II, when he attempted to invade Deccan.

The Chalukyas and Pallavas

In South India, the Chalukyas and the Pallavas gained prominence. Chalukya king Pulakesi II's expansionism started with minor campaign against the Alupas, Gangas and others. He defeated the Pallava king Mahendravarman, and also conquered the Cheras and the Pandyas. His most successful military campaign was his defeat of Harshavardhana (c. 615). However, the war depleted the treasury, so Pulakesi II had to stop his expansionist campaigns.

The Pallava king Narasimhavarman had vowed to avenge Mahendravarman's defeat against Pulakesi II. He invaded Vatapi with an army headed by his general Paranjothi. He successfully defeated Chalukyas, killing Pulakesi II in 642. The clashes between the Chalukyas and the Pallavas continued. The Chalukya king Vikramaditya II won a comprehensive victory against the Pallavas in 740. The Chalukya Empire was overthrown in 750 by the Rashtrakutas. During the 970s, Tailapa II, a scion the Chalukya dynasty, overthrew the Rashtrakutas and recovered most of the Chalukya empire, except for Gujarat. The Chalukyas of this period are known as the Kalyani Chalukyas, as Kalyani was their capital. The Kalyani Chalukyas clashed with the Cholas intermittently. Someshvara I, also known as Ahavamalla, defeated the Chola king Rajadhiraja Chola in 1052.

The Chola Empire

The Cholas were the first rulers in the Indian subcontinent to maintain a fleet and use it to expand their dominion overseas. The Chola king Vijayalaya defeated the Pallavas and captured Thanjavur. In the early 10th century the Chola king Parantaka I defeated the Pandyan king Rajasimha and also invaded Ceylon (Sri Lanka). His son, Rajaditya, was defeated and killed by the Rashtrakuta ruler Krishna III (c.949). It is known through inscriptions that at least from Uttama Chola's time, Chola warriors were provided with waist coats of armor. Hence, one regiment was called Niyayam-Uttama-Chola-tterindaandalakattalar. Paluvettaraiyar Maravan Kandanar is noted as an important general during Uttama Chola reign. He also served under Sundara Chola.

Rajaraja Chola began his military career with the conquest of the Cheras. He defeated the Chera King Bhaskara Ravivarman, destroying his fleet at the port of Kandalur. He also seized Pandya Amara Bhujanga and captured the port of Vilinam, Kerala and a part of Ceylon. In the 14th year of his reign (998-999) he conquered Gangas of Mysore, Nolambas (Bellary and Eastern Mysore), Tadigaipadi (the district of Mysore), Vengi (southern part of Northern Circars), Coorg (Kudamalainadu) and the Pandyas. Next, he conquered the Chalukyas of the Deccan. During the next three years, he subdued Quilon and the northern kingdom of Kalinga with the help of his son Rajendra Chola I.

Rajendra Chola later completed the conquest of Sri Lanka, crossed the Ganges and marched across Kalinga to Bengal, and sent out a great naval expedition that occupied parts of Burma (Myanmar), Java, Malaya, and Sumatra in South East Asia. Cholas were later defeated by the Hoysalas from the west and Pandyas from the south.

The Pratiharas, Palas and Rashtrakutas

In middle of 9th century, the Palas under Devapala attacked Pratiharas. Led by Bhoj, the Pratiharas and their allies defeated Pala king Narayanpala. The Pratiharas' cavalry was described as the finest in 851 by an Arab. There were many battles between Pratiharas under Bhoj and Rashtrakutas under Krishna II with mixed results. When Rashtrakuta king Indra III attacked Kanauj, Mahipala (Bhoj's successor) fled but returned after the left. During the rule of Mahipala, in 915, Al Mas'udi from Baghdad wrote that the Pratiharas were at war with the Muslims in the west and the Rashtrakutas in the south. He wrote that Pratiharas had four armies of about 800,000 men each.

The Rajputs

After Babur's victory over Ibrahim Lodi at the First Battle of Panipat, the Mewar ruler Rana Sanga led a combined Rajput army of 20000, with an intent to defeat Babur and capture Delhi. The Mughals had superior artillery, which prevailed against the Rajput cavalry. A Tomar general betrayed Rana Sanga, resulting in his defeat by Babur at the Battle of Khanua (March 16, 1527). During the reign of Rana Udai Singh II (son of Rana Sanga), Babur's Grandson Akbar conquerod Chittor, the capital of Mewar.

The Battle of Haldighati (June 21, 1576) between Rana Pratap Singh (Rana Udai Singh II's son) and Akbar is one of the most famous battles in the Indian history. The Mughal army of 80,000 was headed by a Rajput, Raja Man Singh and Akbar's son Salim (aka Jahangir). The Rajput army's strength was 20,000. The extremely fierce battle lasted for about four hours.

After most of his soldiers were either killed or captured, Rana Pratap escaped. His legendary horse Chetak was killed in the battle. Rana Pratap was saved by his estranged brother Sakta Singh. Later, Rana Pratap organized a small army of Bhil tribals funded by a businessman called Bhamashah and started a guerrilla war against Akbar. He conquered large parts of Mewar, but was unsuccessful in conquering the capital Chittor.

THE SULTANATE ERA

Delhi Sultanate

The Delhi Sultanate, under the Khilji dynasty, was successful in defeating a number of invasions from the Mongol Empire. Zafar Khan, the general of Alauddin Khilji, was successful against several such invasions. Zafar Khan defeated invading Mongols near Jalandhar in 1297 to secure Alauddin Khilji's throne. Later in 1299, a Mongol army of 200,000 soldiers entered India with the intention of conquest. Zafar Khan showed desperate valor in battle and defeated them, though he did not survive.

Samoothiris of Kozhikode

More famously known as the Zamorin, this small Kingdom welcomed the Portuguese in 1498 as traders and then with the assistance of its naval chief, Kunjali Marakkar, fought several naval wars with them in the 16th century.

Muzzafarid Dynasty

Sultan Muzaffar Shah I, the Governor of Gujarat established the Muzzafarid dynasty in 1391. It expanded rapidly and peaked under Sultan Mahmud I who lost the famous Battle of Diu to the Portuguese in 1509.

Vijayanagar Empire

In 1509, the Bahamani Sultan declared a jehad against Vijaynagar. His large coalition army was defeated by Krishnadevaraya, who also wounded the Sultan. In 1510, Krishnadevaraya launched a counteroffensive against the Sultan at Kovelaconda. In this battle, Yusuf Adil Shahi of Bijapur was killed. In 1512, Krishnadevaraya captured Raichur and Gulbarga after defeating Barid-i-Mamalik, the titular head of the Bahmani Sultanate, who escaped to Bidar. Later, Bidar also fell to Krishnadevaraya. However, he diplomatically restored the Bahmani Sultan to his throne, with an intention to create discord and suspicion in the Bahmani coalition.

In a battle from 1512 to 1514, Krishnadevaraya subjugated the Palaigar of Ummattur, who had rebelled against his brother. While this campaign was halfway, the Gajapati of Orissa attacked Vijayanagar and occupied two northeast provinces, Udayagiri and Kondavidu. In January 1513, Krishnadevaraya launched a campaign recover to Udaygiri. The campaign lasted till 1518, resulting in defeat of Gajapati. On January 26, 1565 the Islamic kingdoms of Ahmednagar, Berar, Bidar, Bijapur and Golconda came together to defeat the Vijayanagar decisively in the Battle of Talikota.

After the battle the remaining Vijaynagar fled with large treasury to re-establish their head quarters at Vellore Fort (in Tamil Nadu and Chandragiri (Present day Andhra Pradesh) near Tirupathi.It would be here where the British sought land grant to establish the English East India CompanyFort St. George in Madras.

Later its southern Telugu governors established their independence and emerging as Gingee Nayaks in Gingee

Fort,Tanjore Nayaks and the famous Nayaks of Madurai all in present day Tamil Nadu.

Effects of the Mongol Wars

Indians made steel weapons that were popular in the ancient world because of their quality and durability. These weapons were forged from wootz steel, which may have existed in India as early as 200 BCE.

The Maratha Empire

The Maratha Empire, also called the Maratha Confederacy, of India was founded by Chatrapati Shivaji in 1674, when he carved an independent Maratha zone around Pune, from the Bijapur Sultanate. Chatrapati Shivaji established an effective civil and military administration. He made it a state policy never to desecrate a mosque or seize women after military raids. He had many loyal Muslim admirers, who served in his army. He was also only the second king in Indian history to have his own active navy. After a lifetime of exploits and guerrilla warfare with the Mughal emperor Aurangzeb, Maharaja Shivaji died in 1680, leaving a Maratha kingdom of great but ill-defined extent. This was followed by a period of unstability which ended with the death of Aurangzeb.

Kanhoji Angre was the first Maratha naval chief under Chattrapati Shahu, Shivaji's grandson. He harassed Dutch, English and Portuguese commercial ships on the Western coast of India in the early 18th century. He remained undefeated until his death in 1729.

Although the descendants of Shivaji continued to rule, the office of the Peshwa, or the Prime Minister, had become the dispensers of Maratha power and patronage. The Peshwas were the effective rulers of the Maratha state and oversaw the period of greatest Maratha expansion, brought to an end by the Maratha's defeat by an Afghan army at the Third Battle of Panipat in 1761. The last Peshwa, Baji Rao II, was defeated by the British in the Third Anglo-Maratha War.

Major wars:

- First Anglo-Maratha War

- Second Anglo-Maratha War
- Third Anglo-Maratha War
- Fourth Anglo-Mysore War
- Third Anglo-Mysore War.

State of Travancore

Raja Marthanda Varma built this Kingdom after inheriting a small state of Venad in 1723. It became one of the most powerful Kingdoms in Southern India until it merged with India in 1956. Raja Varma also led the Battle of Colachel in 1741 which marks one of the first Asian victories over an European naval power with his army called the Nair Brigade.

Kingdom of Mysore

Hyder Ali was instructed by French military officers. He was one of the first Indian rulers to use rockets. He used iron rockets to defeat a top British unit in battle. His son, Tipu Sultan was also instructed by French military officers. Tipu participated in First Anglo-Maratha War of 1775-1779. He defeated the Brathwaite on the banks of the Coleroon in February 1782 in the Second Mysore War. After his father's death in 1782, he decided to check British advances by forming alliances with the Marathas and the Mughals. However, his plan wasn't successful. So, he turned to France. In 1789, he invaded the state of Travancore, a British protectorate. However, he didn't receive expected help from France (the French were embroiled in the French Revolution) and Mysore was defeated in what is now known as the Third Mysore War. Tipu Sultan died in the Fourth Mysore War. Although Horatio Nelson crushed Napoleon's ambitions of advancing to India at the Battle of the Nile, three armies-one from Bombay, and two British (one of which was commanded by Arthur Wellesley), marched into Mysore in 1799 and besieged the capital, Srirangapatnam. On May 4, 1799, the armies broke through the defending walls and Tipu died of a gunshot wound near the gates of his fortress.

Main wars:

- First Mysore War, 1766

- Second Mysore War
- Third Mysore War, 1789-1792
- Fourth Mysore War, 1799.

Punjab

Maharaja Ranjit Singh, also called "Sher-e-Punjab" ("The Lion of the Punjab") (1780-1839) was a Sikh ruler of the sovereign country of Punjab and the Sikh Empire. His Samadhi is located in Lahore, Pakistan. Ranjit Singh was a Sikh born in 1780 in Gujranwala in modern day Pakistan, into the Sansi-Sandhawalia family. At the time much of Punjab was ruled by the Sikhs, who had divided the territory among factions known as misls. Ranjit Singh's father Maha Singh was the commander of the Sukerchakia misl and controlled a territory in west Punjab based around his headquarters at Gujranwala. Ranjit Singh succeeded his father at the young age of 12. After several campaigns, his rivals accepted him as their leader, and he united the Sikh factions into one state and he took the title of Maharaja on April 12, 1801 (to coincide with Baisakhi day), with Lahore having served as his capital from 1799. In 1802 he took the holy city of Amritsar.

Maharaja Ranjit Singh also hired European mercenaries to train his troops, creating a powerful military force whose presence delayed the eventual British colonization of Punjab. He also modernized his army, hiring European mercenaries to create the first modern Indian Army. The effect was to create a powerful and heavily armed state; at this point, Punjab was the only state not controlled by the British. He brought law and order, yet was reluctant to use the death penalty. He stopped Indian non-secular style practises by treating Hindus and Muslims equally. He banned the discriminatory "jizya" tax on Hindus and Sikhs.

Maharaja Ranjit Singh died in 1839 and the state went to his eldest son Kharak Singh.

The Kingdom, that he had worked so hard to build, began to crumble due to poor governance and political mismanagement by his heirs. His successors died through accidents and murder, while the nobility and army struggled for power till the end of the Second Anglo-Sikh War(1848-49), when it was annexed by the British from his youngest son Duleep Singh. However, after the First Anglo-Sikh War(1845-46), Punjab effectively ceased to be an independent state and in 1849 was annexed by the British and all major decisions where made by the British Empire.

- Maharaja Ranjit Singh (b.1780, Coronated April 12, 1801, d.1839)
- Kharak Singh (b.1801, d.1840), Eldest son of Ranjit Singh.
- Nau Nihal Singh (b.1821, d.1840), Grandson of Ranjit Singh.
- Sher Singh (b.1807, d.1843), Son of Ranjit Singh.
- Duleep Singh (b.1838, Coronated 1843, d.1893), Youngest son of Ranjit Singh.

The British Empire annexed Punjab in c.1845-49 AD; after two Anglo Sikh Wars.

The Anglo-Sikhs Wars (1846-1849)

- The First Anglo-Sikh War (1845-1846)
- The Second Anglo-Sikh War (1848-1849).

COMPANY RULE

The British Indian Army was raised to guard the factories. Later, it grew into the army of John Company Bahadur, and subsequently grew into Presidency armies of Bengal, Madras and Bombay in 1795, after the fall of French Pondicherry in 1793. The Dutch trained the military of the princely state of Travancore called the Nair Brigade.

The 1857 Sepoy War

After 1857, the Presidency Armies were abolished. The Queen took over their control.

The British Raj

The Indian Air Force was established in 1932.

The British-Indian Army

The British-Indian army contained members of all the major religious groups in India, it contained Hindus, Sikhs, Christians, and Muslims. The number of Sikhs in the army grew steadily with time because they were considered less biased, less drastic in dealing with the different Indian cultural and religious sects and less likely to challenge their British superiors. This was especially true after the Sepoy Rebellion where they were less active in the rebellion and almost absent from it. The reason for their absence was the recent attacks by the Britishers to take over Punjab and two Sikh Wars (1846 and 1849) in which the Bengalis, Biharis, Purbais and the Marathas helped and abated the British Empire.

THE WORLD WARS

The British Indian Army's strength was about 189,000 in 1939. There were about 3,000 British officers and 1,115 Indian officers. The army was expanded greatly to fight in World War II. By 1945, the strength of the Army had risen to about two and a half million. There were about 34,500 British officers and 15,740 Indian officers. The Army took part in campaigns in France, East Africa, North Africa, Syria, Tunisia, Malaya, Burma, Greece, Sicily and Italy and fought very bravely. It suffered 179,935 casualties in the war (including killed (24,338), wounded (64,354), missing (11,762) and POW (79,481) soldiers).

World War I

During WWI the Sikh battalions fought in Egypt, Palestine, Mesopotamia, Gallipoli and France. The 14th Ferozepore Sikhs were in Gallipoli in April 1915 and fought in a number of battles in the Gallipoli campaign. After Gallipoli the battalion was in the Persian Gulf region and took part in some fierce fighting on the Tigris River. The 15th Ludhiana Sikhs were in France in September 1914 and participated in fighting at Fauquissart, Festubert and Neuve Chapelle.

World War II

India was an active participant in the World War II as a part of the British Empire, and was a major contributor of troops and resources to the war effort. Indian units and troops fought in almost all the major campaigns in which the British were involved, and presented an excellent account of themselves. Of particular significanee were the Chindit operations under Stilwell, and the Burma Camapaign as a whole.

To over come the heavy demands of manpower six new battalions of the Sikh Regiment were raised. They being 6th,7th, 8th, 9th and 25th. Out of the old battalions 1st and 5th saw action in Burma and three others, 2nd, 3rd and 4th fought in the Middle East.

1st Sikh landed in Rangoon in February 1942 and took part in some fierce fighting but the Japanese had built up their strength in the area and pushed the British forces to the Indian border. The battalion was rested and refitted and was back in the war zone on the Indo-Burma border. On March 11, 1943 the battalion was the advance party along the Maungdaw-Buthidaung road. The Japanese were holding a knife-edge hill feature and putting up stiff resistance. The only way to approach the hill was by means of a narrow track. On this track leading the attack was the section commanded by Naik Nand Singh. When the section reached the crest it came under heavy machinegun fire and every man in the section was killed or wounded. Naik Nand Singh dashed forward alone, he was wounded by a grenade as he neared the first Japanese trench. He took out his bayonet and killed the two occupants. Under heavy fire Nand Singh jumped up and charged the second trench, he was again wounded by a grenade and knocked down, but he got up and hurled himself into the trench again killing two Japanese with his bayonet. He then moved on to the third trench and captured it single-handed. With the capture of the third trench the enemy fire started to die away and the rest of the platoon charged the other Japanese positions, killing with bayonet and grenade thirty seven out of the forty Japanese holding it. Naik Nand Singh wounded six times in the assault literally carried the position single-handed. For his valour an immediate award of Victoria Cross was bestowed upon him. The company commander Maj. John Brough was awarded the DSO and the platoon commander Jemadar Mehr Singh the IOM. Two IDSMs were also awarded for this attack.

The battalion then moved to Imphal and took part in the famous battle at Kanglatongbi. After this battle the battalion was among the vanguard in pushing the Japanese back and recapturing Rangoon. During the Second World War the battalions of the Sikh Regiment won 27 battle honours.

Azad Hind Fauj

Azad Hind Fauj, also known as the Indian National Army was led by prominent freedom fighter Netaji Subash Chandra Bose. As repeated promises failed to surface, Bose backed by German and Japanese forces led the liberation of Burma against the wishes of the Allied Powers.

REPUBLIC OF INDIA

The Republic of India has fought three wars and one major incursion battle with Pakistan and one border war with China.

Major Wars

First Indo-Pak War, 1947

Independent India, formed on August 15, 1947, has seen three wars with Pakistan (1947-48, 1965, 1971). The first war took place after Pakistani soldiers and armed tribesmen invaded the independent province of Kashmir. When the forces almost reached the capital Srinagar the Maharaja, Hari Singh, and the democratically elected Prime Minister of Kashmir, Sheikh Abdullah, signed an agreement with India in which all Kashmiri lands were ceded to India. India sent their troops in shortly after and secured a majority of the new Indian state of Jammu and Kashmir. The Indian Air Force carried out Operation Meghdoot in support of the Indian Army and paramilitary forces in Northern Ladakh to secure control of the Siachin glacier.

Sino-Indian War, 1962

India fought a border war against China (1962). China won the war, leading India to revamp the entire military system. After the war ended, the Department of Defence Production was set up to create an indigenous defence production base which is self-reliant and self-sufficient. Since 1962, 16 new ordnance factories have been set up.

Second Indo-Pak War, 1965

The second Indo-Pak war was also fought over Kashmir issue. It ended in with Indian forces gaining chunks of lands all around except Punjab where it was even. USSR interfered and got the truce between the two nations at Tashkent agreement, which also saw the mysterious death of Indian PM Lal Bahadur Shastri. At the same time, there was the possibility of a second Sino-Indian war along the Nathu Pass in Sikkim.

Ten battalions of the Sikh Regiment saw action in the 1965 war. In a bid to seal off routes of infiltrations for the Pakistanis in J&K, 1 Sikh who were in the Tithwal sector attacked Pakistani positions. A company led by Major Somesh Kapur captured Richhmar Ridge on 24 August 1965 and then attacked and captured the Pir Sahiba feature on the night of 25/26 August. From this feature the Indian troops could now overlook an extensive area under Pakistan control. Through out September, Pakistani troops tried hard to recapture this feature but were unsuccessful. 1 Sikh received 3 Vir Chakras (Major Somesh Kapur and L/ Havildar Gurdev Singh and Sepoy Gurmel Singh (posth.)) for these operations. 3 Sikh were in the Keren-Kishanganga sector. A platoon of 22 men under Subedar Sunder Singh withstood attempts by Pakistanis to capture the Pharkian Ki Gali feature. In the end of September the Sikhs blew up the Shahkot Bridge.

Third Indo-Pak War, 1971

In the third Indo-Pak war, India intervened decisively in what was then East Pakistan due to the mass exodus of refugees to India following West Pakistani military action there. The new nation of Bangladesh was created as a result. India succeeded in removing Pakistani soldiers from "EAST PAKISTAN" resulting the formation of Bangladesh.

A number of Sikh battalions fought during the 1971 war, most of them on the Western Front. 8 Sikh were in the Uri sector and 9 Sikh in the nearby Tangdhar sector. Two companies of 9 Sikh attacked and captured Thanda Pani and Kaiyan on 5 December night. The battalion then captured some more positions. At one stage they had advanced so rapidly that they went beyond artillery range. When the Sikhs came under

Pakistani fire, they manhandled a medium gun over the mountains to take on the enemy by direct fire. On 14 December, 9 Sikh then cleared the heights dominating Naukot.

2 Sikh were in the Lahore sector and part of the battalion was defending the Ranian Post, which the Pakistanis seemed determined to capture. They attacked the post repeatedly on 5th, 6th, 7th and 9 December, but each time they were beaten back. At the start of the war the Pakistanis had managed to capture the village of Pulkanjri and had sited 12 BMG's and some 3.5 inch rocket launchers around it. On December 17 and 18th, 2 Sikh attacked and recaptured the Pulkanjri village. During this attack L/Naik Shangara Singh displayed conspicuous gallantry in clearing two machinegun posts which were holding the attack up. Shangara Singh dashed through a minefield and hurled a grenade at one of the post. He then charged the second gun and leaping over the loophole he snatched the gun from its occupants. As he stood with the gun in his hands he received a fatal burst in his abdomen and fell to the ground with the gun still in his hand. He was awarded a posthumous Maha Vir Chakra. N/ Sub. Gian Singh received a posthumous Vir Chakra. The Pakistanis tried to recapture the Pulkanjri village using a company of 43 Punjab and two companies of 15 Punjab. The Sikhs stood firm and inflicted heavy casualties on the enemy's 15 Punjab. In a local counter attack they captured 1 officer and 8 OR's of 43 Punjab and 4 OR's of 15 Punjab. 19 Sikh was in the Ajnala area and captured the border post Budhai Chima on the night of December 5/6.

10 Sikh was in Rajasthan along the Nayachor axis. On December 11, they were part of a brigade attack along with 2 Mahar and 10 Sikh LI to capture Parbat Ali a feature which dominated both the main road and railway line to Nayachor and it was turned into a formidable defensive position by the enemy. In a grim battle working with bayonets and going from trench to trench the feature was cleared by the morning of 13 December. 10 Sikh won 6 Vir Chakras (Major Amrik Singh, Sub. Gurcharn Singh (posth.), Naik Gurjant Singh (posth.), L/Naik Harbhajan Singh, Sep. Mohan Singh) and 3 Sena Medals along with the battle honour Parbat Ali. 4 Sikh fought in the Eastern sector on the Jessore front. The battalion cleared the village of Burinda, which then opened the road to Jessore. The

battalion then continued the advance to Khulna and on December 16, attackedShyamganj and captured it. Naik Mohinder Singh won a posthumous Vir Chakra and the battalion received the battle honour Siramani.

Siachin War, 1984

The Siachin war between India and Pakistan occurred in 1984. The area of the dispute was the Siachen Glacier-the world's highest battlefield. The Glacier was under territorial dispute, but in the late 1970s and early 1980s, Pakistan began organizing several tourist expeditions to the Glacier. India, irked by this development, mounted Operation Meghdoot, and captured the top of the Glacier by establishing a military base which it still maintains to this day at a cost of more than US$1 million per day. Pakistan on the other hand spends just under US$1 million per day, though as % of GDP Pakistan spends 5 times as the Indian Military does to maintain its share of the glacier. Pakistan tried in 1987 and in 1989 to re-take the Glacier but was unsuccessful. A stalemate has arisen where India controls the top part of the Glacier and Pakistan is placed at the bottom of the Glacier.

Kargil War, 1999

India fought a brief border skirmish with Pakistan in the Indian state of Kashmir in 1999. Dubbed the Kargil War, after the infiltration of Pakistani soldiers and paramilitary in the Kargil area, India reclaimed the territory through military and diplomatic channels. More than 500 Soldiers gave their lives for India, most of them sikhs, and 4000 Pakistani soldiers.

During the Kargil Conflict of 1999, two battalions, 8 Sikh and 14 Sikh were inducted into operations. 8 Sikh were tasked to capture Tiger Hill. By 21 May, the 8 Sikh had isolated Tiger Hill from three directions, east, north and south. In order to inflict casualties the enemy positions on Tiger Hill were subjected to artillery and mortar fire. A fresh battalion, 18 Grenadiers was brought in to capture the peak with 8 Sikh holding the firm base. On the night of July 3, 18 Grenadiers captured the eastern slope but further advance was held up due to effective enemy fire from Helmet Top, India Gate features on the western slope.

Other Operations

Sri Lanka Mission, 1987-1990

The Indian Peace Keeping Force (IPKF) carried out a mission in northern and eastern Sri Lanka, comprising of Sikh light Infantary and Sikh Regiment in 1987-1990 to disarm the LTTE as per the Indo-Sri Lanka accord. More than 1200 sikhs gave there lives. In what was labeled as Operation Pawan, the Indian Air Force flew about 70,000 sorties to and within Sri Lanka, without a single aircraft lost or mission aborted.

Operation Cactus, 1988

In November 1988, the Maldives Government appealed India for military help against a mercenary invasion. On the night of November 3, 1988, the Indian Air Force airlifted a parachute battalion group from Agra and flew them non-stop over 2000 km to Maldives. The Indian paratroopers landed at Hulule, secured the airfield and restored the Government rule at Male within hours. The brief, bloodless operation showed the capability of the Indian Air Force in what was labeled as Operation Cactus.

3

Linguistic History of India

Originating over 5,000 years ago, the linguistic history of India describes the evolution and transformation of early human communications techniques-from pictures, pictorial scripts and engravings-to the modern Indian languages that belong to the Indo-Aryan languages and the Dravidian languages.

LANGUAGE OF THE INDUS VALLEY CIVILIZATION

Indo-Aryan Languages

Origins of Sanskrit

The adjective sanskrita-means "refined, consecrated, sanctified". The language referred to as sanskrita vak "the refined language" has by definition always been a 'high' language, used for religious and scientific discourse and contrasted with the languages spoken by the people. The oldest surviving Sanskrit grammar is Panini's Ashtadhyayi dating to ca. the 5th century BC. It is essentially a prescriptive grammar, i.e., an authority that defines (rather than describes) correct Sanskrit, although it contains descriptive parts, mostly to account for Vedic forms that had already passed out of use in Panini's time.

When the term arose in India, "Sanskrit" was not thought of as a specific language set apart from other languages (the people of the time regarded languages more as dialects), but rather as a particularly refined or perfected manner of speaking. Knowledge of Sanskrit was a marker of social class and educational attainment and was taught mainly to Brahmins through close analysis of Sanskrit grammarians such as Panini.

Sanskrit is a descendent of the Proto-Indo-European language. It belongs to the Indo-Aryan sub-family of the Indo-European family of languages. It belongs to the Satem group of Indo-European languages, which also includes the Iranian branch and the Balto-Slavic branch. The categorization may be shown as: Indo-European, Indo-Iranian, Indo-Aryan (i.e., Sanskrit and its descendants).

Technically, Sanskrit is the oldest of the Old Indo-Aryan languages. Its "daughter languages" include the Prakrits of ancient India, Hindi, Bengali, Kashmiri, Urdu, Marathi, Gujarati, Assamese, Nepali, Punjabi and Romany (spoken by the European Roma people).

Vedic Sanskrit

Sanskrit, as defined by Panini, had evolved out of the earlier "Vedic" form, and scholars often distinguish Vedic Sanskrit and Classical or "Paninian" Sanskrit as separate dialects. However, they are extremely similar in many ways and differ mostly in a few points of phonology, vocabulary, and grammar. Classical Sanskrit can therefore be considered a seamless evolution of the earlier Vedic language. Vedic Sanskrit is the language of the Vedas, a large collection of hymns, incantations, and religio-philosophical discussions which form the earliest religious texts in India and the basis for much of the Hindu religion. Modern linguists consider the metrical hymns of the Rigveda Samhita to be the earliest, composed by many authors over centuries of oral tradition. The end of the Vedic period is marked by the composition of the Upanishads, which form the concluding part of the Vedic corpus in the traditional compilations. The current hypothesis is that the Vedic form of Sanskrit survived until the middle of the first millennium BC. It is around this time that Sanskrit began the transition from a first language to a second language of religion and learning, marking the beginning of the Classical period.

It is interesting to note that orthodox Hinduism believes that the language of the Vedas is eternal and revealed. Evidence for this belief is found in the Vedas itself, where in the Upanishads they are described as the very "breath of God" (nihsvasitam brahma). The Vedas are therefore considered "the language of reality", so to speak, and are unauthored, even by God, the rishis or seers ascribed to them being merely individuals gifted with a special insight into reality with the power of perceiving these eternal sounds. Orthodox Hindus, while accepting the linguistic development of Sanskrit as such, do not admit any historical stratification within the Vedic corpus itself, except for the Rig/Sama/Yajur/Atharva order.

This belief is of significant consequence in Indian religious history, as the very sacredness and eternality of the language encouraged exact memorization and transmission and discouraged textual learning via written propagation. Each word is believed to have innate mystic and eternal meaning.

Erroneous learning of repetition of the Veda was considered a grave sin with potentially negative consequences. Consequently, Vedic learning by rote was encouraged and prized, particularly among Brahmins, where learning of one's own Vedic texts was a mandated duty. Vedic Sanskrit differs from Classical Sanskrit in as much as Homeric Greek differs from Classical Greek. The important differences are:

- Vedic Sanskrit had a voiceless bilabial fricative (called upamadhamiya) and a voiceless velar fricative (called jihvamuliya)-which used to occur when the breath visarga appeared before labial and velar consonants respectively. Both of them were lost in Classical Sanskrit.
- Vedic Sanskrit had a retroflex lateral approximant, which was lost in Classical Sanskrit.
- Vedic Sanskrit had a pitch accent which was completely lost sometime around the 6th century ACE (about the same time when Classical Greek also lost its pitch accent)-preserved only in the Vedic chantings.
- The subjunctive tense of Vedic Sanskrit was also lost in Classical Sanskrit.
- More than 12 ways of forming infinitives in Vedic Sanskrit became redundant and clubbed under a single infinitive in Classical Sanskrit.
- A large number of Indo-European words were lost in Classical Sanskrit, and a large number of loanwords

were incorporated from neighboring language families (Dravidian, Munda), and also from now lost substrate languages.

- There was wide-ranging simplification of inflected noun forms for athematic nouns (those not ending in the theme vowel 'a'). Many of the athematic consonant-final nouns were reanalyzed in thematic form (ending with 'a').
- Word order became more standardized on the SOV (Subject-Object-Verb) pattern, whereas in Vedic Sanskrit word order was more variable.
- Verbal affixes in Classical Sansrkit like 'vi', 'upa', etc. became cemented to the verbs they corresponded to, whereas in Vedic Sanskrit these could occur anywhere in the sentence structure.

Other than these, many significant linguistic changes have occurred in Classic Sanskrit to distinguish it from Vedic Sanskrit during the millennia that it evolved due to both internal change, and also due to influences from neighboring language families with whom its speakers had intense contact.

PALI

Pali is sometimes believed to be the same language as Magadhi, but other scholars believe the language to be a slightly different but closely related descendant language.

Emergence of Prakrits

Prakrit (Sanskrit prakrita), "original, natural, artless, normal, ordinary, usual", i.e. "vernacular", in contrast to samskrta "excellently made", both adjectives elliptically referring to vak "speech") refers to the broad family of the Indic languages and dialects spoken in ancient India. The Prakrits became literary languages, generally patronized by kings identified with the ksatriya caste, but were regarded as illegitimate by the Brahmin orthodoxy. The earliest extant use of Prakrit are the inscriptions of Asoka, emperor of Northern India, and while the various Prakrit languages are associated with different patron dynasties, with different religions and different literary traditions, none of them were at any time an informal "mother tongue" in any area of India. In Sanskrit drama, kings speak in Prakrit when addressing women or servants, in contrast to the Sanskrit used in reciting more formal poetic monologues. The three Dramatic Prakrits-Sauraseni, Magadhi, Maharashtri, as well as Jain Prakrit each represent a distinct tradition of literature within the history of India. Other Prakrits are reported in historical sources, but have no extant corpus (e.g., Paisaci).

Prakrit is foremost a native term, designating "vernaculars" as opposed to the artificial Sanskrit. Some modern scholars follow this classification by including all Middle Indo-Aryan languages under the rubric of "Prakrits", while others emphasise the independent development of these languages, often separated from the history of Sanskrit by wide divisions of caste, religion, and geography. Ardhamagadhi, which was used extensively to write Jain scriptures, is the definitive form of Prakrit, while others are considered variants.

THE APABHRAMSHAS

The Prakrits (which includes Pali) were gradually transformed into Apabhramshas which were used until about 13th century. The term Apabhramsha refers to the dialects of North India before the rise of modern North Indian languages. The term apabhramsha implies a corrupt or non-standard language. A significant amount of Apabhramsha literature has been found in Jain libraries. While Amir Khusro and Kabir were writing in a language quite similar to modern Hindi, many poets, specially in regions that were still ruled by Hindu kings, continued to write in Apabhramsha. The Apabhramsha authors include Sarahapad of Kamarupa, Devasena of Dhar (9th c. CE), Pushpadanta of Manyakhet (9th c. CE), Dhanapal, Muni Ramsimha, Hemachandra of Patan, Raighu of Gwalior (15th CE). An early example of the use of Apabhramsha is in Vikramuurvashiiya of Kalidasa, when Pururava asks the animals in the forest about his beloved who had disappeared.

DRAVIDIAN LANGUAGES

The origins of the Dravidian languages, as well as their subsequent development and the period of their differentiation, are unclear, and the situation is not helped by the lack of comparative linguistic research into the Dravidian languages. Inconclusive attempts have also been made to link the family with the Japonic languages, Basque, Korean, Sumerian, the Australian Aboriginal languages and the unknown language of the Indus valley civilisation.

Legends common to many Dravidian-speaking groups speak of their origin in a vast, now-sunken continent far to the south. Many linguists, however, tend to favour the theory that speakers of Dravidian languages spread southwards and eastwards through the Indian subcontinent, based on the fact that the southern Dravidian languages show some signs of contact with linguistic groups which the northern Dravidian languages do not. Proto-Dravidian is thought to have differentiated into Proto-North Dravidian, Proto-Central Dravidian and Proto-South Dravidian around 1500 BC, although some linguists have argued that the degree of differentiation between the sub-families points to an earlier split.

The existence of the Dravidian language family was first suggested in 1816 by Alexander D. Campbell in his Grammar of the Teloogoo Language, in which he and Francis W. Ellis argued that Tamil and Telugu were descended from a common, non-Indo-European ancestor. However, it was not until 1856 that Robert Caldwell published his Comparative grammar of the Dravidian or South-Indian family of languages, which considerably expanded the Dravidian umbrella and established it as one of the major language groups of the world. Caldwell coined the term "Dravidian" from the Sanskrit dravida, which was used in a 7th century text to refer to the languages of the south of India. The publication of the Dravidian etymological dictionary by T. Burrow and M. B. Emeneau was a landmark event in Dravidian linguistics.

Origins of Tamil

The origins of Tamil, like the other Dravidian languages, but unlike most of the other established literary languages of India, are independent of Sanskrit. Tamil has the oldest literature amongst the Dravidian languages (Hart, 1975), but dating the language and the literature precisely is difficult.

Literary works in India or Sri Lanka were preserved either in palm leaf manuscripts (implying repeated copying and recopying) or through oral transmission, making direct dating impossible. External chronological records and internal linguistic evidence, however, indicates that the oldest extant works were probably composed sometime between the 5th century BCE and the 2nd century CE.

The earliest extant text in Tamil is the Tolkappiyam, a work on poetics and grammar which describes the language of the classical period, the oldest portions of this book may date back to around 200 BCE (Hart, 1975). Preliminary results from archaeological excavations in 2005 suggest that the oldest inscriptions in Tamil may date at least to around 500 BCE. Apart from these, the earliest examples of Tamil writing we have today are rock inscriptions from the 3rd century BCE, which are written in an adapted form of the Brahmi script (Mahadevan, 2003).

Many Tamils argue in favour of a much earlier date for the literature by referring to Tamil legends of a lost continent, or by positing links to the Indus valley civilisation, the Sumerian Tammuz, and the Australian Kamilaroi, but none of these theories have been recognised by the mainstream scholarly community.

Linguists categorise Tamil literature and language into three periods: ancient (500 BCE to 700 CE), medieval (700 CE to 1500 CE) and modern (1500 CE to the present). During the medieval period, a number of Sanskrit loan words were absorbed by Tamil, which many 20th century purists, notably Parithimaar Kalaignar and Maraimalai Adigal, later sought to remove. This movement was called thanith thamizh iyakkam (meaning pure Tamil movement). As a result of this, Tamil in formal documents, public speeches and scientific discourses is largely free of Sanskrit loan words. Between 800 and 1300 CE, Malayalam is believed to have evolved into a distinct language.

AUSTROASIATIC LANGUAGES

The Austroasiatic family of languages includes the Santal and Munda languages of eastern India, Nepal, and Bangladesh, along with the Mon-Khmer languages spoken in Myanmar,

Thailand, Laos, Cambodia, Vietnam, and southern China. The Austroasiatic languages are thought to have been spoken throughout the Indian subcontinent by hunter-gatherers who were later assimilated first by the agriculturalist Dravidian settlers and later by the Indo-Europeans from Central Asia.

The Austroasiatic family is thought to be the first to be spoken in ancient India. Some believe the family to be a part of an Austric superstock of languages, along with the Austronesian language family.

EVOLUTION OF SCRIPTS

Indus Script

The term Indus script refers to short strings of symbols associated with the Harappan civilization of ancient India (most of the Indus sites are distributed in present day North West India and Pakistan) used between 2600-1900 BC, which evolved from an early Indus script attested from around 3500-3300 BC. They are most commonly associated with flat, rectangular stone tablets called seals, but they are also found on at least a dozen other materials. The first publication of a Harappan seal dates to 1875, in the form of a drawing by Alexander Cunningham. Since then, well over 4000 symbol-bearing objects have been discovered, some as far afield as Mesopotamia. After 1500 BC, use of the symbols ends, together with the final stage of Harappan civilization. Some early scholars, starting with Cunningham in 1877, thought that the script was the archetype of the Brahmi script used by Ashoka. Today Cunningham's claims are rejected by a majority of researchers, but a minority of mostly Indian scholars continue to argue for the Indus script as the predecessor of the Brahmic family. There are over 400 different signs, but many are thought to be slight modifications or combinations of perhaps 200 'basic' signs.

Over the years, numerous decipherments have been proposed, but none has been accepted by the scientific community at large. The following factors are usually regarded as the biggest obstacles for a successful decipherment:

- The substrate language has not been identified, nor the language family to which it belongs.

- The average length of the inscriptions is less than five signs, the longest being one of only 26 signs.
- No bilingual texts have been found.

The Finnish Indologist Asko Parpola, who has edited a multivolumed corpus of the inscriptions, surmises that the symbols represent a logo-syllabic script, with an underlying Dravidian language as the most likely linguistic substrate.

If the signs are purely ideographical, they may contain no information about the language spoken by their creators, and cannot be called a script in the true sense of the word. A recent paper by Steve Farmer, Richard Sproat, and Michael Witzel-a comparative historian, computational linguist, and Indologist respectively-offers evidence that the symbols were not coupled to oral language, which in part explains the extreme brevity of the inscriptions. For their paper, see the external links.

A number of writers associated with Hindutva have attempted to prove that the script encodes Vedic Sanskrit. R.S. Rajaram and N. Jha made one such claim. D. B. Kasar has compared the Indus script to Germanic runes and claims that IVC inscriptions contain Rigvedic hymns. These theories are not accepted by most scholars.

Brahmi Script

The best known inscriptions in Brahmi are the rock-cut edicts of Ashoka, dating to the 3rd century BC. These were long considered the earliest examples of Brahmi writing, but recent archeological evidence in Sri Lanka and Tamil Nadu suggest the dates for the earliest use of Brahmi to be around the 6th century BC, dated using radiocarbon and thermoluminescence dating methods.

This script is ancestral to most of the scripts of South Asia, Southeast Asia, Tibet, Mongolia, Manchuria, and perhaps even Korean Hangul. The Brahmi numeral system is the ancestor of the Hindu-Arabic numerals, which are now used world-wide.

Brahmi is generally believed to be derived from a Semitic script such as the Imperial Aramaic alphabet, as was clearly the case for the contemporary Kharosthi alphabet that arose in a part of northwest Indian under the control of the

Achaemenid Empire. Rhys Davids suggests that writing may have been introduced to India from the Middle East by traders. Another possibility is with the Achaemenid conquest in the late 6th century BC. It was often assumed that it was a planned invention under Ashoka as a prerequiste for the his edicts. Compare the much better documented parallel of the Hangul script.

Older examples of the Brahmi script appear to be on fragments of pottery from the trading town of Anuradhapura in Sri Lanka, which have been dated to the early 5th century BC. Even earlier evidence of the Brahmi script has been discovered on pieces of pottery in Adichanallur, Tamil Nadu. Radio-carbon dating has established that they belonged to the 6th century BC.

A minority position holds that Brahmi was a purely indigenous development, perhaps with the Indus script as its predecessor; these include the English scholars G.R. Hunter and Raymond Allchin.

Kharosthi Script

The Kharoshti script, also known as the Gandhari script, is an ancient abugida (a kind of alphabetic script) used by the Gandhara culture of historic northwest India to write the Gandhari and Sanskrit languages. It was in use from the 4th century BC until it died out in its homeland around the 3rd century AD. It was also in use along the Silk Road where there is some evidence it may have survived until the 7th century in the remote way stations of Khotan and Niya.

Scholars are not in agreement as to whether the Kharoshti script evolved gradually, or was the work of a mindful inventor. An analysis of the script forms shows a clear dependency on the Aramaic alphabet but with extensive modifications to support the sounds found in Indic languages. One model is that the Aramaic script arrived with the Achaemenid conquest of the region in 500 BC and evolved over the next 200+ years to reach its final form by the 3rd century BC. However, no intermediate forms have yet been found to confirm this evolutionary model, and rock and coins inscriptions from the 3rd century BC onward show a unified and mature form.

The study of the Kharoshti script was recently invigorated by the discovery of the Gandharan Buddhist Texts, a set of birch-bark manuscripts written in Kharoshti, discovered near the Afghanistan city of Hadda just west of the Khyber Pass. The manuscripts were donated to the British Library in 1994. The entire set of manuscripts are dated to the 1st century AD making them the oldest Buddhist manuscripts in existence.

Gupta Script

The Gupta script was used for writing Sanskrit and is associated with the Gupta Empire of India which was a period of material prosperity and great religious and scientific developments. The Gupta script was descended from Brahmi and gave rise to the Siddham script.

Siddham Script

Siddham (Sanskrit, accomplished or perfected), descended from the Brahmi script via the Gupta script, which also gave rise to the Devanagari script as well as a number of other Asian scripts such as Tibetan script. Siddham is an abugida or alphasyllabary rather than an alphabet because each character indicates a syllable. If no other mark occurs then the short 'a' is assumed. Diacritic marks indicate the other vowels, the pure nasal, and the aspirated vowel. A special mark can be used to indicate that the letter stands alone with no vowel which sometimes happens at the end of Sanskrit words.

The writing of mantras and copying of Sutras using the Siddham script is still practiced in Shingon Buddhism in Japan but has died out in other places. It was Kukai who introduced the Siddham script to Japan when he returned from China in 806, where he studied Sanskrit with Nalanda trained monks including one known as Prajña. Sutras that were taken to China from India were written in a variety of scripts, but Siddham was one of the most important. By the time Kukai learned this script the trading and pilgrimage routes over land to India, part of the Silk Road, were closed by the expanding Islamic empire of the Abbasids. Then in the middle of the 9th century there were a series of purges of "foreign religions" in China. This meant that Japan was cut off from the sources of Siddham texts. In time other scripts, particularly Devanagari replaced it in India, and so Japan was left as the only place where Siddham was preserved, although it was, and is only used for writing mantras and copying sutras.

Siddham was influential in the development of the Kana writing system, which is also associated with Kukai-while the Kana shapes derive from Chinese characters, the princlple of a syllable-based script and their systematic ordering was taken over from Siddham.

LITERATURE

Indian literature is generally acknowledged, but not wholly established, as the oldest in the world. India has 22 officially recognized languages, and a huge variety of literature has been produced in these languages over the years. In Indian literature, oral and written forms are both important. Hindu literary traditions dominate a large part of Indian culture. Apart from the Vedas which are a sacred form of knowledge, there are other works such as the Hindu epics Ramayana and Mahabharata, treatises such as Vaastu Shastra in architecture and town planning, and Arthashastra in political science. Devotional Hindu drama, poetry and songs span the subcontinent. Muslim literary traditions also dominate a large part of Indian culture. In the medieval period, during which time India was mostly under Muslim rule, Indian Muslim literature flourished.

Vedic Literature

Examples of early works written in Vedic Sanskrit include the holy Hindu texts, such as the core Vedas and the Upanishads. Other examples include the Sulba Sutras, which are some of the earliest texts on geometry.

Epic Sanskrit Literature

Vyasa's Mahabharata and Valmiki's Ramayana written in Epic Sanskrit are regarded as the greatest Indian epics. The famous poet and playwright Kalidasa also wrote two epics: Raghuvamsha (Dynasty of Raghu) and Kumarasambhava (Birth of Kumar Kartikeya), though they were written in Classical Sanskrit rather than Epic Sanskrit.

Classical Sanskrit Literature

Examples of works written in Classical Sanskrit include the Panini's Ashtadhyayi which standardized the grammar and phonetics of Classical Sanskrit. The Laws of Manu is an important text in Hinduism. Kalidasa is often considered to be the greatest playwright in Sanskrit literature, and one of the greatest poets in Sanskrit literature, whose Recognition of Shakuntala and Meghaduuta are the most famous Sanskrit plays. He occupies the same position in Sanskrit literature that Shakespeare occupies in English literature. Some other famous plays were Mricchakatika by Shudraka, Svapna Vasavadattam by Bhasa, and Ratnavali by Sri Harsha. Later poetic works include Geeta Govinda by Jayadeva. Some other famous works are Chanakya's Arthashastra and Vatsyayana's Kamasutra.

Prakrit Literature

The most notable Prakrit language was Pali. Many of Ashvaghosha's plays were written in Shaurseni Prakrit. Another major work in Shaurseni was Karpoormanjari. Kalidasa, Harsha and Haal used Maharashtrian Prakrit in some of their plays and poetry. Many Shwetambar Jain works are also written in the Maharashtri Prakrit. Many plays (like those of Ashvaghosha) and Jain works were written in the Ardha Magadhi Prakrit.

Pali literature

The Pali Canon is mostly of Indian origin. Later Pali literature however was mostly produced outside the Indian subcontinent, particularly in East Asia, Southeast Asia and Central Asia. Pali literature includes Buddhist philosophical works, poetry and some grammatical works. Major works in Pali are Jataka tales, Dhammapada, Addhakatha, and Mahavansha. Some of the major Pali grammarians were Kachvaayan, Moggalaan and Varruchi (who wrote Prakrit Prakash).

Bengali Literature

The most internationally famous Bengali writer is Nobel laureate Rabindranath Tagore, who received the Nobel Prize for Literature; but another poet, one generation younger is equally popular, valuable, and influential in his country, though virtually unknown in foreign countries: Kazi Nazrul Islam. Other famous Indian Bengali writers were Sharat Chandra Chattopadhyay and Bankim Chandra Chattopadhyay. Bengali is the second most commonly spoken language in India (after Hindi). As a result of the Bengal Renaissance in the 19th and 20th centuries, many of India's most famous, and relatively recent, literature, poetry, and songs are in Bengali.

Hindi Literature

Hindi literature started as religious and philosophical poetry in medieval periods in dialects like Avadhi and Brij. The most famous figures from this period are Kabir and Tulsidas. In modern times, the Khadi dialect became more prominent and a variety of literature was produced in Sanskrit. Chandrakanta, written by Devaki Nandan Khatri, is considered to be the first work of prose in Hindi. Munshi Premchand was the most famous Hindi novelist. The chhayavadi poets include Surya Kant Tripathi "Nirala", Jaishankar Prasad, Sumitranandan Pant, and Mahadevi Varma. Other renowned poets include Maithili Sharan Gupt, Agyey, Harivansh Rai Bachchan, and Dharmveer Bharti. The progressive poets of Hindi were: Kedarnath Agrawal, Shamsher, Gajanan Madhav "Muqtibodh", Ramdhari Singh "Dinkar", Nagarjun, Raghuveer Sahai, and Kedar Nath Singh. Notable poets of the young generation include Kumar Vikal, Dinesh Shukla, Uday Prakash, Mohan Daheria, Shailendra Chauhan, and Vinod Padraj. This young generation is very much extrovert in expressions and much aware of global changes.

Kannada Literature

Kannada literature dates back to 5th century with earliest reported work being Halmidi inscription. The first available complete literary work in Kannada is Kavirajamarga written in 8th century by Amoghavarsha Nrpatunga. The history of Kannada literature is usually studied under three phases: Halegannada, Nadugannada and Kannada literature, Hosagannada. Halegannada mainly consists of Jain religious literature. The most famous poet of this period is Adikavi Pampa. Nadugannada period played a prominent role in the advancement of Kannada literature. It gave birth to several genres in Kannada literature, with new forms of composition coming into use, including Ragale, Vachana, Sangatya, Desi and Bhakti literature. Basava, Kumara Vyasa and Purandaradasa are some big names from that period. The works of this period are based on Jain, Hindu principles. Hosagannada can be seen as the reincarnation of Kannada literature after a period of dormancy in the face of British occupation of India. Kannada poetry and novels found a new beginning and meaning. Presently Kannada literature has the distinction of winning Jnanpeeth award seven times, the highest for any Indian language.

Marathi Literature

Marathi literature began with saint-poets like Dnyaneshwar, Tukaram, Ramdas, and Eknath. Modern Marathi literature was marked by a theme of social reform. Well-known figures from this phase include Mahatma Jyotiba Phule, Lokhitwadi, and others. Prominent modern literary figures include Vishnu Sakharam Khandekar, P.L. Deshpande, Vijay Tendulkar, and Vishnu Vaman Shirvadakar (Kavi Kusumagraj).

Tamil Literature

Tamil literature has a rich and long literary tradition spanning more than 2000 years. Tolkaappiyam has been credited as the oldest work in Tamil available today. The history of Tamil literature follows the history of Tamil Nadu, closely following the social and political trends of various periods. The secular nature of the early Sangam poetry gave way to works of religious and didactic nature during the Middle Ages. Tirukkural is a fine example of such work on human behaviour and political morals. A wave of religious revival helped generate a great volume of literary output by Saivite and Vaishnavite authors. Jain and Buddhist authors during the medieval period and Muslim and European authors later also contributed to the growth of Tamil literature.

A revival of Tamil literature took place from the late nineteenth century when works of religious and philosophical nature were written in a style that made it easier for the common people to enjoy. Nationalist poets began to utilise the power of poetry in influencing the masses. Short stories and novels began to appear. The popularity of Tamil Cinema has also provided opportunities for modern Tamil poets to emerge.

Telugu Literature

Telugu, the third largest language spoken in India, is rich in literary traditions. The earliest written literature dates back to the seventh century. The epic literary tradition started with Nannayya who is acclaimed as Telugu's Aadikavi meaning the first poet. He belongs to tenth or eleventh century. Vemana who lived in the fourteenth century wrote in the language of the common man. He wrote poems in a simple style. He questioned the prevailing pseudo values and conventions and religious practices in his poems. His philosophy made him a unique poet of the masses. Viswanadha Satyanarayana (veyi padagalu), a doyen of conventional yet creative literature, was the first to receive Jnanpith Award for Telugu followed by C. Narayana Reddy. Unnava laxminarayana (malapalli), Bucchi babu, tripuraneni gopichand and many more had profound impact on telugu literature.

Urdu Literature

Among other traditions, Urdu poetry is a fine example of linguistic and cultural synthesis. Arab and Persian vocabulary based on the Hindi language resulted in a vast and extremely beloved class of ghazal literature, usually written by Muslims in contexts ranging from romance and society to philosophy and devotion to Allah. Urdu soon became the court language of the Mughals and in its higher forms was once called the "Kohinoor" of Indian languages.

Indian English Literature

In the last century, several Indian writers have distinguished themselves not only in traditional Indian languages but also in English. India's only Nobel laureate in literature was the Bengali writer Rabindranath Tagore. Other major writers in English who are either Indian or of Indian origin and derive much inspiration from Indian themes are R. K. Narayan, Vikram Seth, Salman Rushdie, Arundhati Roy, Raja Rao, Amitav Ghosh, Vikram Chandra, Mukul Kesavan, Khushwant Singh, Shashi Tharoor, Nayantara Sehgal, Anita

Desai, Ashok Banker, Shashi Deshpande, Jhumpa Lahiri, Kamala Markandaya, Gita Mehta, Manil Suri, and Bharati Mukherjee.

In the 1950s, the Writers Workshop collective in Calcutta was founded by the poet and essayist P. Lal to advocate and publish Indian writing in English. The press was the first to publish Pritish Nandy, Sasthi Brata, and others; it continues to this day to provide a forum for English writing in India.

In recent years, English-language writers of Indian origin are being published in the West at an increasing rate. In June 1997, a special fiction issue of The New Yorker magazine devoted much space to essays by Amitav Ghosh and Abraham Verghese, a short story by Vikram Chandra, and poems by Jayanta Mahapatra and A. K. Ramanujan. John Updike profiled R.K. Narayan and Arundhati Roy's "A God of Small Things." Moncy Pothen's Beneath the Clouds and Coconut Leaves was published in USA, in March 2006.

Indo-Persian Literature

During the early Muslim period, Persian became the lingua franca of the subcontinent, used by most of the educated and the government. Although Persian literature from Persia itself was popular, several Indians became major Persian poets, the most notable being Amir Khusro and in more modern times Allama Iqbal. Much of the older Sanskrit literature was also translated into Persian. For a time, it remained the court language of the Mughals, soon to be replaced by Urdu. Persian still held its status, despite the spread of Urdu, well into the early years of the British rule in India. Most British officials had to learn Persian on coming to India and concluded their conversations in Persian. In the early 19th century, however, the British, in an effort to expand their influence, made a government ruling to discontinue the use of Persian and commence the use of English instead. Thus started the decline of Persian as the subcontinent's lingua franca, a position to be taken up by the new language of the British Raj, English. Many modern Indian languages still show signs of heavy Persian influence, most notably Urdu and Hindi.

4

Kingdoms of Ancient India

Ancient or Epic India as described in the itihasas is divided into a large number of independent kingdoms, spanning the whole of the Indian subcontinent.

INTRODUCTION

Much of the political and geographical mosaic of Ancient India can be derived from the epic Mahabharata. The other great Indian epic Ramayana is yet another source. From the Vedas, notably Rig Veda, we get the geo-political information of the Ancient India, that predates the Mahabharata-period. The Puranas forms a window to the geo-political scenario of Ancient India during the post-Mahabharata period.

The time coordinates in which these kingdoms existed is not exactly known. The classical "Golden Age" of Ancient India spans the 1st millennia BCE and CE, historical kingdoms arising from ca. 700 BCE with the Mahajanapadas. Glimpses of prehistoric political entities may be glimpsed from the early Vedic texts, in particular the Rigveda (dated to from around 1500 BC). The earliest parts of the epic Mahabharata date to around 500 BC and Ramayana around 400 BC. These early kingdoms lasted until the rise of the Maurya Empire in 321 BC, from which period the term Middle kingdoms of India may be used.

BOUNDARIES OF THE KINGDOMS

The kingdoms mentioned below existed when territorial boundaries were less important, due to the limited human population and sparse human settlements. Often rivers formed the boundaries of two neighbouring kingdoms, as was the case between northern and southern Panchala and the western (Pandava's Kingdom) and eastern (Kaurava's Kingdom) Kuru. Sometimes, large forests, which were larger than the kingdoms themselves, formed their boundaries as was the case of the Naimisha forest between Panchala and Kosala kingdoms. Mountain ranges like Himalaya, Vindhya and Sahya also formed their boundaries.

THE CITIES AND VILLAGES IN THE KINGDOMS

Some kingdoms possessed a main city that served as its capital. For example, the capital of Pandava's Kingdom was Indraprastha and the Kaurava's Kingdom was Hastinapura. Ahichatra was the capital of Northern Panchala where as Kampilya was the capital of Southern Panchala. Kosala Kingdom had its capital as Ayodhya. Apart from the main city or capital, where the palace of the ruling king was situated, there were small towns and villages spread in a kingdom. Tax was collected by the officers appointed by the king from these villages and towns. What the king offered in return to these villages and towns was, protection from the attack of other kings and robber tribes as well as from invading foreign nomadic tribes. The king also enforced law and order in his kingdom by punishing the guilty.

INTERACTIONS BETWEEN KINGDOMS

There were no border security for a kingdom and border disputes were very rare. One king may conduct a military-campaign (often designated as Digvijaya meaning victory over all the directions) and defeat another king in a battle, lasting for a day. The defeated king would acknowledge the supremacy of the victorious king. The defeated king might some times be asked to give a tribute to the victorious king. Tribute will be collected only once, not in a periodic basis. The defeated king, in most cases, is free to rule his own kingdom, without maintaining any contact with the victorious king. There was no annexation of one kingdom by another kingdom. Often a military general makes these campaigns on behalf of his king. A military-campaign and tribute collection is often associated with a great sacrifice (like Rajasuya or Aswamedha) conducted in the kingdom of the campaigner king. The defeated king also was invited to attend these sacrifice ceremonies, as a friend and ally.

NEW KINGDOMS

New kingdoms were formed when a major clan produces more than one kings in a generation. The Kuru clan of kings and Ikshwaku clan of kings were very successful in spreading all over north India with their numerous kingdoms, formed after each successive generations. Similarly the Yadava clan of kings spread numerous kingdoms in the central India.

CULTURAL DIFFERENCES IN THE KINGDOMS

Western parts of India were dominated by tribes who had a slightly different culture that was considered as non-vedic by the mainstream Vedic culture prevailed in the Kuru and Panchala kingdoms. Probably these were due to the influence of Iranian cultures. Similarly tribes ruling south India were also considered as non-Vedic by the Kuru, Panchalas, though the differences were not so significant. This may be due to the Dravidian nature of these tribes. Similarly there were some tribes in the eastern regions of India, considered to be in this category. Tribes with a different culture was collectively termed by the Vedic tribes by the name Mlechcha. Very little was mentioned in the ancient Indian literature, about the kingdoms to the north, beyond Himalayas. China was mentioned as a kingdom known as Chin, some times grouped with Mlechcha kingdoms. An astonishing fact is that, some other kingdoms in the north were mentioned with high respect and a sense of mystery.

Prominent among them was the kingdom with the name Northern Kuru or Uttara Kuru. Some text mentions it as the dominion of Devas, the gods of ancient Indian people. Sometimes it was mentioned as just another kingdom, sometimes as a kingless country, sometimes as a republic. The similarity in the name, with the Kuru Kingdom in India, make them related to the Kurus (Kauravas and Pandavas) of India. Some historians argues that they were the forefathers of the Kuru's of India, that the Kuru clan originated in Northern Kuru (identified as Kyrgistan and Tajikistan) and spread to India, establishing their kingdoms in Haryana and Uttar Pradesh states of India.

MAIN KINGDOMS OF THE PURU CLAN

Puru clan was the main clan of Ancient Indian kings belonging to the Lunar Dynasty or the Chandra Vamsa. It was founded by Puru the son of Yayati who himself was the grand grandson of Pururavas Aila the first king of the Lunar Dynasty.

Kuru Kingdom	Kingdom of Kauravas and Pandavas
Panchala Kingdom	Native kingdom of Panchali, the wife of Pandavas
Vatsa Kingdom	

MAIN KINGDOMS OF IKSHWAKU CLAN

Ikswaku clan was the main clan of Ancient Indian kings belonging to the Solar Dynasty or the Surya Vamsa.

Kosala Kingdom	Kingdom of Raghava Rama
Kasi Kingdom	Kingdom of the grandmothers of Pandavas and Kauravas
Videha Kingdom	Native kingdom of Sita wife of Raghava Rama
Dakshina Kosala Kingdom	Native kingdom of Raghava Rama's mother
Malla Kingdom	Ruled by Ikshwaku Kings

YADAVA KINGDOMS

Yadava Kingdoms were ruled by the Yadava clan of kings founded by Yadu the elder brother of Puru.

Surasena Kingdom	Native kingdom of Vasudeva Krishna
Dwaraka Kingdom	Kingdom founded by Vasudeva Krishna
Kunti Kingdom	Native kingdom of Kunti, the mother of the elder Pandavas, viz Yudhisthira, Bhima and Arjuna
Saurashtra Kingdom	

Heheya Kingdom	Kingdom of the Yadava king Kartavirya Arjuna
Nishadha Kingdom	Kingdom of king Nala
Gurjara Kingdom	
Karusha Kingdom	Kingdom of Dantavakra, enemy of Vasudeva Krishna
Chedi Kingdom	Kingdom of Sisupala, enemy of Vasudeva Krishna
Dasarna Kingdom	allied with the Pandavas
Avanti Kingdom	Kingdom of Vinda and Anuvinda, allies of Duryodhana
Malava Kingdom	
Anarta Kingdom	
Youdheya Kingdom	Kingdom of Yadava hero Satyaki

MATSYA KINGDOMS

Matsya Kingdom	Kingdom of Virata ally of the Pandavas
Trigarta Kingdom	Kingdom of the enemy of Virata

WESTERN KINGDOMS

Saubha Kingdom	Kingdom of king Salwa, enemy of Vasudeva Krishna
Madra Kingdom	Native kingdom of Madri, the mother of the Pandava twins younger to Arjuna, viz Nakula and Sahadeva
Sindhu Kingdom	Kingdom of Jayadratha, ally of Duryodhana
Sauvira Kingdom	
Sivi Kingdom	
Kekeya Kingdom	Native kingdom of Kaikeyi, the second wife of Dasaratha, father of Raghava Rama
Gandhara Kingdom	Kingdom of Sakuni, uncle of Duryodhana
Pahlava Kingdom	

NORTH WESTERN KINGDOMS

Bahlika Kingdom
Parama Kamboja Kingdom
Uttara Madra Kingdom
Uttara Kuru Kingdom
Parada Kingdom
Parasika Kingdom
Yavana Kingdom
Tushara Kingdom
Khasa Kingdom
Saka Kingdom

NORTHERN KINGDOMS

Kasmira Kingdom
Kamboja Kingdom
Darada Kingdom
Huna Kingdom
Hara Huna Kingdom
Rishika Kingdom
China Kingdom
Parama China Kingdom

EASTERN KINGDOMS

Magadha Kingdom	Kingdom of Jarasandha, ally of Duryodhana
Kikata Kingdom	
Anga Kingdom	Kingdom of Karna, ally of Duryodhana
Kamarupa Kingdom	Kingdom of Bhagadatta, ally of Duryodhana
Sonita Kingdom	
Lauhitya Kingdom	
Pundra Kingdom	
Suhma Kingdom	

Vanga Kingdom	
Odra Kingdom	
Utkala Kingdom	

KINGDOMS SOUTH TO VINDHYA RANGES

Vidarbha Kingdom	Native kingdom of Rukmini, wife of Vasudeva Krishna
Anupa Kingdom	
Surparaka Kingdom	
Nasikya Kingdom	
Konkana Kingdom	
Asmaka Kingdom	
Danda Kingdom	Kingdom ruled by Ravana's governor general Khara
Kalinga Kingdom	Native kingdom of the wife of Duryodhana

KINGDOMS OF EXTREME SOUTH

Telinga Kingdom	
Andhra Kingdom	
Kishkindha Kingdom	Kingdom of Vanaras
Gomanta Kingdom	
Karnata Kingdom	
Dravida Kingdom	
Kanchi Kingdom	
Chola Kingdom	
Pandya Kingdom	
Mahisha Kingdom	Kingdom of Asura Mahisha
Tulu Kingdom	
Mushika Kingdom	
Satyaputra Kingdom	
Kerala Kingdom	
Sinhala Kingdom	
Lanka Kingdom	Kingdom of Ravana

SARASWATI VALLEY KINGDOMS

Saraswata Kingdom

Abhira Kingdom

Sudra Kingdom

Nishada Kingdom

HIMALAYAN KINGDOMS

The table lands and valleys of the great Himalayan Mountain Ranges, which were almost inaccessible to the people settled in the Ganga, Saraswati and Sindhu river valleys, were inhabited by tribes who had very little interactions with the rest of the world. The Vedic people of the plains considered these tribes to be super-human and in later periods considered them even as natural-spirits. The domains of these exotic tribes are listed below:

To know about the mythological aspects of these exotic tribes see Hindu mythology. To know about the historical significance of these tribes see the Exotic Tribes of Ancient India.

Kimpurusha Kingdom

Pisacha Kingdom

Naga Kingdom

Kinnara Kingdom

Rakshasa Kingdom

Yaksha Kingdom

Gandharva Kingdom

Kirata Kingdom

Himalaya Kingdom

Parvata Kingdom

Nepa Kingdom

MAHAJANAPADAS

Mahajanapadas literally means "Great kingdoms" (from Sanskrit Maha = great, Janapada = foothold of tribe = country). Ancient Buddhist texts like Anguttara Nikaya (I. p 213; IV. pp

252, 256, 261) make frequent reference to sixteen great kingdoms and republics (Solas Mahajanapadas) which had evolved and flourished in the northern/north-western parts of the Indian sub-continent prior to rise of Buddhism in India.

Overview

The political process among the ancient Indo-Aryans appears to have originally started with semi-nomadic tribal units called Jana (meaning subjects). Early Vedic texts attest several Janas or tribes of the Aryans, living in semi-nomadic tribal state, fighting among themselves and with other Non-Aryan tribes for cows, sheep and green pastures. These early Vedic Janas later coalesced into Janapadas of the Epic Age.

Term "Janapada" literally means the foothold of a tribe. The derivative meaning of Janapada from Jana points to an early stage of land-taking by the Jana (tribe) for a settled way of life. This process of first settlement on land had completed its final stage prior to the times of Buddha and Panini. The Pre-Buddhist North-west region of Indian sub-continent was divided into several Janapadas demarcated from each other by boundaries. In Panini, Janapada stands for country and Janapadin for its citizenry. These Janapadas were named after the tribes or the Janas who had settled in them. By circa 600 BCE, many of these Janapadas had further evolved into larger political entities by the process of land-grabbing which eventually led to the formation of kingdoms known in Buddhist traditions as the Mahajanapadas or the great nations (Sanskrit: Maha = great, Janapada = country).

The Buddhist and other texts only incidentally refer to sixteen great nations (Solasa Mahajanapadas) which were in existence before the time of Buddha. They do not give any connected history except in the case of Magadha. The Buddhist Anguttara Nikaya, at several places, gives a list of sixteen nations:

1. Kasi
2. Kosala
3. Anga
4. Magadha

5. Vajji (or Vriji)
6. Malla
7. Chedi
8. Vatsa (or Vamsa)
9. Kuru
10. Panchala
11. Machcha (or Matsya)
12. Surasena
13. Assaka
14. Avanti
15. Gandhara
16. Kamboja

Another Buddhist text Digha Nikaya mentions only first twelve Mahajanapadas and omits the last four in the above list (Digha Nikaya, Vol II, p 200).

Chulla-Niddesa, another ancient text of the Buddhist canon, adds Kalinga to the list and substitutes Yona for Gandhara, thus listing the Kamboja and the Yona as the only Mahajanapadas from Uttarapatha.

The Jaina Bhagvati Sutra gives slightly different list of sixteen Mahajanapadas viz: Anga, Banga (Vanga), Magadha, Malaya, Malavaka, Accha, Vaccha, Kochcha, Padha, Ladha (Lata), Bajji (Vajji), Moli (Malla), Kasi, Kosala, Avaha and Sambhuttara. Obviously, the author of Bhagvati has a focus on the countries of Madhydesa and of far east and south only. He omits the nations from Uttarapatha like the Kamboja and Gandhara. The more extended horizon of the Bhagvati and the omission of all countries from Uttarapatha clearly shows that the Bhagvati list is of later origin and therefore less reliable (Political History of Ancient India, 1996, p 86; History & Culture of Indian People, Age of Imperial Unity, p 15-16).

The main idea in the minds of those who drew up the Janapada lists was basically more tribal than geographical, since the lists include names of the people and not the countries. As the Buddhist and Jaina texts only casually refer to the

Mahajanapadas with no details on history, the following few isolated facts, at best, are gleaned from them and other ancient texts about these ancient nations.

Kasi

The Kasis were Aryan people who had settled in the region around Varanasi (modern Banaras). The capital of Kasi was at Varanasi. The city was bounded by rivers Varuna and Asi on north and south which gave Varanasi its name. Before Buddha, Kasi was the most powerful of the sixteen Mahajanapadas. Several Jatakas bear witness to the superiority of its capital over other cities of India and speaks high of its prosperity and opulence. The Jatakas speak of long rivalry of Kasi with Kosala, Anga and Magadha. A struggle for supremacy went on among them for a time. Kasi was later incorporated into Kosala during Buddha's time. The Kasis along with the Kosalas and Videhans find mention in Vedic texts and appear to have been a closely allied people. Matsya Purana and Alberuni read Kasi as Kausika and Kaushaka respectively. All other ancient texts read Kasi.

Kosala

The country of Kosalas was located to the north-west of Magadha with its capital at Savathi (Sravasti). It was located about 70 miles to north-west of Gorakhpur and comprised territory corresponding to the modern Awadh (or Oudh) in Uttar Pradesh. It had river Ganga for its southern, river Gandhak for its eastern and the Himalaya mountains for its northern boundaries. The kingdom was ruled by king Prasenjit followed by his son Vidudabha. There was struggle for supremacy between king Prasenjit and king Ajatasatru of Magadha which was finally settled once the confederation of Lichchavis became aligned with Magadha. Kosala was ultimately merged into Magadha when Vidudabha was Kosala's ruler. Ayodhya, Saketa and Sravasti were the three chief cities of Kosala.

Anga

The first reference to the Angas is found in the Atharva-Veda where they find mention along with the Magadhas, Gandharis and the Mujavats apparently as a despised people.

The Jaina Prajnapana ranks Angas and Vangas in the first group of Aryan peoples. Based on Mahabharata evidence, the country of Anga roughly corresponded to the region of Bhagalpur and Monghyr in Bihar. River Champa formed the boundaries between the Magadha in the west and Anga in the east. Anga was bounded by river Ganga on the north. Its capital Champa, formerly known as Malini, was located on the right bank of river Ganga, near its junction with river Champa. It was one of the very flourishing cities and is referred to as one of six principal cities of ancient India (Digha Nikaya). It was also a great center of trade and commerce and its merchants regularly sailed to distant Suvarnabhumi. Anga was annexed by Magadha in the time of Bimbisara.

Magadha

The first reference to the Magadhas occurs in the Atharva-Veda where they are found listed along with the Angas, Gandharis and the Mujavats as a despised people. The bards of Magadha are, however, referred to in early Vedic literature and are spoken of in terms of contempt. The Vedic dislike of the Magadhas in early times was due to the fact that the Magadhas were not yet wholly Brahmanised.

Rigveda mentions a king Pramaganda as a ruler of Kikata. Yasaka declares that Kikata was a non-Aryan country. Later Vedic literature refers to Kikata as synonym of Magadha.

With the exception of Rigvedic Pramaganda, no other king of Magadha appears to be mentioned in Vedic literature. According to Mahabharata and the Puranas, the earliest ruling dynasty of Magadha was founded by king Brihadratha, but Magadha came into prominence only under king Bimbisara and his son Ajatasatru. In the war of supremacy which went on for long between the nations of Majjhimadesa, kingdom of Magadha finally emerged victorious and became a predominant empire in Mid India.

The kingdom of the Magadhas roughly corresponded to the modern districts of Patna and Gaya in southern Bihar, and parts of Bengal in the east. It was bounded on the north by river Ganga, on the east by the river Champa, on the south by Vindhya mountains and on the west by river Sona. During

Buddha's time, its boundaries included Anga. Its earliest capital was Girivraja or Rajagriha modern Rajgir in Patna district of Bihar. The other names for the city were Magadhapura, Brihadrathapura, Vasumati, Kushagrapura and Bimbisarapuri. It was an active center of Jainism in ancient times. The first Buddhist council was held in Rajagriha in the Vaibhara Hills. Later on, Pataliputra became the capital of Magadha.

Vajji or Vriji

The Vajjians or Virijis included eight or nine confederated clans of whom the Lichchhavis, the Vedehans, the Jnatrikas and the Vajjis were the most important. Mithila (modern Janakpur in district of Tirhut) was the capital of Vedeha which became the important center of political and cultural activities of northern India. It was in the time of king Janaka that Vedeha came into prominence. The last king of Vadeha was Kalara who is said to have perished along with his kingdom on account of his attempt on a Brahmin maiden. On the ruins of his kingdom arose the republics of Lichchhavis, Vadehans and seven other small republics. The Lichchhavis were very independent people. Mother of Mahavira was a Lichchhavi princess. The Vaisali (modern Basarh in Muzzaferpur district of North Bihar) was the capital of Lichchhavis and the political headquarters of powerful Varijian confederacy. Vaisali was located 25 miles north of river Ganga and 38 miles from Rajagriha and was a very prosperous town. The second Buddhist council was held at Vaisali. The Lichchhavis were followers of Buddha. Buddha is said to have visited Lichchavis on many occasions. The Lichchhavis were closely related by marriage to the Magadhas and are said to be the ancestors of the royal family of Nepal. The Lichchavis are represented as (Vratya) Kshatriyas in Manusmriti. The Vaisali, the headquarters of the powerful Vajji republic and the capital of Lichchavis was defeated by king Ajatasatru of Magadha.

Malla

The Mallas are frequently mentioned in Buddhist and Jain works. They were a powerful people dwelling in Eastern India. Panduputra Bhimasena is said to have conquered the chief of the Mallas in course of his expedition of Eastern India.

Mahabharata mention Mallas along with the Angas, Vangas, and Kalingas as eastern tribes. The Mallas were republican people with their dominion consisting of nine territories (Kalpa Sutra; Nirayavali Sutra), one of eaeh of the nine confederated clans. Two of these confederations...one with Kusinara (modern Kasia near Gorakhpur) as its capital, second with Pava (modern Padrauna, 12 miles from Kasia) as the capital, had become very important at the time of Buddha. Kusinara and Pava are very important in the history of Buddhism since Buddha took his last meal and was taken ill at Pava and breathed his last at Kusinara. The Mallas, like the Lichchhavis, are mentioned by Manusmriti as Vratya Kshatriyas. They are called Vasishthas (Vasetthas) in the Mahapparnibbana Suttanta. The Mallas originally had a monarchical form of government but later they switched to Samgha (republic) of which the members called themselves rajas. The Mallas were a brave and warlike people. Jainism and Buddhism found many followers among the Mallas. The Mallas appeared to have formed alliance with Lichchhavis for self defense. They however, lost their independence not long after Buddha's death and their dominions were annexed to the Magadhan empire.

Chedi or Cheti

The Chedis, Chetis or Chetyas had two distinct settlements of which one was in the mountains of Nepal and the other in Bundelkhand near Kausambi. According to old authorities, Chedis lay near Yamuna midway between the kingdom of Kurus and Vatsas. In the mediaeval period, the southern frontiers of Chedi extended to the banks of river Narmada. Sotthivatnagara, the Sukti or Suktimati of Mahabharata, was the capital of Chedi. The Chedis were an ancient peoples of India and are mentioned in the Rigveda. A Branch of Chedis found a royal dynasty in the kingdom of Kalinga according to the Hathigumpha Inscription of Kharvela.

Vamsa or Vatsa

The Vatsas, Vamsas or Vachchas are stated to be an offshoot from the Kurus. The Vatsa or Vamsa country corresponded with territory of modern Allahabad in Uttar Pradesh. It had monarchical form of government with its capital at Kausambi (identified with village Kosam, 38 miles from Allahabad). Kausambi had been very prosperous city where large number of millionaire merchants resided. It was most important entreport of goods and passengers from north-west and south. Udyana was the ruler of Vatsa in sixth century BCE at the time of Buddha. He was very powerful, warlike and found of hunting. Initially king Udyana was opposed to Buddhism but later on he became follower of Buddha and made Buddhism the state religion.

Kuru

The Puranas trace the origin of Kurus from Puru-Bharata family. Aitareya Brahmana locates the Kurus in Madhyadesha and also refers to the Uttarakurus as living beyond the Himalayas. According to Buddhist text Sumangavilasini (II. p 481), the people of Kururashtra (the Kurus) came from the Uttarakuru. Vayu Purana attests that Kuru, son of Samvarsana of the Puru lineage, was the eponymous ancestor of the Kurus and the founder of Kururashtra (Kuru Janapada) in Kurukshetra. The country of the Kurus roughly corresponded to the modern Thaneswer, union territory of Delhi and Meerut district of Uttar Pradesh. According to Jatakas, the capital of Kurus was Indraprastha (Indapatta) near modern Delhi which extended on seven leagues. At Buddha's time, the Kuru country was ruled by a titular chieftain (king consul) named Korayvya. The Kurus of Buddhist period did not occupy the same position as they did in the Vedic period but they continued to enjoy their ancient reputation for deep wisdom and sound health. The Kurus had matrimonial relations with Yadavas, the Bhojas and the Panchalas. There is a Jataka reference to king Dhananjaya introduced as prince from the race of Yudhishtra. Though a well known monarchical people in earlier period, the Kurus are known to have switched to republic form of government during sixth/fifth century BCE. Fourth century BCE Kautiliya's Arthashastra also attests the Kurus following the Rajashabdopajivin (king consul) constitution.

Panchala

The Panchalas occupied the country to the east of the Kurus between the mountains and river Ganga. It roughly corresponded to modern Budaun, Farrukhabad and the adjoining districts of Uttar Pradesh. The country was divided into Uttara-Panchala and Dakshina-Panchala.

The northern Panchala had its capital at Adhichhatra or Chhatravati (modern Ramnagar in the Bareilly District), while southern Panchala had it capital at Kampilya or Kampil in Farrukhabad District. The famous city of Kanyakubja or Kanauj was situated in the kingdom of Panchala. Originally a monarchical clan, the Panchals appear to have switched to republican corporation in the sixth and fifth century BCE. Fourth century BCE Kautiliya's Arthashastra also attests the Panchalas as following the Rajashabdopajivin (king consul) constitution.

Machcha or Matsya

Country of Matsya or Machcha tribe lied to south of the Kurus and west of the Yamuna which separated them from the Panchalas, It roughly corresponded to former state of Jaipur in Rajasthan, and included the whole of Alwar with portions of Bharatpur. The capital of Matsya was at Viratanagara (modern Bairat) which is said to have been named after its founder king Virata. In Pali literature, the Matsyas are usually associated with the Surasenas. The western Matsya was the hill tract on the north bank of Chambal. A branch of Matsya is also found in later days in Vizagapatam region. The Matsyas had not much political importance of their own during the times of Buddha. King Sujata ruled over both the Chedis and Matsyas thus showing that Matsya once formed a part of Chedi kingdom.

Surasena

Country of the Surasenas lied to south-west of Matsya and west of Yamuna. It had its capital at Madhura or Mathura. Avantiputra, the king of Surasena was the first among the chief disciples of Buddha through whose help, Buddhism gained ground in Mathura country. The Andhakas and Vrishinis of Mathura/Surasena are referred to in the Ashtadhyayi of Panini. In Kautiliya's Arthashastra, the Vrishinis are described as Samgha or republic. The Vrishinis, Andhakas and other allied tribes of the Yadavas formed a Samgha and Vasudeva (Krishna) is described as the Samgha-mukhya. Mathura, the capital of Surasena was also known at the time of Megasthenes as the centre of Krishna worship. The Surasena kingdom had lost its independence on annexation by Magadhan empire.

Assaka or Ashmaka

The Country of Assaka or Ashmaka tribe was located in Dakshinapatha or a southern India. In Buddha's time, Assakas were located on the banks of river Godavari (south of Vindhya mountains). The capital of Assakas was Potana or Potali which corresponds to Paudanya of Mahabharata. The Ashmakas are also mentioned by Panini. They are placed in the north-west in the Markendeya Purana and the Brhat Samhita. River Godavari separated the country of Assakas from that of the Mulakas (or Alakas). The commentator of Kautiliya's Arthashastra identifies Ashmaka with Maharashtra. The country of Assaka lay outside the pale of Madhyadesa. It lied on a southern high road or the Dakshinapatha. At one time, Assaka included Mulaka and their country abutted with Avanti (Dr Bhandarkaar).

Avanti

Country of the Avantis was an important kingdom of western India and was one of the four great monarchies in India when Buddhism arose, the other three being Kosala, Vatsa and Magadha. Avanti was divided into north and south by river Vetravati. Initially, Mahissati (Sanskrit Mahishamati) was the capital of Southern Avanti, and Ujjaini (Sanskrit Ujjayini) was of northern Avanti, but at the times of Mahavira and Buddha, Ujjaini was the capital of integrated Avanti. The country of Avanti roughly corresponded to modern Malwa, Nimar and adjoining parts of the Madhya Pradesh. Both Mahishmati and Ujjaini stood on the southern high road called Dakshinapatha extending from Rajagriha to Pratishthana (modern Paithan). Avanti was an important center of Buddhism and some of the leading theras and theris were born and resided there. King Nandivardhana of Avanti was defeated by king Shishunaga of Magadha. Avanti later became part of Magadhan empire.

Gandhara

The wool of Gandharis is referred to in the Rigveda. The Gandharis, along with the Mujavantas, Angas and the Magadhas, are also mentioned in the Atharvaveda, but apparently as a despised people. Gandharas are included in the Uttarapatha division of Puranic and Buddhistic traditions. Aitareya Brahmana refers to king Naganajit of Gandhara who was contemporary of raja Janaka of Videha. According to Dr Zimmer, Gandharas were settled since the Vedic times on the south bank of river Kubha (Kabol) up to its mouth into Indus itself. Later the Gandhras crossed Indus and expanded into parts of north-west Panjab. Gandharas and their king figure prominently as strong allies of the Kurus against the Pandavas in Mahabharata war.

The Gandharas were a furious people, well trained in the art of war. According to Puranic traditions, this Janapada was founded by Gandhara, son of Aruddha, a descendant of Yayati. The princes of this country are said to have come from the line of Druhyu who was a famous king of Rigvedic period. The river Indus watered the lands of Gandhara. Taksashila and Pushklavati, the two cities of this Mahajanapada, are said to have been named after Taksa and Pushkara, the two sons of Bharata, a prince of Ayodhya. According to Vayu Purana (II.36.107), the Gandharas were destroyed by Pramiti aka Kalika, at the end of Kalyuga. Panini has mentioned both Vedic form Gandhari as well as the later form Gandhara in his Ashtadhyayi.

The Gandhara kingdom sometimes also included Kashmira (Jataka No 406). Hecataeus of Miletus (549-468) refers to Kaspapyros (Kasyapura i.e Kashmira) as Gandaric city. According to Gandhara Jataka, at one time, Gandhara formed a part of the kingdom of Kashmir. Jataka also gives another name Chandahara for Gandhara. Gandhara Mahajanapada of Buddhist traditions included territories of east Afghanistan, and north-west of the Panjab (modern districts of Peshawar (Purushapura) and Rawalpindi). Its capital was Takshasila (Prikrit Taxila). The Taxila University was a renowned center of learning in ancient times, where scholars from all over the world came to seek higher education. Panini, the Indian genius of grammar and Kautiliya are the world renowned products of Taxila University. King Pukkusati or Pushkarasarin of Gandhara in middle of sixth century BCE was the contemporary of king Bimbisara of Magadha. Gandhara was located on the grand northern high road (Uttarapatha) and was a centre of international commercial activities. It was an important channel of communication with ancient Iran and Central Asia. According to some scholars, the Gandharas and Kambojas were same ethnic stock.

Kamboja

Kambojas are also included in the Uttarapatha. In ancient literature, the Kamboja is variously associated with the Gandhara, Darada and the Bahlika (Bactria). Ancient Kamboja is known to have comprised regions on either side of the Hindukush. The original Kamboja was located in eastern Oxus country as neighbor to Bahlika, but with time, some clans of Kambojas appear to have crossed Hindukush and planted colonies on its southern side also. These latter Kambojas are associated with the Daradas and Gandharas in Indian literature and also find mention in the Edicts of Ashoka. The evidence in Mahabharata and in Ptolemy's Geography distinctly supports two Kamboja settlements. The cis-Hindukush region from Nurestan up to Rajori in southwest of Kashmir sharing borders with the Daradas and the Gandharas constituted the Kamboja country (MBH VII.4.5; II.27.23). The capital of Kamboja was probably Rajapura (modern Rajori) in south-west of Kashmir. The Kamboja Mahajanapada of the Buddhist traditions refers to this cis-Hindukush branch of ancient Kambojas.

The trans-Hindukush region including Pamirs and Badakhshan which shared borders with the Bahlikas (Bactria) in the west and the Lohas and Rishikas of Sogdiana/Fergana in the north, constituted the Parama-Kamboja country.

The trans-Hindukush branch of the Kambojas remained pure Iranian but the Kambojas of cis-Hindukush appear to have come under Indian cultural influence. The Kambojas are known to have had both Iranian as well as Indian affinities. The Kambojas were also a well known republican people since Epic times. Mahabharata refers to several Ganah (or Republics) of the Kambojas (MBH 7/91/39). Kautiliya's Arthashastra (11/1/4) and Ashoka's Edict No. XIII also attest that the Kambojas followed republican constitution. Panini's Sutras (IV.1.168-175), though tend to convey that the Kamboja of Panini was a Kshatriya Monarchy, but the special rule and the exceptional form of derivative he gives to denote the ruler of the Kambojas implies that the king of Kamboja was a titular head (king consul) only.

According to Buddhist texts, the first fourteen of the above Mahajanapadas belong to Majjhimadesa (Mid India) while the last two belong to Uttarapatha or the north-west division of Jambudvipa.

In a struggle for supremacy that followed in the sixth/fifth century BCE, the growing state of Magadhas emerged as the most predominant power in ancient India annexing several of the Janapadas of the Majjhimadesa. A bitter line in the Brahmin Puranas laments that Magadhan emperor Mahapadama Nanda exterminated all Kshatriyas, none worthy of the name Kshatrya being left thereafter. This obviously refers to the Kasis, Kosalas, Kurus, Panchalas, Vatsyas and other neo-Vedic tribes of the east Panjab of whom nothing was ever heard except in the legend and poetry.

The Kambojans and Gandharans, however, never came into direct contact with Magadhan state until Chandragupta and Kautiliya arose on the scene. But these nations also fell a prey to the Achaemenids of Persia during the reign of Cyrus (558-530 BCE) or in the first year of Darius. Kamboja and Gandhara formed the twentieth and richest strapy of Achaemenid Empire. Cyrus I is said to have destroyed the famous Kamboja city called Kapisi (modern Begram) in Paropamisadae.

Magadha

The actual extent of the Kingdom of Magadha is unknown. Shown here is the approximate extent of Magadha in 500 BCE. Magadha was an ancient Indo-Aryan kingdom of Mahajanapadas in Ancient India, mentioned in both the Ramayana and the Mahabharata. It was also one of the four main kingdoms of India at the time of the Buddha, having risen to power during the reigns of Bimbisara (c. 544-491 BCE) and his son Ajatashatru (c. 491-460 BCE). The core of the kingdom was that portion of Bihar lying south of the Ganges, with its capital at Rajagriha (modern Rajgir). Magadha expanded to include most of Bihar and Bengal with the conquest of Anga, and then expanded up the Ganges valley annexing Kosala and Kashi. Magadha formed one of the sixteen so-called Mahajanapadas (Sanskrit, 'great country'). The Magadha empire included republican communities such as Rajakumara. Villages had their own assemblies under their local chiefs called Gramakas. Their administrations were divided into executive, judicial, and military functions. Bimbisara was friendly to both Jainism and Buddhism and suspended tolls at the river ferries for all ascetics after the Buddha was once stopped at the Ganges River for lack of money.

There is little certain information available on the early rulers of Magadha. The most important sources are the Buddhist Chronicles of Sri Lanka, the Puranas, and various Buddhist and Jain holy texts. Based on these sources, it appears that Magadha was ruled by the Sisunaga dynasty for some 200 years, c. 550-350 B.C.E. The Sisunaga dynasty was overthrown by Ugrasena Mahapadma Nanda, the first of the so-called nine Nandas (a.k.a. the Nanda or Nava Nanda dynasty). He was followed by his eight sons, whose names were (according to the Mahabodhivamsa) Panduka, Pandugati, Bhutapala, Ratthapala, Govisanaka, Dasasiddhaka, Kevatta, and Dhana Nanda. According to the Sri Lankan Chronicles, the Nanda dynasty was in power for mere 22 years, while the Puranas state that Mahapadma ruled for 28 years and his eight sons for only 12.

King Bimbisara of the Shishunaga dynasty led an active and expansive policy, conquering Anga in what is now West Bengal.

Siddhartha Gautama himself was born a prince of Kapilavastu in Kosala around 563 BCE. As the scene of many incidents in his life, Magadha was a holy land.

After the death of Bimbisara at the hands of his son, Ajatashatru, the widowed princess of Kosala also died of grief, causing King Prasenajit to revoke the gift of Kashi and triggering a war between Kosala and Magadha. Ajatashatru was trapped by an ambush and captured with his army; but in a peace treaty he, his army, and Kashi were restored to Magadha, and he married Prasenajit's daughter.

Accounts differ slightly as to the cause of Ajatashatru's war with the Licchavi republic. It appears that Ajatashatru sent a minister, who for three years worked to undermine the unity of the Licchavis at Vaishali. To launch his attack across the Ganga River (Ganges), Ajatashatru had to build a fort at a new capital called Pataliputra, which the Buddha prophesied would become a great center of commerce. Torn by disagreements the Licchavis were easily defeated once the fort was constructed. Jain texts tell how Ajatashatru used two new weapons-a catapult and a covered chariot with swinging mace that has been compared to modern tanks.

In 326 BCE, the army of Alexander the Great approached the boundaries of the Magadhan Empire. The army, exhausted and frightened by the prospect of facing another giant Indian army at the Ganges River, mutinied at the Hyphasis (modern Beas) and refused to march further East. Alexander, after the meeting with his officer, Coenus, was convinced that it was better to return, and turned south, conquering his way down the Indus to the Ocean.

A short while later, Magadha was the seat of the powerful Maurya dynasty, founded by Chandragupta, which extended over most of Southern Asia under Asoka; and, later, of the powerful Gupta Empire. The capital of the Mauryan Empire, Pataliputra (modern Patna), was begun as a Magadhan fortress and became the capital sometime after Ajatashatru's reign. Chandragupta destroyed the Nanda dynasty around 321 BCE, and became the first king of the great Mauryan Empire.

Magadha Empire

Amongst the sixteen Mahajanapadas, the kingdom of Magadha rose to prominence under a number of dynasties that peaked in power under the reign of Asoka Maurya, one of India's most legendary and famous emperors. The kingdom of Magadha had emerged as a major power following the subjugation of two neighbouring kingdoms, and possessed an unparalleled military.

Brihadratha Dynasty

According to the Puranas,the Magadha Empire was established by the Brihadratha Dynasty, who was the sixth in line from Emperor Kuru of the Bharata dynasty through his eldest son Sudhanush.The first prominent Emperor of the Magadhan branch of Bharathas was Emperor Brihadratha.His son Jarasandha appears in popular legend and is slain by Bhima in the Mahabharatha.Vayu Purana mentions that the Brihadrathas ruled for 1000 years.

Pradyota Dynasty

The Brihadrathas were succeeded by the Pradyotas who according to the Vayu Purana ruled for 138 years.

Shishunaga Dynasty

According to tradition, the Shishunaga dynasty founded the Magadha Empire in 684 BCE, whose capital was Rajagriha, later Pataliputra, near the present day Patna. This dynasty lasted till 424 BCE, when it was overthrown by the Nanda dynasty. This period saw the development of two of India's major religions. Gautama Buddha in the 6th or 5th century BCE was the founder of Buddhism, which later spread to East Asia and South-East Asia, while Mahavira founded Jainism.

Nanda Dynasty

The Nanda dynasty was established by an illegitimate son of the king Mahanandin of the previous Shishunaga dynasty. Mahapadma Nanda died at the age of 88, ruling the bulk of this 100-year dynasty. The Nandas were followed by the Maurya dynasty.

Maurya Dynasty

In 321 BCE, exiled general Chandragupta Maurya founded the Maurya dynasty after overthrowing the reigning king Dhana Nanda to establish the Maurya Empire. During this time, most of the subcontinent was united under a single government for the first time. Capitalising on the destabilization of northern India by the Persian and Greek incursions, the Mauryan empire under Chandragupta would not only conquer most of the Indian subcontinent, but also push its boundaries into Persia and Central Asia, conquering the Gandhara region. Chandragupta was succeeded by his son Bindusara, who expanded the kingdom over most of present day India, barring the extreme south and east, which may have held tributary status.

The kingdom was inherited by his son Ashoka The Great who initially sought to expand his kingdom. In the aftermath of the carnage caused in the invasion of Kalinga, he renounced bloodshed and pursued a policy of non-violence or ahimsa after converting to Buddhism.

The Edicts of Ashoka are the oldest preserved historical documents of India, and from Ashoka's time, approximate dating of dynasties becomes possible.

The Mauryan dynasty under Ashoka was responsible for the proliferation of Buddhist ideals across the whole of East Asia and South-East Asia, fundamentally altering the history and development of Asia as a whole. Ashoka the Great has been described as one of the greatest rulers the world has seen.

Approximate Dates of Mauryan Dynasty

Emperor	Reign start	Reign end
Chandragupta Maurya	322 BCE	298 BCE
Bindusara	297 BCE	272 BCE
Asoka The Great	273 BCE	232 BCE
Dasaratha	232 BCE	224 BCE
Samprati	224 BCE	215 BCE
Salisuka	215 BCE	202 BCE
Devavarman	202 BCE	195 BCE
Satadhanvan	195 BCE	187 BCE
Brihadratha	187 BCE	185 BCE

Greatest extent of the Sunga Empire (185 BCE-73 BCE) It should be possible to replace this fair use image with a freely licensed one. If you can, please do so as soon as is practical.

Shunga Dynasty

The Sunga dynasty was established in 185 BCE, about fifty years after Ashoka's death, when the king Brihadratha, the last of the Mauryan rulers, was brutally murdered by the then commander-in-chief of the Mauryan armed forces, Pusyamitra Sunga, while he was taking the Guard of Honour of his forces. Pusyamitra Sunga then ascended the throne.

Kanva Dynasty

The Kanva dynasty replaced the Shunga dynasty, and ruled in the eastern part of India from 71 BCE to 26 BCE. The last ruler of the Sunga dynasty was overthrown by Vasudeva of the Kanva dynasty in 75 BC.

The Kanva ruler allowed the kings of the Sunga dynasty to continue to rule in obscurity in a corner of their former dominions. Magadha was ruled by four Kanva rulers. In 30 BC, the southern power swept away both the Kanvas and Sungas and the province of Eastern Malwa was absorbed within the dominions of the conqueror. Following the collapse of the Kanva dynasty, the Satavahana dynasty of the Andhra kindgom replaced the Magandhan kingdom as the most powerful Indian state.

Kings of Magadha

A list of kings according to the Sri Lankan Chronicles follows:

1. Bimbisara (ruled for 52 years)
2. Ajatasatru (32 years; The Buddha is thought to have died in the 8th year of Ajatasatru's reign.)
3. Udayin or Udayibhadra (16 years)
4. Anuruddha (c. 4 years)
5. Munda (c. 4 years)
6. Nagadasaka (24 years)
7. Sisunaga (18 years)
8. Kalasoka (28 years)

9. Ten sons of Kalasoka, Nandivardhana being the most prominent (22 years). The names for the other eight are given in the Mahabodhivamsa as follows: Bhaddasena, Korandavanna, Mangura, Sabbañjaha, Jalika, Ubhaka, Sañjaya, Korabya, and Pañcamaka.

The Puranas give a rather different list with long reigns, making the Sisunaga dynasty 321 years long:

1. Sisunaga (ruled for 40 years)
2. Kakavarna (26 years)
3. Ksemadharman (36 years)
4. Ksemajit or Ksatraujas (24 years)
5. Bimbisara (28 years)
6. Ajatasatru (27 years)
7. Darsaka (24 years)
8. Udayin (33 years)
9. Nandivardhana (40 years)
10. Mahanandin (43 years)

MIDDLE KINGDOMS OF INDIA

- Nanda empire
- Maurya Empire
- Satavahana empire
- Sunga Empire
- Kuninda Kingdom
- Kalinga
- Gupta Empire
- Pala Empire
- Solanki
- Sena dynasty
- Pandyan Kingdom
- Chera
- Cholas
- Kalabhras

- Pallava
- Chalukya

Rashtrakuta

(Persian rule)

(Greek conquests)

- Indo-Greeks
- Indo-Scythians
- Indo-Parthians
- Kushan Empire
- Western Kshatrapas
- Indo-Sassanians
- Kidarite Kingdom
- Indo-Hephthalites

(Islamic invasion of India)

- Shahi

5

Maurya Empire

The Maurya Empire, ruled by the Mauryan dynasty, was the largest and most powerful political and military empire of ancient India.

ORIGIN

Originating from the kingdom of Magadha in the Indo-Gangetic plains of modern Bihar and Bengal, and with its capital city of Pataliputra (near modern Patna), the Empire was founded in 321 BCE by Chandragupta Maurya, who had overthrown the Nanda Dynasty and begun expanding his power across central and western India. The Empire stretched to the north along the natural boundaries of the Himalayas, and to the east stretching into what is now Assam. To the west, it reached beyond modern Pakistan and included Baluchistan in Persia and significant portions of what is now Afghanistan, including the modern Herat and Kandahar provinces. The Empire was expanded into India's central and southern regions by Emperor Bindusara, but it excluded a small portion of unexplored tribal and forested regions near Kalinga.

Following the conquest of Kalinga in a major war, Ashoka the Great ended the military expansion of the empire. The kingdoms of Pandya and Cheras in southern India thus preserved their independence, accepting the supremacy of the Mauryan emperor. The Mauryan Empire was perhaps the greatest empire to rule the Indian subcontinent until the arrival of the British. Its decline began fifty years after Ashoka's rule ended, and it dissolved in 185 BCE with the foundation of the Sunga Dynasty in Magadha.

Under Chandragupta, the Mauryan Empire liberated the trans-indus region, which was under Macedonian occupation. Chandragupta then defeated the invasion led by Seleucus I, a Greek general from Alexander's army. Under Chandragupta and his successors, both internal and external trade, and agriculture and economic activities, all thrived and expanded across India thanks to the creation of a single and efficient system of finance, administration and security. After the Kalinga War, the Empire experienced half a century of peace and security under Ashoka: India was a prosperous and stable empire of great economic and military power whose political influence and trade extended across Western and Central Asia and Europe. Mauryan India also enjoyed an era of social harmony, religious transformation, and expansion of the sciences and of knowledge. Chandragupta Maurya's embrace of Jainism increased social and religious renewal and reform across his society, while Ashoka's embrace of Buddhism was the foundation of the reign of social and political peace and non-violence across all of India. Ashoka sponsored the spreading of Buddhist ideals into Sri Lanka, Southeast Asia, West Asia and Mediterranean Europe.

The Lion Capital of Ashoka, erected around 250 BCE. It is the emblem of India.

Chandragupta's minister Kautilya Chanakya wrote the Arthashastra, one of the greatest treatises on economics, politics, foreign affairs, administration, military arts, war, and religion ever produced in the East. Archaeologically, the period of Mauryan rule in South Asia falls into the era of Northern Black Polished Ware (NBPW). The Arthashastra and the Edicts of Ashoka are primary sources of written records of the Mauryan times. The Mauryan empire is considered one of the most significant periods in Indian history. The Lion Capital of Asoka at Sarnath, is the emblem of India.

Although Alexander set up a Macedonian garrison and satrapies (vassal states) in Northwest India, ruled by the previous Indian kings Ambhi of Taxila and Porus of Pauravas, and the Greek generals Eudemus and Peithon until around 316 BCE, the disruptive nature of his invasion and subsequent retreat left the region in a state of instability. It was in this context that Chandragupta Maurya and his advisor, Chanakya, were able to drive away the occupying forces and consolidate the region under the control of his newly-occupied seat of power in Magadha.

CHANAKYA AND CHANDRAGUPTA MAURYA

Following Alexander's advance into the Punjab, a brahmin named Chanakya (real name Vishnu Gupta, also known as Kautilya) Chanakya traveled to Magadha, a kingdom that was large and militarily-powerful and feared by its neighbors, but was dismissed by its king Dhana, of the Nanda Dynasty. However, the prospect of battling Magadha in a major war was one of the factors that caused the refusal of Alexander's troops to go further east: he returned to Babylon, and he re-deployed most of his troops west of the Indus river. When Alexander died in Babylon, soon after in 323 BCE, his empire fragmented, and local kings declared their independence.

Chandragupta Maurya's rise to power is shrouded in mystery and controversy. On the one hand, a number of ancient Indian accounts, such as the drama Mudrarakshasa (Poem of Rakshasa-Rakshasa was the prime minister of Magadha) by Visakhadatta, describe his royal ancestry and even link him with the Nanda family. A kshatriya tribe known as the Maurya's are referred to in the earliest texts Buddhist texts, Mahaparinibbana Sutta. However, any conclusions are hard to make without further historical evidence. Chandragupta first emerges in Greek accounts as "Sandrokottos". As a young man he is said to have met Alexander. He is also said to have met the Nanda king, angered him, and made a narrow escape.

Chanakya's original intentions were to train a guerilla army under Chandragupta's command. Gathering young men and ex-soldiers from across central India, including Yavana (Greek), Scythian and Persian troops, Chandragupta's forces attacked and vanquished the Nanda dynasty. In the northwest, sometime after the departure of the Greek satraps Peithon and Eudemus in 317 BCE, Chandragupta vanquished the remnants of Greek forces. Under principles outlined in the Arthashastra, Maurya built an extensive intelligence network, the first of its kind in India-a network of spies and informers who betrayed enemy plans, and mis-informed the enemy themselves of Maurya's true designs.

Conquest of Magadha

Chanakya encouraged Chandragupta and his army to take over the throne of Magadha. Using his intelligence network, Chandragupta gathered many young men from across Magadha and other provinces, men upset over the corrupt and oppressive rule of king Dhana, plus resources necessary for his army to fight a long series of battles. These men included the former general of Taxila, other accomplished students of Chanakya, the representative of King Porus of Kakayee, his son Malayketu, and the rulers of small states.

Preparing to invade Pataliputra, Maurya hatched a plan. A battle was announced and the Magadhan army was drawn from the city to a distant battlefield to engage Maurya's forces. Maurya's general and spies meanwhile bribed the corrupt general of Nanda. He also managed to create an atmosphere of civil war in the kingdom, which culminated in the death of the heir to the throne. Chanakya managed to win over popular sentiment. Ultimately Nanda resigned, handing power to Chandragupta, and went into exile and was never heard of again. Chanakya contacted the prime minister, Rakshasas, and made him understand that his loyalty was to Magadha, not to the Magadha dynasty, insisting that he continue in office. Chanakya also reiterated that choosing to resist would start a war that would severely affect Magadha and destroy the city. Rakshasa accepted Chanakya's reasoning, and Chandragupta Maurya was legitimately installed as the new King of Magadha. Rakshasa became Chandragupta's chief advisor, and Chanakya assumed the position of an elder statesman.

The actual extent of the Kingdom of Magadha is unknown. Shown here is the approximate extent of Magadha in 500 BCE. Chandragupta extended the borders of Magadha towards Selucid Persia after conquering the Gangetic plains. Bindusara is thought to have extended the borders of the empire southward into the Deccan. Ashoka extended into the Kalinga Kingdom during the Kalinga War and established superiority over the southern kingdoms.

BUILDING INDIA'S FIRST EMPIRE

Having become the king of one of India's most powerful states, Chandragupta invaded the Punjab. One of Alexander's satraps, Peithon, satrap of Media, had tried to raise a coalition against him. Chandragupta managed to conquer the Punjab capital of Taxila, one of ancient India's most important cities, increasing his power and consolidating his control.

EMPEROR CHANDRAGUPTA

Approximate Dates of Mauryan Dynasty

Emperor	Reign start	Reign end
Chandragupta Maurya	322 BCE	298 BCE
Bindusara	297 BCE	272 BCE
Asoka The Great	273 BCE	232 BCE
Dasaratha	232 BCE	224 BCE
Samprati	224 BCE	215 BCE
Salisuka	215 BCE	202 BCE
Devavarman	202 BCE	195 BCE
Satadhanvan	195 BCE	187 BCE
Brihadratha	187 BCE	185 BCE

Chandragupta was again in conflict with the Greeks when Seleucus I, ruler of the Seleucid Empire, tried to reconquer the northwestern parts of India, during a campaign in 305 BCE, but failed. The two rulers finally concluded a peace treaty: a marital treaty (Epigamia) was concluded, implying either a marital alliance between the two dynastic lines or a recognition of marriage between Greeks and Indians, Chandragupta received the satrapies of Paropamisadae (Kamboja and Gandhara), Arachosia (Kandhahar) and Gedrosia (Balochistan), and Seleucus I received 500 war elephants that were to have a decisive role in his victory against western Hellenistic kings at the Battle of Ipsus in 301 BCE. Diplomatic relations were established and several Greeks, such as the historian Megasthenes, Deimakos and Dionysius resided at the Mauryan court.

Chandragupta established a strong centralized state with a complex administration at Pataliputra, which, according to Megasthenes, was "surrounded by a wooden wall pierced by 64 gates and 570 towers-(and) rivaled the splendors of contemporaneous Persian sites such as Susa and Ecbatana." Chandragupta's son Bindusara extended the rule of the Mauryan empire towards central and southern India. He also had a Greek ambassador at his court, named Deimachus (Strabo 1-70).

ASHOKA THE GREAT

Chandragupta's great grandson Ashokavardhan Maurya, better known as Ashoka the Great (ruled 273-232 BCE), is considered by contemporary historians to have been perhaps the greatest of Indian monarchs.

As a young prince, Ashoka was a brilliant commander who crushed revolts in Ujjain and Taxila. As monarch he was ambitious and aggressive, re-asserting the Empire's superiority in southern and western India. But it was his conquest of Kalinga which proved to be the pivotal event of his life. Although Ashoka's army succeeded in overwhelming Kalinga forces of royal soldiers and civilian units, an estimated 100,000 soldiers and civilians were killed in the furious warfare, including over 10,000 of Ashoka's own men. Hundreds of thousands of people were adversely affected by the destruction and fallout of war. When he personally witnessed the devastation, Ashoka began feeling remorse, and he cried 'what have I done?'. Although the annexation of Kalinga was completed, Ashoka embraced the teachings of Gautama Buddha, and renounced war and violence. For a monarch in ancient times, this was an historic feat.

Ashoka implemented principles of ahimsa by banning hunting and violent sports activity and ending indentured and forced labor (many thousands of people in war-ravaged Kalinga had been forced into hard labor and servitude). While he maintained a large and powerful army, to keep the peace and maintain authority, Ashoka expanded friendly relations with states across Asia and Europe, and he sponsored Buddhist missions. He undertook a massive public works building campaign across the country. Over 40 years of peace, harmony and prosperity made Ashoka one of the most successful and famous monarchs in Indian history. He remains an idealized figure of inspiration in modern India.

The Edicts of Ashoka, set in stone, some of them written in Greek and Aramaic, refer to the Greeks, Kambojas, and Gandharas as peoples forming a frontier region of his empire. They also attest to Ashoka's having sent envoys to the Greek rulers in the West as far as the Mediterranean. The edicts precisely name each of the rulers of the Hellenic world at the time such as Amtiyoko (Antiochus), Tulamaya (Ptolemy), Amtikini (Antigonos), Maka (Magas) and Alikasudaro Alexander as recipients of Ashoka's prozelitism. The Edicts also accurately locates their territory "600 yojanas away" (a yojanas being about 7 miles), corresponding to the distance between the center of India and Greece (roughly 4,000 miles).

Administration

The Empire was divided into four provinces, with the imperial capital at Pataliputra. From Ashokan edicts, the names of the four provincial capitals are Tosali (in the east), Ujjain in the west, Suvarnagiri (in the south), and Taxila (in the north). The head of the provincial administration was the Kumara (royal prince), who governed the provinces as king's representative. The kumara was assisted by Mahamatyas and council of ministers. This organizational structure was reflected at the imperial level with the Emperor and his Mantriparishad (Council of Ministers).

Historians theorize that the organization of the Empire was in line with the extensive bureaucracy described by Kautilya in the Arthashastra: a sophisticated civil service governed everything from municipal hygiene to international trade. The expansion and defense of the empire was made possible by what appears to have been the largest standing army of its time. According to Megasthenes, the empire wielded a military of 600,000 infantry, 30,000 cavalry, and 9,000 war elephants. A vast espionage system collected intelligence for both internal and external security purposes. Having renounced offensive warfare and expansionism, Ashoka nevertheless continued to maintain this large army, to protect the Empire and instill stability and peace across West and South Asia.

Economy

For the first time in South Asia, political unity and military security allowed for a common economic system and enhanced trade and commerce, with increased agricultural productivity. The previous situation involving hundreds of kingdoms, many small armies, powerful regional chieftains, and internecine warfare, gave way to a disciplined central authority. Farmers were freed of tax and crop collection burdens from regional kings, paying instead to a nationally-administered and strict-but-fair system of taxation as advised by the principles in the Arthashastra.

Chandragupta Maurya established a single currency across India, and a network of regional governors and administrators and a civil service provided justice and security for merchants, farmers and traders. The Mauryan army wiped out many gangs of bandits, regional private armies, and powerful chieftains who sought to impose their own supremacy in small areas. Although regimental in revenue collection, Maurya also sponsored many public works and waterways to enhance productivity, while internal trade in India expanded greatly due to newfound political unity and internal peace.

Under the Indo-Greek friendship treaty, and during Ashoka's reign, an international network of trade expanded. The Khyber Pass, on the modern boundary of Pakistan and Afghanistan, became a strategically-important port of trade and intercourse with the outside world. Greek states and Hellenic kingdoms in West Asia became important trade partners of India.

Trade also extended through the Malay peninsula into Southeast Asia. India's exports included silk goods and textiles, spices and exotic foods. The Empire was enriched further with an exchange of scientific knowledge and technology with Europe and West Asia. Ashoka also sponsored the construction of thousands of roads, waterways, canals, hospitals, rest-houses and other public works. The easing of many overly-rigorous administrative practices, including those regarding taxation and crop collection, helped increase productivity and economic activity across the Empire.

Religion

Emperor Chandragupta Maurya became the first major Indian monarch to initiate a religious transformation at the highest level when he embraced Jainism, a religious movement resented by orthodox Hindu priests who usually attended the imperial court. At an older age, Chandragupta renounced his throne and material possessions to join a wandering group of Jain monks. However, his successor, Emperor Bindusara, preserved Hindu traditions and distanced himself from Jain and Buddhist movements.

But when Ashoka embraced Buddhism, following the Kalinga War, he renounced expansionism and aggression, and the harsher injunctions of the Arthashastra on the use of force, intensive policing, and ruthless measures for tax collection and against rebels. Ashoka sent a mission led by his son and daughter to Sri Lanka, whose king Tissa was so charmed with Buddhist ideals that he adopted them himself and made Buddhism the state religion.

Ashoka sent many Buddhist missions to West Asia, Greece and South East Asia, and commissioned the construction of monasteries, schools and publication of Buddhist literature across the empire. He is believed to have built as many as 84,000 stupas across India, and he increased the popularity of Buddhism in Afghanistan. Ashoka helped convene the Third Buddhist Council of India and South Asia's Buddhist orders, near his capital, a council that undertook much work of reform and expansion of the Buddhist religion.

While himself a Buddhist, Ashoka retained the membership of Hindu priests and ministers in his court, and he maintained religious freedom and tolerance although the Buddhist faith grew in popularity with his patronage. Indian society began embracing the philosophy of ahimsa, and given the increased prosperity and improved law enforcement, crime and internal conflicts reduced dramatically. Also greatly discouraged was the caste system and orthodox discrimination, as Hinduism began to absorb the ideals and values of Jain and Buddhist teachings. Social freedom began expanding in an age of peace and prosperity.

Contacts with the Hellenistic World

Foundation of the Empire

Relations with the Hellenistic world may have started from the very beginning of the Maurya Empire. Plutarch reports that Chandragupta Maurya met with Alexander the Great, probably around Taxila in the northwest:

"Androcottus, when he was a stripling, saw Alexander himself, and we are told that he often said in later times that Alexander narrowly missed making himself master of the country, since its king was hated and despised on account of his baseness and low birth."

The Macedonians (described as Yona or Yavana in Indian sources) may also have participated, together with other groups, to the armed uprising of Chandragupta against the Nanda Dynasty. The Mudrarakshasa of Visakhadutta as well as the Jaina work Parisishtaparvan talk of Chandragupta's alliance with the Himalayan king Parvatka, often identified with Porus. This Himalayan alliance gave Chandragupta a composite and powerful army made up of Yavanas (Greeks), Kambojas, Shakas (Scythians), Kiratas (Nepalese), Parasikas (Persians) and Bahlikas (Bactrians) who took Pataliputra (also called Kusumapura, "The City of Flowers"):

"Kusumapura was besieged from every direction by the forces of Parvata and Chandragupta: Shakas, Yavanas, Kiratas, Kambojas, Parasikas, Bahlikas and others, assembled on the advice of Canakya"

With the help of these frontier martial tribes from Central Asia, Chandragupta was apparently able to defeat the Nanda/ Nandin rulers of Magadha so as to found the powerful Maurya empire in northern India.

Reconquest of the Northwest (c. 310 BCE)

Chandragupta ultimately occupied Northwestern India, in the territories formerly ruled by the Greeks, where he fought the satraps (described as "Prefects" in Western sources) left in place after Alexander (Justin), among whom may have been Eudemus, ruler in the western Punjab until his departure in 317 BCE or Peithon, son of Agenor, ruler of the Greek colonies along the Indus until his departure for Babylon in 316 BCE, and possibly Sophytes, who may have ruled in the Punjab until around 294 BCE (although it is also conjectured he may have ruled in Bactria instead).

"India, after the death of Alexander, had assassinated his prefects, as if shaking the burden of servitude. The author of this liberation was Sandracottos, but he had transformed liberation in servitude after victory, since, after taking the throne, he himself oppressed the very people he has liberated from foreign domination" Justin XV.4.12-13.

"Later, as he was preparing war against the prefects of Alexander, a huge wild elephant went to him and took him on his back as if tame, and he became a remarkable fighter and war leader. Having thus acquired royal power, Sandracottos possessed India at the time Seleucos was preparing future glory." Justin XV.4.19.

Conflict and Alliance with Seleucus (303 BCE)

Silver coin of Seleucus I Nicator, who fought Chandragupta Maurya, and later made an alliance with him. Seleucus I Nicator, the Macedonian satrap of the Asian portion of Alexander's former empire, conquered and put under his own authority eastern territories as far as Bactria and the Indus (Appian, History of Rome, The Syrian Wars 55), until in 305 BCE he entered in a confrontation with Chandragupta:

"Always lying in wait for the neighboring nations, strong in arms and persuasive in council, he [Seleucus] acquired Mesopotamia, Armenia, 'Seleucid' Cappadocia, Persis, Parthia, Bactria, Arabia, Tapouria, Sogdia, Arachosia, Hyrcania, and other adjacent peoples that had been subdued by Alexander, as far as the river Indus, so that the boundaries of his empire were the most extensive in Asia after that of Alexander. The whole region from Phrygia to the Indus was subject to Seleucus." Appian, History of Rome, The Syrian Wars 55.

Marital Alliance

A matrimonial alliance was also agreed upon (called Epigamia in ancient sources, meaning either the recognition of marriage between Indians and Greeks, or a dynastic alliance):

"He (Seleucus) crossed the Indus and waged war with Sandrocottus [Maurya], king of the Indians, who dwelt on the banks of that stream, until they came to an understanding with each other and contracted a marriage relationship." Appian, History of Rome, The Syrian Wars 55.

Since there are no records of an Indian princess in the abundant Classical literature on the Seleucid, it is generally thought that the alliance went the other way around, and that a Seleucid princess may have been bethrothed to the Mauryan Dynasty. This practice in itself was quite common in the Hellenistic world to formalize alliances. There is thus a possibility that the descendants of Chandragupta were partly of Hellenic descent, whether Chandragupta married the Seleucid princess, or his son Bindusara, and that the Maurya dynasty was considered as closely connected to the Seleucid one. Bindusara himself, born earlier around 320 BCE, could not have been the result of such a union, but he may have been the one who married the Seleucid princess, just before his rise as Emperor in 298 BCE.

The marriage arrangement has led some to suggest that Ashoka may have been a product of this union although the general view is that Ashoka was born from a Brahmin mother who was a minor queen of Bindusara, based on the account of the 2nd century CE Ashokavadana ("Legend of Ashoka"). The practice of Mauryan rulers to have harems is repeatedly mentionned in sources such as the Ashokavadana however, which would suggest a multiplicity of bloodlines and a numerous descent for each king.

At the very least, this treaty on "Epigamia" implies lawfull marriage between Greeks and Indians was recognized at the State level, although it is unclear whether it occurred among dynastic rulers or common people, or both.

Exchange of Ambassadors

Seleucus dispatched an ambassador, Megasthenes, to Chandragupta, and later Deimakos to his son Bindusara, at the Mauryan court at Pataliputra (Modern Patna in Bihar state). Later Ptolemy II Philadelphus, the ruler of Ptolemaic Egypt and contemporary of Ashoka, is also recorded by Pliny the

Elder as having sent an ambassador named Dionysius to the Mauryan court.

Exchange of Presents

Classical sources have also recorded that following their treaty, Chandragupta and Seleucus exchanged presents, such as when Chandragupta sent various aphrodisiacs to Seleucus:

"And Theophrastus says that some contrivances are of wondrous efficacy in such matters [as to make people more amorous]. And Phylarchus confirms him, by reference to some of the presents which Sandrakottus, the king of the Indians, sent to Seleucus; which were to act like charms in producing a wonderful degree of affection, while some, on the contrary, were to banish love" Athenaeus of Naucratis, "The deipnosophists" Book I, chapter 32.

His son Bindusara 'Amitraghata' (Slayer of Enemies) also is recorded in Classical sources as having exchanged present with Antiochus I:

"But dried figs were so very much sought after by all men (for really, as Aristophanes says, "There's really nothing nicer than dried figs"), that even Amitrochates, the king of the Indians, wrote to Antiochus, entreating him (it is Hegesander who tells this story) to buy and send him some sweet wine, and some dried figs, and a sophist; and that Antiochus wrote to him in answer, "The dry figs and the sweet wine we will send you; but it is not lawfull for a sophist to be sold in Greece" Athenaeus, "Deipnosophistae" XIV.67.

Buddhist Missions to the West (c.250 BCE)

Also, in the Edicts of Ashoka, Ashoka mentions the Hellenistic kings of the period as a recipient of his Buddhist prozelitism, although no Western historical record of this event remain:

"The conquest by Dharma has been won here, on the borders, and even six hundred yojanas (5,400-9,600 km) away, where the Greek king Antiochos rules, beyond there where the four kings named Ptolemy, Antigonos, Magas and Alexander rule, likewise in the south among the Cholas, the Pandyas, and as far as Tamraparni (Sri Lanka)." (Edicts of Ashoka, 13th Rock Edict, S. Dhammika).

Ashoka also claims that he encouraged the development of herbal medicine, for men and animals, in their territories:

"Everywhere within Beloved-of-the-Gods, King Piyadasi's [Ashoka's] domain, and among the people beyond the borders, the Cholas, the Pandyas, the Satiyaputras, the Keralaputras, as far as Tamraparni and where the Greek king Antiochos rules, and among the kings who are neighbors of Antiochos, everywhere has Beloved-of-the-Gods, King Piyadasi, made provision for two types of medical treatment: medical treatment for humans and medical treatment for animals. Wherever medical herbs suitable for humans or animals are not available, I have had them imported and grown. Wherever medical roots or fruits are not available I have had them imported and grown. Along roads I have had wells dug and trees planted for the benefit of humans and animals." 2nd Rock Edict.

The Greeks in India even seem to have played an active role in the propagation of Buddhism, as some of the emissaries of Ashoka, such as Dharmaraksita, are described in Pali sources as leading Greek ("Yona") Buddhist monks, active in Buddhist proselytism (the Mahavamsa, XII).

Subhagsena and Antiochos III (206 BCE)

Sophagasenus was an Indian Mauryan ruler of the 3rd century BCE, described in ancient Greek sources, and named Subhagsena or Subhashsena in Prakrit. His name is mentionned in the list of Mauryan princes, and also in the list of the Yadava dynasty, as a descendant of Pradyumana. He may have been a grandson of Ashoka, or Kunala, the son of Ashoka. He ruled an area south of the Hindu Kush, possibly in Gandhara. Antiochos III, the Seleucid king, after having made peace with Euthydemus in Bactria, went to India in 206 BCE and is said to have renewed his friendship with the Indian king there:

"He (Antiochus) crossed the Caucasus and descended into India; renewed his friendship with Sophagasenus the king of the Indians; received more elephants, until he had a hundred and fifty altogether; and having once more provisioned his troops, set out again personally with his army: leaving Androsthenes of Cyzicus the duty of taking home the treasure which this king had agreed to hand over to him." Polybius 11.39

Decline

Ashoka was followed for 50 years by a succession of weaker kings. Brhadrata, the last ruler of the Mauryan dynasty, held territories that had shrunk considerably from the time of emperor Ashoka, although he still upheld the Buddhist faith.

Sunga Coup (185 BCE)

He was assassinated in 185 BCE during a military parade, by the commander-in-chief of his guard, the Brahmin general Pusyamitra Sunga, who then took over the throne and established the Sunga dynasty. The assassination of Brhadrata and the rise of the Sunga empire led to a wave of persecution for Buddhists, and a resurgence of Hinduism.

ESTABLISHEMENT OF THE INDO-GREEK KINGDOM

The fall of the Mauryas left the Khyber Pass unguarded, and a wave of foreign invasion followed. The Greco-Bactrian king, Demetrius, capitalized on the break-up of pan-Indian power, and he conquered southern Afghanistan and parts of northwestern India around 180 BCE, forming the Indo-Greek Kingdom.

The Indo-Greeks would maintain holdings on the trans-Indus region, and make forays into central India, for about a century. Under them, Buddhism was able to flourish, and one of their kings Menander became a famous figure of Buddhism. However, the extent of their domains and the lengths of their rule are subject to much debate. Numismatic evidence indicates that they retained holdings in the subcontinent right up to the birth of Christ.

Although the extent of their successes against indigenous powers such as the Sungas, Satavahanas, and Kalingas are unclear, what is clear is that Scythian tribes, renamed Indo-Scythians, brought about the demise of the Indo-Greeks from around 70 BCE and retained lands in the trans-Indus, the region of Mathura, and Gujarat.

The Empire to Modern Indians

Having been India's first major empire, the Maurya Empire holds a special place in the minds of Indian people: Indians feel pride in recalling the great political and military power the Empire held in its day, and the spirituality and piety of Ashoka, who kept war and violence away from his people. The media in India also has produced works based upon Mauryan times:

- Chanakya (early 1990s) was a Hindi television series that depicted the life and philosophy of Kautilya Chanakya, from fighting Alexander's invasion to the coronation of Chandragupta Maurya.
- Asoka (2001) is a Hindi film by Santosh Sivan starring Shahrukh Khan as the Emperor Ashoka, depicting his aggressive youth, early impetuous rule, and his transformation following the war in Kalinga. The film, however, does not claim that its portrayal of Ashoka's life is historically accurate.

HISTORICAL COMPARISON

While Chandragupta toppled the last Nanda king Dhanananda and established the Mauryan Empire, c. 321 BC, the first unified Chinese empire only arose a century later in 221 BC when the King of Qin, in the words of the Tang dynasty poet Li Bai, "swept up the Six States", thereby ending the Warring States Period and establishing himself as the First Emperor of China.

Although the Maurya and Qin both contended with vast populations and lands newly-unified by one centralized state, the rapid decline of the latter in fourteen years versus the much longer duration of the former (Maurya dynasty c.321-181 BC) may in part be explained by the brutal Legalist philosophy associated with Qin rule.

Whereas both empires recognized the ruler and his ministers as the basis of social order, the first great emperor of India recognized that he had a dharma (duty) to protect his people; his reign was not supported by brute force alone. Indeed, Emperor Asoka (the third Mauryan ruler) would be so troubled by the violent war in Kalinga that he would become a believer in Buddhism and emphasize non-violence, while endorsing freedom of religion in his empire.

Similarly, where Qin law emphasized strengthening the state by weakening the people through strict laws and punishments, Mauryan law had its basis in both protecting the people and maintaining order in the state. While Qin condemnation of individual rights would lead to hundreds of thousands of persons being forced into becoming state laborers, and hundreds more executed for engaging in prohibited scholarship, the Arthashastra of Kautilya urged conciliation as the best method to end popular unrest.

The First and Second Qin Emperors, who were neither benevolent nor conciliatory, implemented harsh laws that fomented much social unrest. Thus, Han dynasty historians, such as Sima Qian and Jia Yi, have insisted that in ruling through fear and coercion the First Emperor built both his empire's tomb and his own. In contrast, the greater order and more benign social philosophy implemented in Mauryan India may have helped stabilize the empire against severe internal and external pressures.

INDO-GREEK KINGDOM

The Indo-Greek Kingdom (or sometimes Graeco-Indian Kingdom) covered various parts of the northwest and northern Indian subcontinent from 180 BCE to around 10 CE, and was ruled by a succession of more than thirty Hellenistic kings, often in conflict with each other. The kingdom was founded when the Greco-Bactrian king Demetrius invaded India in 180 BCE, ultimately creating an entity which seceded from the powerful Greco-Bactrian Kingdom centered in Bactria (today's northern Afghanistan). Since the term "Indo-Greek Kingdom" loosely describes a number of various dynastic polities, it had numerous capitals, but the city of Taxila in northern Pakistan was probably among the earliest seats of local Hellenic rulers, though cities like Pushkalavati and Sagala (apparently the largest of such residences) would house a number of dynasties in their times-based on Ptolemy's Geography and the nomenclature of later kings, a certain Theophila in the south was also probably a satrapal or royal seat at some point.

During the two centuries of their rule, the Indo-Greek kings combined the Greek and Indian languages and symbols, as seen on their coins, and blended ancient Greek, Hindu and Buddhist religious practices, as seen in the archaeological remains of their cities and in the indications of their support of Buddhism. The Indo-Greek kings seem to have achieved a level of cultural syncretism with no equivalent in history, the consequences of which are still felt today, particularly through the diffusion and influence of Greco-Buddhist art.

The Indo-Greeks ultimately disappeared as a political entity around 10 CE following the invasions of the Indo-Scythians, although pockets of Greek populations probably remained for several centuries longer under the subsequent rule of the Indo-Parthians and Kushans.

Background

Preliminary Greek Presence in India

In 326 BCE Alexander the Great conquered the northwestern part of the Indian subcontinent as far as the Hyphasis River, and established satrapies as well as several cities, such as Bucephala, until his troops refused to go further east. The Indian satrapies of the Punjab were left to the rule of Porus and Taxiles, who were confirmed again at the Treaty of Triparadisus in 321 BCE, and remaining Greek troops in these satrapies were left under the command of the general Eudemus. Sometime after 321 Eudemus toppled Taxiles, until he left India in 316 BCE. Another general also ruled over the Greek colonies of the Indus: Peithon, son of Agenor, until his departure for Babylon in 316 BCE, and a last one, Sophytes, seems to have ruled in northern Punjab until around 294 BCE.

According to Indian sources, Greek ("Yavana") troops seem to have assisted Chandragupta Maurya in toppling the Nanda Dynasty and founding the Mauryan Empire. By around 312 BCE Chandragupta had established his rule in large parts of the northwestern Indian territories as well.

In 303 BCE, Seleucus I led an army to the Indus, where he encountered Chandragupta. The confrontation ended with a peace treaty, and "an intermarriage agreement", meaning either a dynastic marriage or an agreement for intermarriage between Indians and Greeks. Accordingly, Seleucus ceded to Chandragupta his northwestern territories as far as Arachosia and received 500 war elephants (which played a key role in the victory of Seleucus at the Battle of Ipsus):

"The Indians occupy [in part] some of the countries situated along the Indus, which formerly belonged to the Persians: Alexander deprived the Ariani of them, and established there settlements of his own. But Seleucus Nicator gave them to Sandrocottus in consequence of a marriage contract, and received in return five hundred elephants." Strabo 15.2.1(9). Also several Greeks, such as the historian Megasthenes followed by Deimakos and Dionysius, were sent to reside at the Mauryan court. Presents continued to be exchanged between the two rulers.

On these occasions, Greek populations apparently remained in the northwest of the Indian subcontinent under Mauryan rule. Chandragupta's grandson Ashoka, who had converted to the Buddhist faith declared in the Edicts of Ashoka, set in stone, some of them written in Greek, that Greek populations within his realm also had converted to Buddhism:

"Here in the king's domain among the Greeks, the Kambojas, the Nabhakas, the Nabhapamkits, the Bhojas, the Pitinikas, the Andhras and the Palidas, everywhere people are following Beloved-of-the-Gods' instructions in Dharma." Rock Edict Nb13 (S. Dhammika).

In his edicts, Ashoka claims he sent Buddhist emissaries to Greek rulers as far as the Mediterranean (Edict No13), and that he developed herbal medicine in their territories, for the welfare of humans and animals (Edict No2).

The Greeks in India even seem to have played an active role in the propagation of Buddhism, as some of the emissaries of Ashoka, such as Dharmaraksita, are described in Pali sources as leading Greek ("Yona") Buddhist monks, active in Buddhist proselytism (the Mahavamsa, XII). It is also thought that Greeks contributed to the sculptural work of the Pillars of Ashoka.

Again in 206 BCE, the Seleucid emperor Antiochus led an army into India, where he received war elephants and presents from the king Sophagasenus:

"He (Antiochus) crossed the Caucasus (Hindu Kush) and descended into India; renewed his friendship with Sophagasenus the king of the Indians; received more elephants, until he had a hundred and fifty altogether; and having once more provisioned his troops, set out again personally with his army: leaving Androsthenes of Cyzicus the duty of taking home the treasure which this king had agreed to hand over to him." Polybius 11.39.

Greek Rule in Bactria

Alexander also had established in neighbouring Bactria several cities (Ai-Khanoum, Begram) and an administration that were to last more than two centuries under the Seleucids and the Greco-Bactrians, all the time in direct contact with Indian territory.

The Greco-Bactrians maintained a strong Hellenistic culture at the door of India during the rule of the Mauryan empire in India, as exemplified by the archaeological site of Ai-Khanoum. When the Mauryan empire was toppled by the Sungas around 185 BCE, the Greco-Bactrians expanded into India, where they established the Indo-Greek kingdom.

Rise of the Sungas (185 BCE)

In India, the Maurya Dynasty was overthrown around 185 BCE when Pusyamitra Sunga, the commander-in-chief of Mauryan Imperial forces and a Brahmin, assassinated the last of the Mauryan emperors Brhadrata. Pusyamitra Sunga then ascended the throne and established the Sunga Empire, which extended its control as far west as the Punjab. Buddhist sources, such as the Asokavadana, affirm that Pusyamitra was hostile towards Buddhists and allegedly persecuted the Buddhist faith. A large number of Buddhist monasteries (viharas) were allegedly converted to Hindu temples, in such places as Nalanda, Bodhgaya, Sarnath or Mathura.

Establishment of the Indo-Greek Kingdom

The invasion of northern India, and the establishment what would be known as the "Indo-Greek kingdom", started around 180 BCE when Demetrius, son of the Greco-Bactrian king Euthydemus I, led his troops across the Hindu Kush. In the process of the invasion, the Greeks seem to have occupied territory as far as the capital of Pataliputra, before ultimately retreating and stabilizing their rule in northwestern India. Apollodotus, seemingly a relative of Demetrius, led the invasion to the south, while Menander, one of the generals of Demetrius, led the invasion to the east. Following his conquests, Demetrius received the title, a title never given to any king before.

Written evidence of the initial Greek invasion survives in the Greek writings of Strabo and Justin, and in Sanskrit in the records of Patanjali, Kalidasa, and in the Yuga Purana, among others. Coins and architectural evidence also attest to the extent of the initial Greek campaign.

Evidence of the Initial Invasion

Greco-Roman Sources

The founder of the Indo-Greek Kingdom Demetrius I "the Invincible" (205-171 BCE), wearing the scalp of an elephant, symbol of his conquests in India.

According to Strabo, Greek advances temporarily went as far as the Sunga capital Pataliputra (today Patna) in eastern India:

"Those who, after Alexander, advanced beyond the Hypanis, to the Ganges and Pataliputra." (Strabo, 15-1-27)

The 1st century BCE Greek historian Apollodorus, quoted by Strabo, affirms that the Bactrian Greeks, led by Demetrius I and Menander, conquered India and occupied a larger territory than the Macedonians under Alexander the Great, going beyond the Hypanis towards the Himalayas.

The Roman historian Justin also mentioned the Indo-Greek conquests, describing Demetrius as "King of the Indians" ("Regis Indorum"), and explaining that after vanquishing him Eucratides in turn "put India under his rule" ("Indiam in potestatem redegit"). Although "India" only meant the upper Indus for Alexander the Great, since the embassies of Megasthenes in the 3rd century BCE "India" meant to the Greeks most of the northern half of the Indian subcontinent. Greek and Indian sources tend to indicate that the Greeks campaigned as far as Pataliputra until they were forced to retreat following the coup staged by Eucratides back in Bactria circa 170 BCE, suggesting an occupation period of about eight years.

To the south, the Greeks occupied the areas of the Sindh and Gujarat down to the region of Surat (Greek: Saraostus) near Mumbai (Bombay), including the strategic harbour of Barigaza (Bharuch), as attested by several writers (Strabo 11; Periplus of the Erythraean Sea, Chap. 41/47) and as evidenced by coins dating from the Indo-Greek ruler Apollodotus I:

"The Greeks... took possession, not only of Patalena, but also, on the rest of the coast, of what is called the kingdom of Saraostus and Sigerdis." (Strabo 11.11.1)

The 1st century CE Periplus of the Erythraean Sea describes numerous Greek buildings and fortifications in Barigaza, although mistakenly attributing them to Alexander, and the circulation of Indo-Greek coinage in the region:

"The metropolis of this country is Minnagara, from which much cotton cloth is brought down to Barygaza. In these places there remain even to the present time signs of the expedition of Alexander, such as ancient shrines, walls of forts and great wells." Periplus, Chap. 41.

"To the present day ancient drachmae are current in Barygaza, coming from this country, bearing inscriptions in Greek letters, and the devices of those who reigned after Alexander, Apollodorus (sic) and Menander." Periplus Chap. 47.

From ancient authors (Pliny, Arrian, Ptolemy and Strabo), a list of provinces, satrapies, or simple regional designations, and Greek cities from within the Indo-Greek Kingdom can be discerned (though others have been lost), ranging from the Indus basin to the upper valley of the Ganges.

Indian Sources

Various Indian records describe Greek (called Yavana) attacks on Mathura, Panchala, Saketa, and Pataliputra. Patanjali, a grammarian and commentator on Panini around 150 BCE, describes in the Mahabhasya, the invasion in two examples using the imperfect tense of Sanskrit, denoting a recent event:

- "Arunad Yavanah Saketam" ("The Yavana [Greeks] were besieging Saketa")
- "Arunad Yavano Madhyamikam" ("The Yavana were besieging Madhyamika (the "Middle country").

The Anushasanaparava of the Mahabharata affirms that the country of Mathura, the heartland of India, was under the joint control of the Yavanas and the Kambojas. Accounts of battles between the Greeks and the Sunga in Central India are also found in the Malavikagnimitram, a play by Kalidasa which describes a battle between Greek forces and Vasumitra, the grandson of Pushyamitra, during the latter's reign. Also the Brahmanical text of the Yuga Purana, which describes Indian historical events in the form of a prophecy, relates the attack of the Indo-Greeks on the capital Pataliputra, a magnificent fortified city with 570 towers and 64 gates according to Megasthenes, and describes the ultimate destruction of the city's walls: "Then, after having approached Saketa together with the Panchalas and the Mathuras, the Yavanas, valiant in battle, will reach Kusumadhvaja ("The town of the flower-standard", Pataliputra). Then, once Puspapura (another name of Pataliputra) has been reached and its celebrated mud[-walls] cast down, all the realm will be in disorder." (Yuga Purana, Paragraph 47-48, 2002 edition.)

According to the Yuga Purana a situation of complete social disorder follows, in which the Yavanas rule and mingle with the people, and the position of the Brahmins and the Sudras is inverted: "Sudras will also be utterers of bho (a form of address used towards an equal or inferior), and Brahmins will be utterers of arya (a form of address used towards a superior), and the elders, most fearful of dharma, will fearlessly exploit the people. And in the city the Yavanas, the princes, will make this people acquainted with them: but the Yavanas, infatuated by war, will not remain in Madhyadesa." (Yuga Purana, Paragraph 55-56, 2002 edition.)

Archaeological Remains

Urban Remains

The city of Sirkap, today in northwestern Pakistan near Taxila, was built according to the "Hippodamian" grid-plan characteristic of Greek cities, and was a Hellenistic fortress of considerable proportions, with a 6,000 meter wall on the circonference, of a height of about 10 meters. The houses of the Indo-Greek level are "the best planned of all the six strata, and the rubble masonry of which its walls are built is also the most solid and compact". It is thought that the city was built by Demetrius.

Artifacts

Main archaeological artifacts from the Indo-Greek strata at Taxila. From top, left:

- Fluted vase with bead and reel design (Bhir Mound, stratum 1)
- Cup with rosace and decoratice scroll (Bhir Mound, stratum 1)
- Stone palette with individual on a couch being crowned by standing woman, and served (Sirkap, stratum 5)
- Handle with double depiction of a philosopher (Sirkap, stratum 5/4)
- Woman with smile (Sirkap, stratum 5)
- Man with moustache (Sirkap, stratum 5)

(Source: John Marshall "Taxila, Archaeological excavations").

Several Hellenistic artifacts have been found, in particular coins of Indo-Greek kings, stone palettes representing Greek mythological scenes, and small statuettes. Some of them are purely Hellenistic, others indicate an evolution of the Greco-Bactrian styles found at Ai-Khanoum towards more indianized styles. For example, accessories such as Indian ankle bracelets can be found on some representations of Greek mythological figures such as Artemis.

The excavations of the Greek levels at Sirkap were however very limited and made in peripheral areas, out of respect for the more recent archeological strata (those of the Indo-Scythian and especially Indo-Parthian levels) and the remaining religious buildings, and due to the difficulty of excavating extensively to a depth of about 6 meters. The results, although interesting, are partial and cannot be considered as exhaustive. Beyond this, no extensive archaeological excavation of an Indo-Greek city has ever really been done.

Stupas

When the Indo-Greeks settled in the area of Taxila, large Buddhist structures were already present, such as the stupa of Dharmarajika built by Ashoka in the 3rd century BCE. These structures were reinforced in the following centuries, by building rings of smaller stupas and constructions around the original ones. Several coins of the Indo-Greek king Zoilos II were found under the foundation of such a 1st century BCE stupa. Also, various Buddhist structures, such as the Butkara Stupa in the area of Swat were decorated with Hellenistic architectural elements from the 2nd century BCE.

Consolidation

Tetradrachm of Menander I (160-135 BCE) in Greco-Bactrian style (Alexandria-Kapisa mint).

Obv: King Menander throwing a spear.

Rev: Athena with thunderbolt. Greek legend: BASILEOS SOTEROS MENANDROU "Of King Menander, the Saviour".

Retreat from Eastern Regions

The first invasion was completed by 175 BCE, as the Indo-Greeks apparently contained the Sungas to the area eastward of Pataliputra, and established their rule on the new territory. Back in Bactria however, around 170 BCE, an usurper named Eucratides managed to topple the Euthydemid dynasty. He took for himself the title of king and started a civil war by invading the Indo-Greek territory, forcing the Indo-Greeks to retreat from their easternmost possessions and establish their new oriental frontier at Mathura, to confront this new threat:

"The Yavanas, infatuated by war, will not remain in Madhadesa (the Middle Country). There will be mutual agreement among them to leave, due to a terrible and very dreadful war having broken out in their own realm." (Yuga Purana, paragraphs 56-57, 2002 edition).

The Hathigumpha inscription, written by the king of Kalinga, Kharavela, also describes the presence of the Greek king "Demetrius" with his army in eastern India, apparently as far as the city of Rajagriha about 70 km southeast of Pataliputra and one of the foremost Buddhist sacred cities, but claims that Demetrius ultimately retreated to Mathura on hearing of Kharavela's military successes further south:

"Then in the eighth year, (Kharavela) with a large army having sacked Goradhagiri causes pressure on Rajagaha (Rajagriha). On account of the loud report of this act of valour, the Yavana (Greek) King Dimi[ta] retreated to Mathura having extricated his demoralized army and transport." Hathigumpha inscription, in Epigraphia Indica, Vol. XX.

In any case, Eucratides seems to have occupied territory as far as the Indus, between ca 170 BCE and 150 BCE. His advances were ultimately checked by the Indo-Greek king Menander I (Milinda), previously a general of Demetrius, who asserted himself in the Indian part of the empire, apparently conquered Bactria as indicated by his issue of coins in the Greco-Bactrian style, and even began the last expansions eastwards.

Consolidation and Rise of Menander I

Detail of Asia in the Ptolemy world map. The "Menander Mons" are in the center of the map, at the east of the Indian subcontinent, beyond the Ganges, right above the Malaysian Peninsula.

Menander (Milinda), originally a general of Demetrius, is considered as probably the most successful Indo-Greek king, and the conqueror of the vastest territory. The finds of his coins are the most numerous and the most widespread of all the Indo-Greek kings. In Antiquity, from at least the 1st century CE, the "Menander Mons", or "Mountains of Menander", came to designate the mountain chain at the extreme east of the Indian subcontinent, today's Naga hills and Arakan, as indicated in the Ptolemy world map of the 1st century CE geographer Ptolemy. Menander is also remembered in Buddhist literature (the Milinda Panha) as a convert to Buddhism: he became an arhat whose relics were enshrined in a manner reminiscent of the Buddha. He also introduced a new coin type, with Athena Alkidemos ("Protector of the people") on the reverse, which was adopted by most of his successors in the East. Conquests east of the Punjab region were most likely made during the second half of the century by the king Menander I.

Following Menander's reign, about twenty Indo-Greek kings are known to have ruled in succession in the eastern parts of the Indo-Greek territory. Upon his death, Menander was succeeded by his queen Agathokleia, who for some time acted as regent to their son Strato I.

Greco-Bactrian Encroachments

From 130 BCE, the Scythians and then the Yuezhi, following a long migration from the border of China), started to invade Bactria from the north. Around 125 BCE the Greco-Bactrian king Heliocles, son of Eucratides, was probably killed during the invasion and the Greco-Bactrian kingdom proper ceased to exist. Heliocles may have been survived by his relative Eucratides II, who ruled south of the Hindu Kush, in areas untouched by the invasion. Other Indo-Greek kings like Zoilos I, Lysias and Antialcidas may possible have been relatives of either the Eucratid or the Euthydemid dynasties; they struck both Greek and bilingual coins and established a kingdom of their own.

A stabilizing alliance with the Yuezhi then seems to have followed, as hinted on the coins of Zoilos I, who minted coins showing Heracles' club together with a steppe-type recurve bow inside a victory wreath.

The Indo-Greeks thus suffered encroachments by the Greco-Bactrians in their western territories. The Indo-Greek territory was divided into two realms: the house of Menander retreated to their territories east of the Jhelum River as far as Mathura, whereas the Western kings ruled a larger kingdom of Paropamisadae, western Punjab and Arachosia to the south.

Ideology

Bilingual silver drachm of Menander I (160-135 BC). With obverse and reverse legends in Greek "BASILEOS SOTEROS MENANDROY" and Kharosthi "MAHARAJA TRATASA

MENADRASA": "Of The Saviour King Menander". Reverse shows Athena advancing right, with thunderbolt and shield.

Buddhism flourished under the Indo-Greek kings, and their rule, especially that of Menander, has been remembered as benevolent. It has been suggested, although direct evidence is lacking, that their invasion of India was intended to show their support for the Mauryan empire which had a long history of marital alliances, treaties of friendship, and exchange of ambassadors and religious emissaries with the Greeks, to protect Greek populations in India, and to protect the Buddhist faith from the religious persecutions of the Sungas. The city of Sirkap founded by Demetrius combines Greek and Indian influences without signs of segregation between the two cultures.

Alternatively, the Greek invasions in India are also sometimes described as purely materialistic, only taking advantage of the ruin of the Mauryan Empire to acquire territory and wealth.

The first Greek coins to be minted in India, those of Menander I and Appolodotus I bear the mention "Saviour king" (BASILEOS SOTHROS), a title with high value in the Greek world which indicated an important deflective victory. For instance, Ptolemy I had been Soter (saviour) because he had helped save Rhodes from Demetrius the Besieger, and Antiochus I because he had saved Asia Minor from the Gauls. The title was also inscribed in Pali as ("Tratarasa") on the reverse of their coins. Menander and Apollodotus may indeed have been saviours to the Greek populations residing in India, and to some of the Indians as well.

Also, most of the coins of the Greek kings in India were bilingual, written in Greek on the front and in Pali (in the Kharoshthi script) on the back, a tremendous concession to another culture never before made in the Hellenic world. From the reign of Apollodotus II, around 80 BCE, Kharoshthi letters started to be used as mintmarks on coins in combination with Greek monograms and mintmarks, suggesting the participation of local technicians to the minting process. Incidentally, these bilingual coins of the Indo-Greeks were the key in the decipherment of the Kharoshthi script by James Prinsep (1799-1840). Kharoshthi became extinct around the 3rd century CE.

In Indian literature, the Indo-Greeks are described as Yavanas (transliteration of "Ionians"). Direct epigraphical evidence involves the Indo-Greek kings, such as the mention of the "Yavana king" Antialcidas on the Heliodorus pillar in Vidisha, or the mention of Menander I in the Buddhist text of the Milinda Panha. In the Harivamsa the "Yavana" Indo-Greeks are qualified, together with the Sakas, Kambojas, Pahlavas and Paradas as Kshatriya-pungava i.e foremost among the Warrior caste, or Kshatriyas. The Majjhima Nikaya explains that in the lands of the Yavanas and Kambojas, in contrast with the numerous Indian castes, there were only two classes of people, Aryas and Dasas (masters and slaves). The Arya could become Dasa and vice versa.

Armed Forces

The coins of the Indo-Greeks provide rich clues on their uniforms and weapons. Typical Hellenistic uniforms are depicted, with helmets being either round in the Greco-Bactrian style, or the flat kausia of the Macedonians (coins of Apollodotus I).

Military Technology

Their weapons were spears, swords, longbow (on the coins of Agathokleia) and arrows. Interestingly, around 130 BCE the Central Asian recurve bow of the steppes with its gorytos box starts to appear for the first time on the coins of Zoilos I, suggesting strong interactions (and apparently an alliance) with nomadic peoples, either Yuezhi or Scythian. The recurve bow becomes a standard feature of Indo-Greek horsemen by 90 BCE, as seen on some of the coins of Hermaeus.

Generally, Indo-Greek kings are often represented riding horses, as soon as the reign of Antimachus II around 160 BCE. The equestrian tradition probably goes back to the Greco-Bactrians, who are said by Polybius to have faced a Seleucid invasion in 210 BCE with 10,000 horsemen. Although war elephants are never represented on coins, a harness plate (phalera) dated to the 3-2nd century BCE, today in the Hermitage Museum, depicts a helmetted Greek combatant on an Indian war elephant, and would be either Greco-Bactrian or Indo-Greek work. Indian war elephants were a standard feature of Hellenistic armies, and this would naturally have been the case for the Indo-Greeks as well.

Indo-Greek officer (on a coin of Menander II), circa 90 BCE. He is equipped with a cuirass, lamellar armour for the thighs, and leg protections.

Size of Indo-Greek Armies

The Greco-Bactrian king Eucratides (171-145 BCE) is said to have vanquished 60,000 Indo-Greeks, before being himself defeated by Menander.

The armed forces of the Indo-Greeks during their invasion of India must have been quite considerable, as suggested by their ability to topple local rulers, but also by the size of the armed reaction of some Indian rulers. The ruler of Kalinga, Kharavela, claims in the Hathigumpha inscription that he led a "large army" in the direction of Demetrius' own "army" and "transports", and that he induced him to retreat from Pataliputra to Mathura. A "large army" for the state of Kalinga must indeed have been quite considerable. The Greek ambassador Megasthenes took special note of the military strength of Kalinga in his Indica in the middle of the 3rd century BCE:

"The royal city of the Calingae (Kalinga) is called Parthalis. Over their king 60,000 foot-soldiers, 1,000 horsemen, 700 elephants keep watch and ward in "procinct of war." (Megasthenes fragm. LVI. in Plin. Hist. Nat. VI. 21. 8-23. 11.).

That this kind of military strength was needed to confront the Indo-Greeks is indicative of the Indo-Greeks' own military commitment.

Indo-Greek cavalryman, circa 80 BCE, according to coins of Hermaeus. He wears a cuirass for the upper body and lamellar armour for the thighs, as well as a cape, boots and a round crested helmet. His weapons are a recurve bow, stowed in a gorytos, and a straight sword with round pommel. The flowing headband indicates royalty.

An account by the Roman writer Justin gives another hint of the size of Indo-Greek armies, which, in the case of the conflict between the Greco-Bactrian Eucratides and the Indo-Greek Demetrius II, he numbers at 60,000 (although they allegedly lost to 300 Greco-Bactrians):

"Eucratides led many wars with great courage, and, while weakened by them, was put under siege by Demetrius, king of the Indians. He made numerous sorties, and managed to vanquish 60,000 enemies with 300 soldiers, and thus liberated after four months, he put India under his rule" (Justin, XLI,6)

These are considerable numbers, as large armies during the Hellenistic period typically numbered between 20,000 to 30,000.

However, the military strength of nomadic tribes from Central Asia (Yuezhi and Scythians) probably constituted a significant threat to the Indo-Greeks. According to Zhang Qian, the Yuezhi represented a considerable force of between 100,000 and 200,000 mounted archer warriors, with customs identical to those of the Xiongnu.

Finally, the Indo-Greek seem to have combined forces with other "invaders" during their expansion into India, since they are often referred to in combination with others (especially the Kambojas), in the Indian accounts of their invasions.

Religion

In addition to the worship of the Classical pantheon of the Greek deities found on their coins (Zeus, Herakles, Athena, Apollo...), the Indo-Greeks were involved with local faiths, particularly with Buddhism, but also with Hinduism and Zoroastrianism.

Buddhism

After the Greco-Bactrians militarily occupied parts of northern India from around 180 BCE, numerous instances of interaction between Greeks and Buddhism are recorded.

The Conversion of Menander

A Hellenistic-style Buddhist stupa in the Indo-Greek city of Sirkap, northern Pakistan, 1st century CE. It combines the sculptures of three temple-fronts: Greek (hidden from view, on the left), Hindu (center) and Buddhist (right) with Hellenistic columns. Wider view with the three temples Photo.

Menander I, the "Saviour king", seems to have converted to Buddhism, and is described in Buddhist texts as a great benefactor of the religion, on a par with Ashoka or the future Kushan emperor Kanishka. He is famous for his dialogues with the Buddhist monk Nagasena, transmitted to us in the Milinda Panha, which explain that he became a Buddhist arhat:

"And afterwards, taking delight in the wisdom of the Elder, he handed over his kingdom to his son, and abandoning the household life for the house-less state, grew great in insight, and himself attained to Arahatship!" (The Questions of King Milinda, Translation by T. W. Rhys Davids)

Plutarch also presents Menander as an example of benevolent rule, and explains that upon his death, the honour of sharing his remains was claimed by the various cities under his rule, and they were enshrined in "monuments" (probably stupas), in a parallel with the historic Buddha:

"But when one Menander, who had reigned graciously over the Bactrians, died afterwards in the camp, the cities indeed by common consent celebrated his funerals; but coming to a contest about his relics, they were difficultly at last brought to this agreement, that his ashes being distributed, everyone should carry away an equal share, and they should all erect monuments to him." (Plutarch, "Political Precepts" Praec. reip. ger. 28, 6).

Buddhist Proselytism

There are records of the involvement of Greeks in Buddhist pilgrimages. During the reign of Menander, the Greek (Pali: Yona, lit: "Ionian") Buddhist monk Mahadhammarakkhita (Sanskrit: Mahadharmaraksita, lit. "Great protector of the Dharma") is said to have come from Alasandra (thought to be Alexandria of the Caucasus, the city founded by Alexander the Great, near today's Kabul) with 30,000 monks for the foundation ceremony of the Maha Thupa ("Great stupa") built by king Dutthagamani at Anuradhapura in Sri Lanka, indicating the importance of Buddhism within Greek communities in northwestern India, and the prominent role Greek Buddhist monks played in them: "From Alasanda the city of the Yonas came the thera (elder) Yona Mahadhammarakkhita with thirty thousand bhikkhus." (Mahavamsa, XXIX)

Lay devotee couple in Hellenistic dress (right, man holding a lamp), and Buddhist monks (shaven, left), circambulating a stupa. Several Buddhist dedications by Greeks in India are recorded, such as that of the Greek meridarch (civil governor of a province) named Theodorus, describing in Kharoshthi how he enshrined relics of the Buddha. The inscriptions were found on a vase inside a stupa, dated to the reign of Menander or one his successors in the 1st century BCE (Tarn, p391):

"Theudorena meridarkhena pratithavida ime sarira sakamunisa bhagavato bahu-jana-stitiye":

"The meridarch Theodorus has enshrined relics of Lord Shakyamuni, for the welfare of the mass of the people" (Swat relic vase inscription of the Meridarkh Theodoros)

Although the spread of Buddhism to Central Asia and Northern Asia is usually associated with the Kushans, a century or two later, there is a possibility that it may have been introduced in those areas from Gandhara "even earlier, during the time of Demetrius and Menander" (Puri, "Buddhism in Central Asia"). There is however some textual evidence to suggest that Buddhism had penetrated much earlier to Central Asia, at least in a limited form: the first two disciples of the Buddha were named Tapassu and Bhallika, from the region of Balhika (the present Balkh, and Sanskrit for Bactria), and though it cannot necessarily be presumed that any extensive prosyletization occurred on their return journey, that the Sanskrit name for Bactria derived from the name of a Bactrian-Buddhist disciple is suggestive of some early influence. Bhallika and Tapassu were both travellers, and if nothing else, the story of their conversion and their home region's Sanskrit nomenclature illustrates the possibility of early transmission via the local trade routes.

Buddhist Symbolism

From around 180 BCE, Agathocles and Pantaleon, probable successors to Demetrius I in the Paropamisadae, and the earliest

Greek kings to issue Indian-standard square bilingual coins (in Brahmi), depicted the Buddhist lion together with the Hindu goddess Lakshmi.

Some coins of Agathocles in the Indian standard also show a six-arched stupa and a tree in a railing, typical symbol of the Bodhi tree in early Buddhism. These coins show an unprecedented willingness to adapt to every aspect of the local culture: shape of the coinage, coinage size, language, and religion. Later, some Indo-Greek coins incorporate the Buddhist symbol of the eight-spoked wheel, such as those of Menander I, as well as his possible grandson Menander II. On these coins, the wheel is associated with the Greek symbols of victory, either the palm of victory, or the victory wreath handed over by the goddess Nike. This symbology has led some to conclude that Menander adopted the Buddhist mantle of a "Chakravartin" during his lifetime; lit., "one for whom the wheel of law turns," translated as "King of the Wheel" in Western texts.

The ubiquitous symbol of the elephant may or may not have been associated with Buddhism. Interestingly, on some coin series of Antialcidas, the elephant holds the same relationship to Zeus and Nike as the Buddhist wheel on the coin of Menander II, tending to suggest a common meaning for both symbols. Some of the earlier coins of king Apollodotus I directly associate the elephant with Buddhist symbolism, such as the stupa hill surmounted by a star, also seen, for example on the coins of the Mauryan Empire or those of the later Kuninda kingdom. Conversely, the bull is probably associated with Shiva, and often described in an erectile state as on the coins of Apollodotus I.

Also, after the reign of Menander I, several Indo-Greek rulers, such as Agathokleia, Amyntas, Nicias, Peukolaos, Hermaeus, Hippostratos and Menander II, depicted themselves or their Greek deities forming with the right hand a symbolic gesture identical to the Buddhist vitarka mudra (thumb and index joined together, with other fingers extended), which in Buddhism signifies the transmission of the Buddha's teaching.

Indian relief of probable Indo-Greek king (Susan Huntington, "The art of ancient India"), with Buddhist triratana symbol on his sword. Bharhut, 2nd century BCE. Indian

Museum, Calcutta (drawing). At precisely the same time, right after the death of Menander, several Indo-Greek rulers also started to adopt on their coins the Pali title of "Dharmikasa", meaning "follower of the Dharma" (the title of the great Indian Buddhist king Ashoka was Dharmaraja "King of the Dharma"). This usage was adopted by Strato I, Zoilos I, Heliokles II, Theophilos, Peukolaos, Menander II and Archebios.

Vitarka Mudra gestures on Indo-Greek coinage. Top: Divinities Tyche and Zeus. Bottom: Depiction of Indo-Greek kings Nicias and Menander II.

Altogether, the conversion of Menander I to Buddhism suggested by the Milinda Panha seems to have triggered the use of Buddhist symbolism in one form or another on the coinage of close to half of the kings who succeeded him. Especially, all the kings after Menander who are recorded to have ruled in Gandhara (apart from the little known Demetrius III) display Buddhist symbolism in one form or another. On the contrary, none of the kings whose rule was limited to Punjab did display Buddhist signs (with the exception of the powerful Hippostratos, who probably took under his protection many Gandharan Greeks fleeing from the Indo-Scythians (Tarn).).

A 2nd century BCE relief from a Buddhist stupa in Bharhut, in eastern Madhya Pradesh (today at the Indian Museum in Calcutta), represents a foreign soldier with the curly hair of a Greek and the royal headband with flowing ends of a Greek king. In his left hand, he hold a branch of ivy, symbol of Dionysos. Also parts of his dress, with rows of geometrical folds, are characteristically Hellenistic in style. On his sword appears the Buddhist symbol of the three jewels, or Triratana.

Representation of the Buddha

The anthropomorphic representation of the Buddha is absent from Indo-Greek coinage, suggesting that the Indo-Greek kings may have respected the Indian aniconic rule for Buddhist depictions, limiting themselves to Buddhist symbolism only. Consistently with this perspective, the actual depiction of the Buddha would be a later phenomenon, usually dated to the 1st century CE, emerging from the sponsorship of the syncretic Kushan Empire and executed by Greek, and, later,

Indian and possibly Roman artists. Datation of Greco-Buddhist statues is generally uncertain, but they are at least firmly established from the 1st century CE.

One of the first known representations of the Buddha, Gandhara, in pure Hellenistic style and technique: Standing Buddha (Tokyo National Museum).

Another possibility is that the Indo-Greeks may not have considered the Buddha strictly as a God, but rather as an essentially human sage or philosopher, in line with the traditional Nikaya Buddhist doctrine. Just as philosophers were routinely represented in statues (but certainly not on coins) in Antiquity, the Indo-Greek may have initiated anthropomorphic representations of the Buddha in statuary only, possibly as soon as the 2nd-1st century BCE, as advocated by Foucher and suggested by Chinese murals depicting Emperor Wu of Han worshipping Buddha statues brought from Central Asia in 120 BCE. Foucher especially considered Hellenistic free-standing Buddhas as "the most beautiful, and probably the most ancient of the Buddhas", assigning them to the 1st century BCE, and making them the starting point of the anthropomorphic representations of the Buddha.

The willingness of ancient Greeks to represent and worship local deities is also attested in Egypt with the creation of the god Serapis in Hellenistic style, an adaptation of the Egyptian god Apis, or in Phrygia with the Hellenistic representation of the heretofore aniconic Cybele. On the contrary, Indian Buddhist art was traditionally aniconic (the Buddha was only represented with symbols), and the Iranian tradition (represented by the 1st century Indo-Parthians) also did not represent their deities in human form. An Indo-Chinese tradition also explains that Nagasena, also known as Menander's Buddhist teacher, created in 43 BCE in the city of Pataliputra a statue of the Buddha, the Emerald Buddha, which was later brought to Thailand.

An Indo-Corinthian capital from the Butkara Stupa, representing a Buddhist devotee within foliage, dated to 20 BCE (Turin City Museum of Ancient Art).

Stylistically, Indo-Greek coins generally display a very high level of Hellenistic artistic realism, which declined drastically around 50 BCE with the invasions of the Indo-Scythians, Yuezhi and Indo-Parthians. The first known statues of the Buddha are also very realistic and Hellenistic in style and are more consistent with the pre-50 BCE artistic level seen on coins. This would tend to suggest that the first statues were created between 130 BCE (death of Menander) and 50 BCE, precisely at the time when Buddhist symbolism appeared on Indo-Greek coinage. From that time, Menander and his successors may have been the key propagators of Buddhist ideas and representations: "the spread of Gandhari Buddhism may have been stimulated by Menander's royal patronage, as may have the development and spread of Gandharan sculpture, which seems to have accompanied it" (Mc Evilly, "The shape of ancient thought", p378)

The representation of the Buddha may also be connected to his progressive deification, which is usually associated with the spread of the Indian principle of Bhakti (personal devotion to a deity). Bhakti is a principle which evolved in the Bhagavata religious movement, and is said to have permeated Buddhism from about 100 BCE, and to have been a contributing factor to the representation of the Buddha in human form. The association of the Indo-Greeks with the Bhagavata movement is documented in the inscription of the Heliodorus pillar, made during the reign of the Indo-Greek king Antialcidas (r.c. 115-95 BCE). At that time relations with the Sungas seem to have improved, and some level of religious exchange seems to have occurred. The point of time when bhakti fervour would have encountered the Hellenistic artistic tradition would then be around 100 BCE.

Most of the early images of the Buddha (especially those of the standing Buddha) are anepigraphic, which makes it difficult to have a definite datation. The earliest known image of the Buddha with approximate indications on date is the Bimaran casket, which has been found buried with coins of the Indo-Scythian king Azes II (or possibly Azes I), indicating a 30-10 BCE date, although this date is not undisputed. Such datation, as well as the general Hellenistic style and attitude of the Buddha on the Bimaran casket (himation dress, contrapposto attitude, general depiction) would made it a possible Indo-Greek work, used in dedications by Indo-Scythians right after the end of Indo-Greek rule in the area of Gandhara. Since it already displays quite a sophisticated iconography (Brahma and Sakra as attendants, Bodhisattvas) in an advanced style, it would suggest much earlier representations of the Buddha were already current by that time, going back to the rule of the Indo-Greeks (Alfred A. Foucher and others):

"It seems highly probable to me that the unknown artist who created the initial model [for the Buddha] was a Yavana, both artist and philosopher, who belonged both to Greece and India." Mario Bussagli, "L'art du Gandhara"

Hinduism

The first known bilingual coins of the Indo-Greeks were issued by Agathocles around 180 BCE. These coins were found in Ai-Khanoum, the great Greco-Bactrian city in northeastern Afghanistan, but introduce for the first time an Indian script (the Brahmi script which had been in use under the Mauryan empire), and the first known representations of Hindu deities, in a very Indian iconography: Krishna-Vasudeva, with his large wheel with six spokes (chakra) and conch (shanka), and his brother Sankarshan-Balarama, with his plough (hala) and pestle (masala), both early avatars of Vishnu. The square coins, instead of the usual Greek round coins, also followed the Indian standard for coinage. The dancing girls on some of the coins of Agathocles and Pantaleon are also sometimes considered as representations of Subhadra, Krishna's sister.

These first issues were in several respects a short-lived experiment. Hindu anthropomorphic deities were never again represented in Indo-Greek coinage (although the bull on the vast quantity of subsequent coins may have symbolized Shiva, as the elephant may have symbolized Buddhism), and the Brahmi script was immediately replaced by the Kharoshti script, derived from Aramaic. The general practice however of minting bilingual coins and combining Greek and Indian iconography, sometimes in the Greek and sometimes in the Indian standard continued for the next two centuries.

In any case, these coins suggest the strong presence of Indian religious traditions in the northwestern Indian subcontinent at that time, and the willingness of the Greeks to acknowledge and even promote them. Artistically, they tend to indicate that the Greeks were not particularly reluctant to make representations of local deities, which has some bearing on the later emergence of the image of the Buddha in Hellenistic style.

The Heliodorus pillar inscription is another epigraphical evidence of the interaction between Greeks and Hinduism. The pillar was erected around 110 BCE in central India at the site of Vidisha, by Heliodorus, a Greek ambassador of the Indo-Greek king Antialcidas to the court of the Sunga king Bhagabhadra. The pillar was surmounted by a sculpture of Garuda and was apparently dedicated by Heliodorus to the temple of Vasudeva.

"This Garuda-standard of Vasudeva (Vishnu), the God of Gods was erected here by the Bhagavata Heliodoros, the son of Dion, a man of Taxila, sent by the Great Greek (Yona) King Antialkidas, as ambassador to King Kasiputra Bhagabhadra, the Savior son of the princess from Benares, in the fourteenth year of his reign." (Heliodorus pillar inscription)

Zoroastrianism

Persian culture and religion seem to have been rather influential among the Western Indo-Greeks, who, located around the Paropamisadae, lived in direct contact with the Central Asian cultural sphere and the eastern reaches of the Parthian empire. Images of the Persian Zoroastrian god Mithra appear extensively on the Indo-Greek coinage of the Western kings, as a god with a radiated phrygian cap.

This Zeus-Mithra god is also the one represented seated (with the rays around the head, and a small protrusion on the top of the head representing the cap) on many coins of Hermaeus, Antialcidas or Heliokles II, or possibly even earlier during the time of Eucratides I, on whose coins the deity is said to be the god of the city of Kapisa.

The future Buddha Maitreya, usually represented seated on a throne Western-style, and venerated both in Mahayana and non-Mahayana Buddhism, is sometimes considered as influenced by the god Mithra. "Some scholars suggest he

(Maitreya) was originally linked to the Iranian saviour-figure Mitra, and that his later importance for Buddhist as the future Buddha residing in the Tusita heaven, who will follow on from Sakyamuni Buddha, derives from this source." (Keown, Dictionary of Buddhism)

Art

Incipient Greco-Buddhist Art

In general, the art of the Indo-Greeks is poorly documented, and few works of art (apart from their coins and a few stone palettes) are directly attributed to them. The coinage of the Indo-Greeks however is generally considered as some of the most artistically brilliant of Antiquity. Traditionally, very few sculptural remains have been attributed to the Indo-Greeks, although their Hellenistic heritage and artistic proficiency would naturally have encouraged such creations (as neighbouring and contemporary Ai-Khanoum abundantly suggests). On the contrary, and rather paradoxically, most Gandharan Hellenistic works of art are usually attributed to the direct successors of the Indo-Greeks in India, such as the Indo-Scythians, the Indo-Parthians and the Kushans, from the 1st century CE, although Kushan Greco-Buddhist art is usually considered as already decadent.

The Buddha with Herakles/Vajrapani (left detail) and Tyche/Hariti (right detail) may be "incipient Buddhist sculpture in Indo-Greek style" (Boardman). Herakles still has his lion skin on the left shoulder, although his club has been replaced by Vajrapani's thunderbolt. Tyche holds a Classical cornucopia, Tapa-i-Shotor, Hadda, eastern Afghanistan (Click on the image for photographic reference).

Coin of the Indo-Greek king Amyntas, 95-90 BCE. Seated Tyche with cornucopia in left hand, and, with the right hand, making a benediction gesture identical to the Buddhist vitarka mudra.

The possibility of a direct connection between the Indo-Greeks and Greco-Buddhist art has been reaffirmed recently as the dating of the rule of Indo-Greek kings has been extended to the first decades of the 1st century CE, with the reign of Strato II in the Punjab. Also, Foucher, Tarn and more recently

Boardman, Bussagli or McEvilley have taken the view that some of the most purely Hellenistic works of northwestern India and Afghanistan, may actually be wrongly attributed to later centuries, and instead belong to a period one or two centuries earlier, to the time of the Indo-Greeks in the 2nd-1st century BCE. This is particularly the case of some purely Hellenistic works in Hadda, Afghanistan, an area which "might indeed be the cradle of incipient Buddhist sculpture in Indo-Greek style". Referring to one of the Buddha triads in Hadda (drawing), in which the Buddha is sided by very Classical depictions of Herakles/Vajrapani and Tyche/Hariti, Boardman explains that both figures "might at first (and even second) glance, pass as, say, from Asia Minor or Syria of the first or second century BC (...) these are essentially Greek figures, executed by artists fully conversant with far more than the externals of the Classical style". Many of the works of art at Hadda can also be compared to the style of the 2nd century BCE sculptures of the Hellenistic world, such as those of the Temple of Olympia at Bassae in Greece, which could also suggest roughly contemporary dates.

Alternatively, it has been suggested that these works of art may have been executed by itinerant Greek artists during the time of maritime contacts with the West from the 1st to the 3rd century CE.

The supposition that such highly Hellenistic and, at the same time Buddhist, works of art belong to the Indo-Greek period would be consistent with the known Buddhist activity of the Indo-Greeks (the Milinda Panha etc...), their Hellenistic cultural heritage which would naturally have induced them to produce extensive statuary, their know artistic proficiency as seen on their coins until around 50 BCE, and the dated appearance of already complex iconography incorporating Hellenistic sculptural codes with the Bimaran casket in the early 1st century CE.

Indo-Greeks in the Art of Gandhara

The Greco-Buddhist art of Gandhara, beyond the omnipresence of Greek style and stylistic elements which might be simply considered as an enduring artistic tradition, offers numerous depictions of people in Greek Classical realistic style, attitudes and fashion (clothes such as the chiton and the himation, similar in form and style to the 2nd century BCE Greco-Bactrian statues of Ai-Khanoum, hairstyle), holding contraptions which are characteristic of Greek culture (amphoras, "kantaros" Greek drinking cups), in situations which can range from festive (such as Bacchanalian scenes) to Buddhist-devotional.

Uncertainties in dating make it unclear whether these works of art actually depict Greeks of the period of Indo-Greek rule up to the 1st century BCE, or remaining Greek communities under the rule of the Indo-Parthians or Kushans in the 1st and 2nd century CE. Greek Buddhist devotees, holding plantain leaves, in purely Hellenistic style, inside Corinthian columns, Buner relief, dated 1st-2nd century CE.

Bacchanalian scene, representing the harvest of wine grapes, Greco-Buddhist art of Gandhara, 1st-2nd century CE.

Devotee couple in Greek dress (right), husband bearing a lamp, circambulating around a stupa. Gandhara frieze. British Museum.

Indo-Corinthian capital representing a Buddhist devotee wearing a Greek cloak attached by a fibula. Dated to the 1st century BCE. Butkara Stupa.

Drinking scene, with Dionysus and Ariadne on his lap, Greek drinking cups, Greek dress. Greco-Buddhist art of Gandhara. Dated 3rd century CE.

"The Great Departure", with the Buddha amid Greek deities and costumes.

Economy

Very little is known about the economy of the Indo-Greeks. The abundance of their coins would tend to suggest large mining operations, particularly in the mountainous area of the Hindu-Kush, and an important monetary economy. The Indo-Greek did strike bilingual coins both in the Greek "round" standard and in the Indian "square" standard, suggesting that monetary circulation extended to all parts of society. The adoption of

Indo-Greek monetary conventions by neighbouring kingdoms, such as the Kunindas to the east and the Satavahanas to the south, would also suggest that Indo-Greek coins were used extensively for cross-border trade.

Tribute Payments

Silver tetradrachm of the Indo-Greek king Philoxenus (100-95 BCE), one example of the coins in the monolingual Attic standard by later Indo Greek kings, thought to have been used for tribute payments (Qunduz hoard).

It would also seem that some of the coins emitted by the Indo-Greek kings, particularly those in the monolingual Attic standard, may have been used to pay some form of tribute to the Yuezhi tribes north of the Hindu-Kush. This is indicated by the coins finds of the Qunduz hoard in northern Afghanistan, which have yielded quantities of Indo-Greek coins in the Hellenistic standard (Greek weights, Greek language), although none of the kings represented in the hoard are known to have ruled so far north. Conversely, none of these coins have ever been found south of the Hindu-Kush.

Trade with China

An indirect testimony by the Chinese explorer Zhang Qian, who visited Bactria around 128 BCE, suggests that intense trade with Southern China was going through northern India, and therefore probably through the contemporary Indo-Greek realm. Zhang Qian explains that he found Chinese products in the Bactrian markets, and that they were transiting through northwestern India, which he incidentially describes as a civilization similar to that of Bactria:

"When I was in Bactria," Zhang Qian reported, "I saw bamboo canes from Qiong and cloth (silk) made in the province of Shu. When I asked the people how they had gotten such articles, they replied: "Our merchants go buy them in the markets of Shendu (northwestern India). Shendu, they told me, lies several thousand li southeast of Bactria. The people cultivate land, and live much like the people of Bactria". (Sima Qian, "Records of the Great Historian", trans. Burton Watson, p236).

Indian Ocean Trade

Maritime relations across the Indian ocean started in the 3rd century BCE, and further developed during the time of the Indo-Greeks together with their territorial expansion along the western coast of India. The first contacts started when the Ptolemies constructed the Red Sea ports of Myos Hormos and Berenike, with destination the Indus delta and the Kathiawar peninsula. Around 130 BCE, Eudoxus of Cyzicus is reported (Strabo, Geog. II.3.4) to have made a successful voyage to India and returned with a cargo of perfumes and gemstones. By the time Indo-Greek rule was ending, up to 120 ships were setting sail every year from Myos Hormos to India (Strabo Geog. II.5.12).

Later History

Eastern Indo-Greek Territories

After around 100 BCE, Indian kings recovered the area of Mathura and Eastern Punjab east of the Ravi River, and started to mint their own coins. The Arjunayanas (area of Mathura) and Yaudheyas mention military victories on their coins ("Victory of the Arjunayanas", "Victory of the Yaudheyas"). During the 1st century BCE, the Trigartas, Audumbaras and finally the Kunindas (closest to Punjab) also started to mint their own coins, usually in a style highly reminiscent of Indo-Greek coinage.

The Western king Philoxenus briefly occupied the whole remaining Greek territory from the Paropamisadae to Western Punjab between 100 to 95 BCE, after what the territories fragmented again. The eastern kings regained their territory as far west as Arachosia.

Around 80 BCE, an Indo-Scythian king named Maues, possibly a general in the service of the Indo-Greeks, ruled for a few years in northwestern India before the Indo-Greeks again took control. King Hippostratos (65-55 BCE) seems to have been one of the most successful subsequent Indo-Greek kings until he lost to the Indo-Scythian Azes I, who established an Indo-Scythian dynasty.

Throughout the 1st century BCE, the Indo-Greeks progressively lost ground against the invasion of the Indo-

Scythians. Although the Indo-Scythians clearly ruled militarily and politically, they remained surprisingly respectful of Greek and Indian cultures. Their coins were minted in Greek mints, continued using proper Greek and Kharoshthi legends, and incorporated depictions of Greek deities, particularly Zeus. The Mathura lion capital inscription attests that they adopted the Buddhist faith, as do the depictions of deities forming the vitarka mudra on their coins. Greek communities, far from being exterminated, probably persisted under Indo-Scythian rule. There is a possibility that a fusion, rather than a confrontation, occured between the Greeks and the Indo-Scythians: in a recently published coin, Artemidoros presents himself as "son of Maues", and the Buner reliefs show Indo-Greeks and Indo-Scythians reveling in a Buddhist context. The Indo-Greeks continued to rule a territory in the eastern Punjab, until the kingdom of the last Indo-Greek king Strato II was taken over by the Indo-Scythian ruler Rajuvula around 10 CE.

Western Indo-Greek Territories

Silver bilingual drachm of Hermaeus (ruled 90-70 BCE) with his wife Kalliope. King on horse, equipped with the recurve bow of the steppes.

Around eight western Indo-Greek kings are known. The last important king was Hermaeus, who reigned until around 70 BCE; soon after his death the Yuezhi took over his areas from neighbouring Bactria. Chinese chronicles (the Hou Hanshu) actually tend to suggest that the Chinese general Wen-Chung had helped negotiate the alliance of Hermaeus with the Yuezhi, against the Indo-Scythians. When Hermaeus is depicted on his coins riding a horse, he is equipped with the recurve bow and bow-case of the steppes.

After 70 BCE, the Yuezhi became the new rulers of the Paropamisadae, and minted vast quantities of posthumous issues of Hermaeus up to around 40 CE, when they blend with the coinage of the Kushan king Kujula Kadphises. The first documented Yuezhi prince, Sapadbizes, ruled around 20 BCE, and minted in Greek and in the same style as the western Indo-Greek kings, probably depending on Greek mints and celators. The Yuezhi expanded to the east during the 1st century CE, to found the Kushan Empire. The first Kushan emperor Kujula Kadphises ostensibly associated himself with Hermaeus on his coins, suggesting that he may have been one of his descendants by alliance, or at least wanted to claim his legacy. The Yuezhi (future Kushans) were in many ways the cultural and political heirs to the Indo-Greeks, as suggested by their adoption of the Greek culture (writing system, Greco-Buddhist art) and their claim to a lineage with the last western Indo-Greek king Hermaeus.

The last known mention of an Indo-Greek ruler is suggested by an inscription on a signet ring of the 1st century CE in the name of a king Theodamas, from the Bajaur area of Gandhara, in modern Pakistan. No coins of him are known, but the signet bears in kharoshthi script the inscription "Su Theodamasa", "Su" being explained as the Greek transliteration of the ubiquitous Kushan royal title "Shau" ("Shah", "King").

Enduring Legacy of the Indo-Greek Kingdom

From the 1st century CE, the Greek communities of central Asia and northwestern India lived under the control of the Kushan branch of the Yuezhi, apart from a short-lived invasion of the Indo-Parthian Kingdom. The Kushans founded the Kushan Empire, which was to prosper for several centuries. In the south, the Greeks were under the rule of the Western Kshatrapas. It is unclear how much longer the Greeks managed to maintain a distinct presence in the Indian sub-continent.

Military Role

At the beginning of the 2nd century CE, the Central India Satavahana king Gautamiputra (r. 106-130 CE) adopted the epithet Satakarni, meaning "Destroyer of Sakas (Western Kshatrapas), Yavanas (Indo-Greeks) and Pahlavas (Indo-Parthians)" in his inscriptions, suggesting a continued presence of the Indo-Greeks until that time.

Around 200 CE, the Manu Smriti describes the downfall of the Yavanas, as well as many others:

"43. But in consequence of the omission of the sacred rites, and of their not consulting Brahmanas, the following tribes of

Kshatriyas have gradually sunk in this world to the condition of Shudras;

44. (Viz.) the Paundrakas, the Chodas, the Dravidas, the Kambojas, the Yavanas, the Shakas, the Paradas, the Pahlavas, the Chinas, the Kiratas, the Daradas and the Khashas." (Manusmritti, X.43-44)

The Brihat-Katha-Manjari text of the Sanskrit poet Kshmendra (11th and 12th centuries) (10/1/285-86) relates that around 400 CE the Gupta king Vikramaditya (Chandragupta II) had "unburdened the sacred earth of the Barbarians" like "the Shakas, Mlecchas, Kambojas, Yavanas, Tusharas, Parasikas, Hunas" etc... by annihilating these "sinners" completely.

Linguistic Legacy

A Greco-Roman-style carnelian seal from the Punjab region, with Brahmi inscription "Kusumadasasya" ("Flower-Servant"). 4-5th century CE. British Museum.

The "Avaca" Kharosthi inscription, found on a Buddhist relic casket, indicates that the old Greek military title of strategos ("commander") had apparently endured the Indo-Scythian invasion and was being used by the Apracarajas of Bajaur during the 1st century CE (the inscription mentions the dedication date of the casket as "the year 63 of the late Maharaja Aya", Aya being the Indo-Scythian ruler Azes I, who started the Vikrama era in 58 BCE, therefore suggesting a date around 5 CE). The dedication mentions "vaga stratego puyaite viyayamitro ya" i.e. "The Lord Commander (Stratego) Viyayamitra is honored too"

The Greek philosopher Apollonius of Tyana is related by Philostratus in Life of Apollonius Tyana to have visited India, and specifically the city of Taxila around 46 CE. He describes constructions of the Greek type, probably referring to Sirkap, and explains that the Indo-Parthian king of Taxila, named Phraotes, received a Greek education at the court of his farther and spoke Greek fluently:

"Tell me, O King, how you acquired such a command of the Greek tongue, and whence you derived all your philosophical attainments in this place?"

"My father, after a Greek education, brought me to the sages at an age somewhat too early perhaps, for I was only twelve at the time, but they brought me up like their own son; for any that they admit knowing the Greek tongue they are especially fond of, because they consider that in virtue of the similarity of his disposition he already belongs to themselves."

Lastly, from the Rabatak inscription we have the following information, tending to indicate that Greek was still in official use until the time of Kanishka (circa 120 CE):

"He (Kanishka) issued an edict in Greek and then he put it into the Aryan language". ...but when Kanishka refers to "the Aryan language" he surely means Bactrian, ..."By the grace of Auramazda, I made another text in Aryan, which previously did not exist". It is difficult not to associate Kanishka's emphasis here on the use of the "Aryan language" with the replacement of Greek by Bactrian on his coinage. The numismatic evidence shows that this must have taken place very early in Kanishka's reign,..."-Prof. Nicholas Sims-Williams (University of London). The Greek script was used not only on coins, but also in manuscripts and stone inscriptions as late as the period of Islamic invasions in the 7th-8th century.

Greek Era

A Greek "Yona" calendar era seems to have been in use in Northwestern Indian for several centuries following the foundation of the Indo-Greek kingdom. A recently discovered inscription in Kharoshthi gives a relationship between several eras of the period:

"In the twenty-seventh-27-year in the reign of Lord Vijayamitra, the King of the Apaca; in the seventy-third-73-year which is called "of Azes", in the two hundred and first-201-year of the Yonas (Greeks), on the eighth day of the month of Sravana; on this day was established [this] stupa by Rukhana, the wife of the King of Apraca, [and] by Vijayamitra, the king of Apraca, [and] by Indravarma (Indravasu), the commander (stratega), [together] with their wives and sons." (Senior 2003)

As the Azes era is usually considered as starting in 58 BCE, the Yona era would correspond to 186 BCE, which falls in the reign of Demetrius I, although dates ranging from 186 to 150 BCE are still debated.

Macedonian Calendar

The names of the months belonging to the Ancient Macedonian calendar remained in use under the Indo-Scythians and the Kushans until around the 2nd century CE. For example, the Dast-i Nawur inscription mentionning the Kushan king Vima Kadphises (reigned circa 90-100 CE) is dated to the 279th year (possibly of the Yona era), and the 15th day of the month of Gorpaios, which is the 11th month of the Macedonian calendar, corresponding to the moon of August.

Astronomy and Astrology

One of the earliest Indian writings on astronomy and astrology (although not the earliest, as the Vedanga Jyotisha is dated to around 1350 BCE), titled the Yavanajataka or "The Saying (Horoscopy to some) of the Greeks", is a translation from Greek to Sanskrit made by "Yavanesvara" ("Lord of the Greeks") in 149-150 CE under the rule of the Western Kshatrapa king Rudrakarman I. The Yavanajataka contains instructions on calculating astrological charts (horoscopes) from the time and place of one's birth. Astrology flourished in the Hellenistic world (particularly Alexandria) and the Yavanajataka reflects astrological techniques developed in the Greek-speaking world. Astronomical mathematical methods, such as the calculate of the 'horoskopos' (zodiac sign on the eastern horizon) was used in the service of astrology.

Another set of treatises, the Paulisa Siddhanta and the Romaka Siddhantas, are attributed to later Greek influence in India. The Paulisa Siddhanta has been tentatively identified with the works of Paulus Alexandrinus, who wrote a well-known astrological hand-book. Indian astronomy is widely acknowledged to be influenced by the Alexandrian school, and its technical nomenclature is essentially Greek: "The Yavanas are barbarians, yet the science of astronomy originated with them and for this they must be reverenced like gods" (The Gargi-Samhita). Several other Indian texts show appreciation for the scientific knowledge of the "Yavana" Greeks.

Influence of Indo-Greek Coinage

Overall, the coinage of the Indo-Greeks remained extremely influential for several centuries throughout the Indian subcontinent: Coin of the Western Kshatrapa ruler Bhratadaman (278-295), with corrupted Greek legend on the obverse and Brahmi legend on the reverse.

A silver coin of the Gupta King Kumara Gupta I (414-455) influenced by Indo-Greek coinage through the Western Kshatrapas, with profile of the ruler and obverse legend in pseudo Greek (succession of letters H and O), and reverse legend is in Brahmi.

- The Indo-Greek weight and size standard for silver drachms was adopted by the contemporary Buddhist kingdom of the Kunindas in Punjab, the first attempt by an Indian kingdom to produce coins that could compare with those of the Indo-Greeks.
- In central India, the Satavahanas (2nd century BCE-2nd century CE) adopted the practice of representing their kings in profile, within circular legends.
- The direct successors of the Indo-Greeks in the northwest, the Indo-Scythians and Indo-Parthians continued displaying their kings within a legend in Greek, and on the obverse Greek deities.
- To the south, the Western Kshatrapas (1st-4th century) represented their kings in profile with circular legends in corrupted Greek.
- The Kushans (1st-4th century) used the Greek language on their coinage until the first few years of the reign of Kanishka, whence they adopted the Bactrian language, written with the Greek script.
- The Guptas (4th-6th century), in turn imitating the Western Kshatrapas, also showed their rulers in profile, within a legend in corrupted Greek, in the coinage of their western territories.

The latest use of the Greek script on coins corresponds to the rule of the Turkish Shahi of Kabul, around 850.

Genetic Contribution

Limited population genetics studies have been made on genetic markers such as mitochondrial DNA in the populations of the Indian subcontinent, to estimate the contribution of the Greeks to the genetic pool. Although some of the markers which are present in a large proportion of Greeks today have not been found, the Greek/European genetic contribution to the Punjab region has been estimated between 0%-15%:

"The political influence of Seleucid and Bactrian dynastic Greeks over northwest India, for example, persisted for several centuries after the invasion of the army of Alexander the Great (Tarn 1951). However, we have not found, in Punjab or anywhere else in India, Y chromosomes with the M170 or M35 mutations that together account for 30% in Greeks and Macedonians today (Semino et al. 2000). Given the sample size of 325 Indian Y chromosomes examined, however, it can be said that the Greek homeland (or European, more generally, where these markers are spread) contribution has been 0%-3% for the total population or 0%-15% for Punjab in particular. Such broad estimates are preliminary, at best. It will take larger sample sizes, more populations, and increased molecular resolution to determine the likely modest impact of historic gene flows to India on its pre-existing large populations." (Kivisild et al. "Origins of Indian Casts and Tribes").

Some pockets of Greek populations probably remained for some time, and to this day, some communities in the Hindu Kush claim to be descendants of the Greeks, such as the Kalasha and Hunza in Pakistan, and the neighbouring Nuristani in Afghanistan. One cannot assume however that the present Greek population is representative of the Macedonian army under Alexander. This army probably contained a large number of Persians and other groups such as Scythians and Thracians.

Greco-Roman Exchanges with India

Although the political power of the Greeks had waned in the north, mainly due to nomadic invasions, trade relations between the Mediterranean and India continued for several centuries. The trade started by Eudoxus of Cyzicus in 130 BCE kept on increasing, and according to Strabo (II.5.12), by the time of Augustus, up to 120 ships were setting sail every year from Myos Hormos to India. So much gold was used for this trade, and apparently recycled by the Kushans for their own coinage, that Pliny (NH VI.101) complained about the drain of specie to India. In practice, this trade was still handled by Greek middlemen, as all the recorded names of ship captains for the period are Greek.

In India, the ports of Barbaricum (modern Karachi), Barygaza, and Muziris and Arikamedu on the southern tip of India were the main centers of this trade. Ptolemy described Muzuris as "a port packed with Greek ships" (VII.I.8), and the Tamil Sangam describes that "fine vessels, masterpieces of Yavana workmanship, arrive with gold and depart with pepper". In the south, the main trading partners were the Tamil dynasties of the Pandyas, Cholas and Cheras.

The 2nd century Periplus of the Erythraean Sea describes Greco-Roman merchants selling in Barbaricum "thin clothing, figured linens, topaz, coral, storax, frankincense, vessels of glass, silver and gold plate, and a little wine" in exchange for "costus, bdellium, lycium, nard, turquoise, lapis lazuli, Seric skins, cotton cloth, silk yarn, and indigo". In Barygaza, they would buy wheat, rice, sesame oil, cotton and cloth. At Cape Comorin and in Sri Lanka, they would buy pearls and gems.

Also various exchanges are recorded between India and Rome during this period. In particular, embassies from India, as well as several missions from "Sramanas" to the Roman emperors are known. Finally, Roman goods and works of art found their way to the Kushans, as archaeological finds in Begram have confirmed.

Artistic Legacy

The "Kanishka casket", dated to the first year of Kanishka's reign in 127 CE, was signed by a Greek artist named Agesilas, who oversaw work at Kanishka's stupas (caitya), confirming the direct involvement of Greeks with Buddhist realizations at such a late date.

Iconographical evolution from the Greek god Herakles to the Japanese god Shukongoshin. From left to right:

(1) Herakles (Louvre Museum).

(2) Herakles on coin of Greco-Bactrian king Demetrius I.

(3) Vajrapani, the protector of the Buddha, depicted as Herakles in the Greco-Buddhist art of Gandhara.

(4) Shukongoshin, manifestation of Vajrapani, as protector deity of Buddhist temples in Japan.

Iconographical evolution of the Wind God.

Left: Greek Wind God from Hadda, 2nd century.

Middle: Wind God from Kizil, Tarim Basin, 7th century.

Right: Japanese Wind God Fujin, 17th century.

Greek representations and artistic styles, with some possible admixtures from the Roman world, continued to maintain a strong identity down to the 3rd-4th century, as indicated by the archaeological remains of such sites as Hadda in eastern Afghanistan. The Greco-Buddhist image of the Buddha was transmitted progressively through Central Asia and China until it reached Japan in the 6th century.

Numerous elements of Greek mythology and iconography, introduced in northwestern India by the Indo-Greeks through their coinage at the very least, were then adopted throughout Asia within a Buddhist context, especially along the Silk Road. The Japanese Buddhist deity Shukongoshin, one of the wrath-filled protector deities of Buddhist temples in Japan, is an interesting case of transmission of the image of the famous Greek god Herakles to the Far-East along the Silk Road. The image of Herakles was introduced in India with the coinage of Demetrius and several of his successors, used in Greco-Buddhist art to represent Vajrapani the protector of the Buddha, and was then used in Central Asia, China and Japan to depict the protector gods of Buddhist temples. Another case of artistic transmission is the Greek Wind God Boreas, transiting through Central Asia and China to become the Japanese Shinto wind god Fujin. In consistency with Greek iconography for Boreas, the Japanese wind god holds above his head with his two hands a draping or "wind bag" in the same general attitude. The abundance of hair have been kept in the Japanese rendering, as well as exaggerated facial features.

Intellectual and Religious Legacy

The impact of the Indo-Greeks on Indian thought and religion is unknown, although many influences have been suggested. Scholars believe that Mahayana Buddhism as a distinct movement began around the 1st century BCE in the North-western Indian subcontinent, corresponding to the time and place of Indo-Greek florescence. Intense multi-cultural influences have indeed been suggested in the appearance of Mahayana: "Key formative influences on the early development of the Mahayana and Pure Land movements, which became so much part of East Asian civilization, are to be sought in Buddhism's earlier encounters along the Silk Road". As Mahayana Buddhism emerged, it received "influences from popular Hindu devotional cults (bhakti), Persian and Greco-Roman theologies which filtered into India from the northwest". Many of the early Mahayana theories of reality and knowledge can be related to Greek philosophical schools of thought: Mahayana Buddhism has been described as "the form of Buddhism which (regardless of how Hinduized its later forms became) seems to have originated in the Greco-Buddhist communities of India, through a conflation of the Greek Democritean-Sophistic-Skeptical tradition with the rudimentary and unformalized empirical and skeptical elements already present in early Buddhism".

List of the Indo-Greek Kings and their Territories

Today 36 Indo-Greek kings are known. Several of them are also recorded in Western and Indian historical sources, but the majority are known through numismatic evidence only. The exact chronology and sequencing of their rule is still a matter of scholarly inquiry, with adjustments regular being made with new analysis and coin finds (overstrikes of one king over another's coins being the most critical element in establishing chronological sequences).

Lastly Theodamas, not mentioned in this list, may have been an Indo-Greek ruler in the Bajaur area in the 1st century CE.

6

Satavahana Dynasty

The Satavahanas, also known as the Andhras, were a dynasty which ruled in Southern and Central India starting from around 230 BCE. Although there is some controversy about when the dynasty came to an end, the most liberal estimates suggest that it lasted about 450 years. The satavahanas are credited for establishing peace in the country from the onslaught of foreigners after the decline of Mauryan empire.

ORIGINS

The first mention of the Andhras is in the Aitareya Brahmana, dating back to the 8th century BCE. Their first capital was Junnar, near Pune which falls in Andar maval region. In the Puranas and on their coins the dynasty is variously referred to as the Andhras, Andhrabhrityas, Satakarnis and Satavahanas. there was a reference of Andhras in Greek traveller Megasthanes's indica that they pocessed 12,00,000 infantry, 2,000 elephants, over 10,000 tanks and other armored vehicles, and had more than 30 well built fortified towns and were in command of all the sea ports from Bengal to all of south India. The Andhras ruled the biggest and most powerful empire of that time in Asia and this was evidenced by establishment of Indian colonies in southeast Asia for the first time in history.

The Satavahanas started out as feudatories to the Mauryan Empire but declared independence soon after the death of Ashoka (232 BCE).

They were the first native Indian rulers to issue their own coins with portraits of their rulers, starting with king

Vashishtiputra Shri Pulumavi (r. 130-158 CE), a practice derived from that of the Indo-Greek kings to the northwest. Their coins give unique indications as to their chronology, language, and even facial features (curly hair, long ears, strong lips). They issued mainly lead and copper coins; their portrait-style silver coins were usually struck over coins of the Western Kshatrapa kings. Their coins also display various traditional symbols, such as elephants, lions, horses, and chaityas (stupas), as well as the "Ujjain symbol", a cross with four circles at the end.the legendary ujjayini emperor Vikramditya on whose name the Vikram Samvat is initiated might be a Satavahana emperor as the ujjayini symbol also appeared on the Satavahana coins.

EARLY RULERS

After becoming independent around 230 BCE, Simuka, the founder of the dynasty, conquered Maharashtra, Malwa and part of Madhya Pradesh. He was succeeded by his brother Kanha (or Krishna) (r. 207-189 BCE), who further extended his kingdom to the west and the south.

His successor Satakarni I defeated the Sunga dynasty of North India, and performed several Vedic sacrifices at huge cost, including the Horse Sacrifice. By this time the dynasty was well established, with its capital at Pratishthanapura (Paithan) in Maharashtra, and its power spreading into all of South India. The Puranas list 30 rulers of this line. Many are known from their coins and inscriptions as well.

CONFLICT WITH THE SHAKAS, YAVANAS AND PAHLAVAS

The first century CE saw the incursion of the Sakas of Central Asia into India, where they formed the dynasty of the Western Kshatrapas. The four immediate successors of Hala (r. 20-24 CE) had short reigns totalling about a dozen years. About this time the kingdom lost some of its territory, including Malwa, to the Western Kshatrapas.

Eventually Gautamiputra (Sri Yagna) Satakarni (r. 106-130 CE) defeated the Western Kshatrapa ruler Nahapana, restoring the prestige of his dynasty by reconquering a large part of the former dominions of the Satavahanas. He was an ardent supporter of the Brahminical religion. He called himself "Destroyer of Shakas (Western Kshatrapas), Yavanas (Indo-Greeks) and Pahlavas (Indo-Parthians)" in his inscriptions.

Gautamiputra Satakarni's son, Vashishtiputra Pulumayi (r. 130-158 CE), succeeded him. He was the first Satavahana king to issue the portrait-type coinage.

His brother, Vashishtiputra Satakarni, married the daughter of Rudradaman I of the Western Kshatrapa dynasty, but was defeated by his father-in-law in battle, with serious effect on Satavahana power and prestige. It was not until the reign of Sri Yajna Satakarni (170-199 CE) that there was another change of fortune for the Satavahanas. He struggled hard against the Shakas and recovered some of the territory lost to them.

CULTURAL ACHIEVEMENTS

Of the Satavahana kings, Hala (r. 20-24 CE) is famous for compiling the collection of Prakrit poems known as the Gaha Sattasai (Sanskrit: Gatha Saptashati), although from linguistic evidence it seems that the work now extant must have been re-edited in the succeeding century or two.

The Satavahana kings are also remarkable for their contributions to Buddhist art and architecture. The great stupas in the Krishna River Valley were built by them, including the stupa at Amaravati in Andhra Pradesh. The stupas were decorated in marble slabs and sculpted with scenes from the life of the Buddha, portrayed in a characteristic slim and elegant style.the greatest achievement of satavahana empire is the colinisation of southeast asia and the spread of indian culture to those parts,mahayana buddism which originated in andhra spread to many parts of asia because of the rich maritime culture of satavahanas.the amaravati style of sculpture spread to southeast asia in this time.

DECLINE

Altough the Satavahanas could resist their enimies, they were ultimateley weakened by continuous Military conflicts and around 220 AD, this Dynasty ended.

Several dynasties divided the lands of the kingdom among themselves. Among them were:

- Abhiras in the northwestern part of the kingdom. They were ultimately to succeed the Satavahānas in their capital Pratishthanapura.
- Chutus in South Maharashtra
- Kadambas of Banavasi in North Karnataka.
- Ikshvakus (or Sriparvatiyas) in the Krishna-Guntur region.

On the boundaries of the old Satavahana Kingdom arose a number of new states, which seized their territory. The most important were the Pallavas of Kanchipuram, of whom the first ruler was Simhavarman I (r. 275-300 CE).

Main Rulers

- Simuka (r. 230-207 BCE)
- Kanha (or Krishna) (r. 207-189 BCE)
- Satakarni I
- Lambodara Trikarna (r. 87-67 BCE)
- Hala (r. 20-24 CE)
- Gautamiputra Satakarni (r. 106-130 CE)
- Vashishtiputra Pulumayi (r. 130-158 CE)
- Vashishtiputra Satakarni
- Sri Yajna Satakarni (r. 170-199 CE)

7

Kushan Empire

The Kushan Empire (c. 1st-3rd centuries) was a state that at its height, about 105-250, stretched from what is now Tajikistan to Afghanistan, Pakistan and down into the Ganges river valley in northern India.

The empire was created by the Kushan tribe of the Yuezhi confederation, an Indo-European people from the eastern Tarim Basin and Gansu, China, possibly related to the Tocharians. They had diplomatic contacts with Rome, Persia and China, and for several centuries were at the center of exchange between the East and the West.

ORIGINS

Chinese sources describe the Guishuang, i.e. the "Kushans", as one of the five aristocratic tribes of the Yuezhi, a loose confederation of Indo-European peoples. The Yuezhi are also generally considered as the easternmost speakers of Indo-European languages, who had been living in the arid grasslands of eastern Central Asia, in modern-day Xinjiang and Gansu, possibly speaking versions of the Tocharian language, until they were driven west by the Xiongnu in 176-160 BCE. The five tribes constituting the Yuezhi are known in Chinese history as Xiumì, Guishuang, Shuangmi, Xidun, and Dumì.

The Yuezhi reached the Hellenic kingdom of Greco-Bactria, in the Bactrian territory (northernmost Afghanistan and Uzbekistan) around 135 BCE, and displaced the Greek dynasties there, who resettled in Indus basin (in present day Pakistan) in the western part of the Indo-Greek Kingdom.

A MULTI-CULTURAL EMPIRE

In the following century, the Guishuang gained prominence over the other Yuezhi tribes, and welded them into a tight confederation under yabgu (Commander) Kujula Kadphises. The name Guishuang was adopted in the West and modified into Kushan to designate the confederation, although the Chinese continued to call them Yuezhi.

Gradually wresting control of the area from the Scythian tribes, the Kushans expanded south into the region traditionally known as Gandhara (An area lying primarily in Pakistan's Pothowar, and NWFP region but going in an arc to include Kabul valley and part of Qandahar in Afghanistan) and established twin capitals near present-day Kabul and Peshawar then known as Kapisa and Pushklavati respectively.

The Kushan writing system used the Greek alphabet, with the addition of the letter Sho (here in majuscule and minuscule), used to represent the Kushan sound "Sh".

The Kushans adopted elements of the Hellenistic culture of Bactria. They adapted the Greek alphabet (often corrupted) to suit their own language (with the additional development of the letter Þ "sh", as in "Kushan") and soon began minting coinage on the Greek model. On their coins they used Greek language legends combined with Pali legends (in the Kharoshthi script), until the first few years of the reign of Kanishka. After that date, they used Kushan language legends (in an adapted Greek script), combined with legends in Greek (Greek script) and legends in Pali (Kharoshthi script).

The Kushans are believed to have been predominantly Zoroastrian and later Buddhist as well. However, from the time of Wima Takto, many Kushans started adopting aspects of Indian culture like the other nomadic groups who had invaded India, principally the Royal clans of Gujjars. Like the Macedonians and Egyptians they absorbed the strong remnants of the Greek Culture of the Hellenistic Kingdoms, becoming at least partly Hellenised. The first great Kushan emperor Wima Kadphises may have embraced Saivism, as surmised by coins minted during the period. The following Kushan emperors represented a wide variety of faiths including Zoroastrianism,

Buddhism, and possibly Saivism. The rule of the Kushans linked the seagoing trade of the Indian Ocean with the commerce of the Silk Road through the long-civilized Indus Valley. At the height of the dynasty, the Kushans loosely oversaw a territory that extended to the Aral Sea through present-day Uzbekistan, Afghanistan, and Pakistan into northern India.

The loose unity and comparative peace of such a vast expanse encouraged long-distance trade, brought Chinese silks to Rome, and created strings of flourishing urban centers.

MAIN KUSHAN RULERS

Silver tetradrachm of Kushan king Heraios (1-30) in Greco-Bactrian style, with horseman crowned by the Greek goddess of victory Nike. Greek legend the Tyrant Heraios, Sanav, the Kushan" (the meaning of "Sanav" is unknown).

Heraios (1-30)

Heraios was probably the first of the Kushan kings. He may have been an ally of the Greeks, and he shared the same style of coinage. Heraios was probably the father of Kujula Kadphises.

Kujula Kadphises (30-80)

According to the Hou Hanshu: "the prince (xihou) of Guishuang (Badakhshan and the adjoining territories north of the Oxus), named Kujula Kadphises ("Qiujiuque") attacked and exterminated the four other princes (xihou). He set himself up as king of a kingdom called Guishuang. He invaded Anxi (Parthia) and took the Gaofu (Kabul) region. He also defeated the whole of the kingdoms of Puda, and Jibin (Kapisha-Gandhara). Qiujiuque (Kujula Kadphises) was more than eighty years old when he died."

These conquests probably took place sometime between 45 and 60, and laid the basis for the Kushan Empire which was rapidly expanded by his descendants.

Vima Taktu (80-105)

Vima Takt[u] (or Tak[to]) is mentioned in the Rabatak inscription, which states that he was the father of Vima

Kadphises, and the grandfather of Kanishka I. He expanded the Kushan Empire into the northwest of the Indian subcontinent. The Hou Hanshu says:

"His [Kujula Kadphises'] son, Yangaozhen (Vima Taktu), became king in his place. He conquered Tianzhu (Northwestern India) and installed a General to supervise and lead it. The Yuezhi then became extremely rich. All the kingdoms call [their king] the Guishuang (Kushan) king, but the Han call them by their original name, Da Yuezhi."

Vima Kadphises (105-127)

Vima Kadphises was the son of Vima Taktu and the father of Kanishka I. He issued an extensive series of coins and inscriptions.

Kanishka I (127-147)

The rule of Kanishka I, the second great Kushan emperor, fifth Kushan king, who flourished for at least 28 years from c. 127, was administered from two capitals: Purushapura (now Peshawar in northern Pakistan) and Mathura, in northern India. He is also credited (along with Raja Dab) for building the massive, ancient Fort at Bathinda (Qila Mubarak), in the modern city of Bathinda, Indian Punjab. The Kushans also had a summer capital in Bagram (then known as Kapisa), where the "Begram Treasure", comprising works of art from Greece to China, has been found. According to the Rabatak inscription, Kanishka was the son of Vima Kadphises, the grandson of Vima Taktu, and the great-grandson of Kujula Kadphises. Kanishka's era is now generally accepted to have begun in 127 on the basis of Harry Falk's ground-breaking research. Kanishka's era was used as a calendar reference by the Kushans for about a century, until the decline of the Kushan realm.

THE KUSHANS AND BUDDHISM

Cultural exchanges also flourished, encouraging the development of Greco-Buddhism, a fusion of Hellenistic and Buddhist cultural elements, that was to expand into central and northern Asia as Mahayana Buddhism. Kanishka is renowned in Buddhist tradition for having convened a great

Buddhist council in Kashmir. Kanishka also had the original Gandhari vernacular, or Prakrit, Buddhist texts translated into the language of Sanskrit. Along with the Indian emperors Ashoka and Harsha Vardhana and the Indo-Greek king Menander I (Milinda), Kanishka is considered by Buddhism as one of its greatest benefactors.

An early Mahayana Buddhist triad. From left to right, a Kushan devotee, the Bodhisattva Maitreya, the Buddha, the Bodhisattva Avalokitesvara, and a Buddhist monk. 2nd-3rd century, Gandhara.

Depiction of Kushan devotees in the art of Gandhara

The art and culture of Gandhara, at the crossroads of the Kushan hegemony, are the best known expressions of Kushan influences to Westerners. Several direct depictions of Kushans are known from Gandhara, where they are represented with a tunic, belt and trousers and play the role of devotees to the Buddha, as well as the Bodhisattva and future Buddha Maitreya.

In the iconography, they are never associated however with the very Hellenistic "Standing Buddha" statues, which might therefore correspond to an earlier historical period. The style of these friezes incorporating Kushan devotees is already strongly Indianized, quite remote from earlier Hellenistic depictions of the Buddha:

Kushan costume.

Detail of the face of a Kushan devotee.

Flaming Buddha with Kushan devotees around Maitreya.

Maitreya, with Kushan devotee couple. 2nd century Gandhara.

Detail of Kushan devotee.

Maitreya, with Kushan devotees, left and right. 2nd century Gandhara.

Maitreya, with Indian (left) and Kushan (right) devotees.

Kushans worshipping the Buddha's bowl. 2nd century Gandhara.

Kushan devotee couple, around the Buddha, Brahma and Indra.

The "Kanishka casket", with the Buddha surrounded by Brahma and Indra, and Kanishka on the lower part, 127.

Buddha triad and kneeling Kushan devotee couple. 3rd century.

CONTACTS WITH ROME

Several Roman sources describe the visit of ambassadors from the Kings of Bactria and India during the 2nd century, probably referring to the Kushans.

Historia Augusta, speaking of Emperor Hadrian (117-138) tells:

"Reges Bactrianorum legatos ad eum, amicitiae petendae causa, supplices miserunt"

"The kings of the Bactrians sent supplicant ambassadors to him, to seek his friendship."

Also in 138, according to Aurelius Victor (Epitome, XV, 4), and Appian (Praef., 7), Antoninus Pius, successor to Hadrian, received some Indian, Bactrian (Kushan) and Hyrcanian ambassadors.

The Chinese Historical Chronicle of the Hou Hanshu also describes the exchange of goods between northwestern India and the Roman Empire at that time: "To the west (Tiazhu, northwestern India) communicates with Da Qin (the Roman Empire). Precious things from Da Qin can be found there, as well as fine cotton cloths, excellent wool carpets, perfumes of all sorts, sugar loaves, pepper, ginger, and black salt."

The summer capital of the Kushan in Begram has yielded a considerable amount of goods imported from the Roman Empire, in particular various types of glassware.

CONTACTS WITH CHINA

The Kushan Buddhist monk Lokaksema, first known translator of Buddhist Mahayana scriptures into Chinese, circa 170.

During the 1st and 2nd century, the Kushan Empire expanded militarily to the north and occupied parts of the Tarim Basin, their original grounds, putting them at the center of the profitable Central Asian commerce with the Roman Empire. They are related to have collaborated militarily with the Chinese against nomadic incursion, particularly when they collaborated with the Chinese general Ban Chao against the Sogdians in 84, when the latter were trying to support a revolt by the king of Kashgar. Around 85, they also assisted the Chinese general in an attack on Turfan, east of the Tarim Basin. In recognition for their support to the Chinese, the Kushans requested, but were denied, a Han princess, even after they had sent presents to the Chinese court. In retaliation, they marched on Ban Chao in 86 with a force of 70,000, but, exhausted by the expedition, were finally defeated by the smaller Chinese force. The Yuezhi retreated and paid tribute to the Chinese Empire during the reign of the Chinese emperor Han He (89-106).

Later, around 116, the Kushans under Kanishka established a kingdom centered on Kashgar, also taking control of Khotan and Yarkand, which were Chinese dependencies in the Tarim Basin, modern Xinjiang. They introduced the Brahmi script, the Indian Prakrit language for administration, and expanded the influence of Greco-Buddhist art which developed into Serindian art. The Kushans are again recorded to have sent presents to the Chinese court in 158-159 during the reign of the Chinese emperor Han Huan.

Following these interactions, cultural exhanges further increased, and Kushan Buddhist missionaries, such as Lokaksema, became active in the Chinese capital cities of Loyang and sometimes Nanjing, where they particularly distinguished themselves by their translation work. They were the first recorded promoters of Hinayana and Mahayana scriptures in China, greatly contributing to the Silk Road transmission of Buddhism.

DECLINE

From the 3rd century the Kushan empire began to fragment. Around 225 Vasudeva I died and the Kushan empire was divided into western and eastern halves. Around 224-240, the Sassanids invaded Bactria and Northern India, where they are known as the Indo-Sassanians.

Around 270, the Kushans lost their territories on the Gangetic plain, where the Gupta Empire was established around 320 and to the Sassanians during Shapur II's reign, notably the area that comprises of Afghanistan.

During the middle of the 4th century a Kushan vassal in Pakistan, named Kidara, rose to power and overthrew the old Kushan dynasty. He created a kingdom known as the Kidarite Kingdom, although he probably considered himself a Kushan, as indicated by the Kushan style of his coins. The Kidarite seem to have been rather prosperous, although on a smaller scale than their Kushan predecessors.

These remnants of the Kushan empire were ultimately wiped out in the 5th century by the invasions of the White Huns, and later the expansion of Islam. The end of the Kushans could be considered the end of Hellenism in India.

Today we find Kushans as a subclan among Gujjars. They are said to be the same Kushans as it is very much known that most of the Gurjar Clans were originated from Yuezhi.

Main Kushan Rulers

- Heraios (c. 1-30), first Kushan ruler, generally Kushan ruling period is disputed
- Kujula Kadphises (c. 30-c. 80)
- Vima Takto, (c. 80-c. 105) alias Soter Megas or "Great Saviour."
- Vima Kadphises (c. 105-c. 127) the first great Kushan emperor
- Kanishka I (127-c. 147)
- Vasishka (c. 151-c. 155)
- Huvishka (c. 155-c. 187)
- Vasudeva I (c. 191-to at least 230), the last of the great Kushan emperors
- Kanishka II (c. 226-240)

- Vashishka (c. 240-250)
- Kanishka III (c. 255-275)
- Vasudeva II (c. 290-310)
    - o Vasudeva III reported son of Vasudeva III,a King,uncertain.
- Vasudeva IV reported possible child of Vasudeva III,ruling in Kandahar,uncertain
- Vasudeva of Kabul reported Possible child of Vasudeva IV,ruling in Kabul,uncertain.
- Chhu (c. 310-325)
- Shaka I (c. 325-345)
- Kipunada (c. 350-375)

8

Gupta Empire

The Gupta Empire was one of the largest political and military empires in ancient India. It was ruled by the Gupta dynasty from around 240 to 550 CE and covered most of northern India and what is now eastern Pakistan and Bangladesh. During the time of the Gupta Empire, Indians enjoyed a "Golden Age" in science, astronomy, religion and philosophy. The peace and prosperity created under leadership of Guptas enabled the pursuit of scientific and artistic endeavors. The decimal numeral system, including the concept of zero, was invented in India during the reign of the Guptas. At the time of its maximum extent, the Gupta empire was considered a Great power. Historians place the Gupta dynasty alongside with the Han Dynasty, Tang Dynasty and Rome as a model of a classical civilization.

ORIGINS

The origins of the Guptas are shrouded in obscurity. The Chinese traveller I-tsing provides the first evidence of the Gupta kingdom in Magadha. He came to India in 672 CE and heard of 'Maharaja Sri-Gupta' who built a temple for Chinese pilgrims near Mrigasikhavana. I-tsing gives the date for this event merely as '500 years before'. This does not match with other sources and hence we can assume that I-tsing's computation was a mere guess. Some scholars link Guptas with abhir ruler mentioned in Bhagwatam. The most likely date for the reign of Sri-Gupta is c. 240-280 CE. His successor Ghatotkacha ruled probably from c. 280-319 CE. In contrast to his successor, he is also referred to in inscriptions as 'Maharaja'.

The most accepted theory about the origins of the Guptas is that the Guptas originated from Bengal. The mention of "Varendra Mrigashihavan Stupa" on a mound in Nepal is a strong evidence that the Guptas originated from Bengal. Maharaja Sri-Gupta probably ruled a portion of Northern/Southern Bengal. Later Chandragupta I established his dominion over Magadha through marital policy with the Licchavis. However the origins of the Guptas is still hotly debated. At the beginning of the 4th century the Guptas established and ruled a few small Hindu kingdoms in Magadha and around modern-day Uttar Pradesh.

THE GUPTAS ASCENDANT

The Gupta dynasty ruled India north of the Vindhya Range during the 4th and 5th centuries. Though not as vast as Mauryan empire, The Gupta era left a deep and wide cultural impact not only in the subcontinent but on the adjacent Asian countries as well. We get plenty of information about this illustrious dynasty through coins, inscriptions, monuments and Sanskrit classics.

The Gupta rulers were great conquerors and good administrators. They checked the infiltration of foreign tribes like Sakas and Hunas and established political stability. Economic prosperity followed and led to cultural expansion.

Sanskrit language and literature reached its peak during the Gupta era. Poets Kalidasa, Dandi, Visakhadatta, Shudraka, and Bharavi all belong to this period. Many puranas and shastras were composed and famous commentaries on sacred works appeared. Buddhist and Jain literature, which was produced earlier in Pali, Ardhamagadhi and other Prakrit languages, began to appear in Sanskrit. The practice of dedicating temples to different deities came into vogue followed by fine artistic temple architecture and sculpture. Most of the twenty-eight Ajanta caves were constructed during this period. Gupta inscriptions, some of them on "victory pillars" provide first hand information not only about royalty but society in general.

Books on medicine, veterinary science, mathematics, astronomy and astrophysics were written. The famous Aryabhata and Varahamihira belong to this age. Overseas trade and commerce flourished. Hindu and Buddhist mythology, architecture, along with religion took root in Burma, Cambodia, Thailand, Indonesia and other countries. The Chinese monk Lui Kang who was in India and Sri Lanka between 399 and 414 noticed general prosperity and peace-loving nature of the people.

This period is regarded as the golden age of Indian culture. The high points of this cultural creativity are magnificent and creative architecture, sculpture, and painting. The wall-paintings of Ajanta Caves in the central Deccan are considered among the greatest and most powerful works of Indian art. The paintings in the cave represent the various lives of the Buddha, but also are the best source we have of the daily life in India at the time.

The Gupta established a strong central government which also allowed a degree of local control. Gupta society was ordered in accordance with Hindu beliefs. This included a strict caste system, or class system. The peace and prosperity created under Gupta leadership enabled the pursuit of scientific and artistic endeavors.

The Gupta Dynasty declined due to weak rulers and a series of invasions, but many of their cultural and intellectual achievements were saved and transmitted to other cultures and live on today. The Gupta period is considered something of a golden age, marked by great achievements in literature, music, art, architecture, and philosophy. Lui Kang wrote of beautiful cities, fine hospitals and universities, and described a content and prosperous people

MAIN GUPTA RULERS

Chandragupta

Ghatotkacha (c. 280-319) CE, had a son named Chandragupta. (Not to be confused with Chandragupta Maurya, founder of the Mauryan Empire.) In a breakthrough deal, Chandragupta was married to a Lichchhavi-the main power in Magadha. With a dowry of the kingdom of Magadha (capital Pataliputra) and an alliance with the Lichchhavis, Chandragupta set about expanding his power, conquering much of Magadha, Prayaga and Saketa. He established a realm stretching from the Ganga River (Ganges River) to Prayaga (modern-day Allahabad) by 320. Chandragupta was the first of the Guptas to be referred to as 'Maharajadhiraja' or 'King of Kings'.

Samudragupta

Chandragupta died in 335 and was succeeded by his son Samudragupta, a tireless conqueror. He took the kingdoms of Shichchhatra and Padmavati early in his reign. He then took the Kingdom of Kota and attacked the tribes in Malvas, the Yaudheyas, the Arjunayanas, the Maduras and the Abhiras. By his death in 380, he had incorporated over twenty kingdoms into his realm, his rule extended from the Himalayas to the river Narmada and from the Brahmaputra to the Yamuna. He gave himself the titles King of Kings and World Monarch. He performed Ashwamedha yajna (horse sacrifice) to underline the importance of his conquest. Samudragupta was not only a warrior but also a great patron of art and literature. The important scholars present in his court were Harishena, Vasubandhu and Asanga. He was a poet and musician himself. He was a firm believer in Hinduism and is known to have worshipped Lord Vishnu. He was considerate of other religions and allowed Sri Lanka's buddhist king to build a monastery at Bodh Gaya. He was succeeded by his son Ramagupta, who was captured by the Saka Satraps (Kshatrapas) and was soon succeeded by his brother Chandragupta II.

Chandragupta II

Chandragupta II, the Sun of Power (Vikramaditya), ruled until 413. He married his daughter Prabhavatigupta to Rudrasena II, the Vakataka king of Deccan, and gained a valuable ally. Only marginally less war-like than his father, he expanded his realm westwards, defeating the Saka Western Kshatrapas of Malwa, Gujarat and Saurashtra in a campaign lasting until 409, but with his main opponent Rudrasimha III defeated by 395, and crushing the Bengal (Vanga) chiefdoms. This extended his control from coast-to-coast, established a second (trading) capital at Ujjain and was the high point of the empire.

Despite the creation of the empire through war, the reign is remembered for its very influential style of Hindu art, literature, culture and science, especially during the reign of Chandra Gupta II. Some excellent works of Hindu art such as the panels at the Dashavatara Temple in Deogarh serve to illustrate the magnificence of Gupta art. Above all it was the synthesis of the sacred and sensual elements that gave Gupta art its distinctive flavour. During this period, the Guptas were supportive of thriving Buddhist and Jain cultures as well, and for this reason there is also a long history of non-Hindu Gupta period art. In particular, Gupta period Buddhist art was to be influential in most of East and Southeast Asia. Much of advances was recorded by the Chinese scholar and traveller Fa-hsien in his diary and published afterwords. The lineage of the Chandra Guptas' can be traced down for generations to the present day, to one Ashok Chandra Gupta.

The court of Chandragupta was made even more illustrious by the fact that it was graced by the navaratna, a group of nine who excelled in the literary arts. Amongst these men was the immortal Kalidasa whose works dwarfed the works of many other literary geniuses, not only in his own age but in the ages to come. Kalidasa was particularly known for his fine exploitation of the sringara (erotic) element in his verse.

Kumaragupta I

Silver coin of the Gupta King Kumara Gupta I (414-455) CE (Western territories).

Obv: Bust of king Rev: Garuda standing facing with spread wings. Brahmi legend: Parama-bhagavata rajadhiraja Sri Kumaragupta Mahendraditya. Chandragupta II was succeeded by his son Kumaragupta I. Known as the Mahendraditya, he ruled until 455. Towards the end of his reign a tribe in the Narmada valley, the Pushyamitras, rose in power to threaten the empire.

Skandagupta

Skandagupta is generally considered the last of the great rulers. He defeated the Pushyamitra threat, but then was faced with invading Hephthalites or "White Huns", known in India as Indo-Hephthalites or Hunas, from the northwest. He repulsed a Huna attack c. 455, But the expense of the wars drained the empire's resources and contributed to its decline. Skandagupta died in 467 and was succeeded by his son Narasimhagupta Baladitya.

MILITARY ORGANIZATION

The Imperial Guptas could not have achieved their successes through force of arms without an efficient martial system. Historically, the best accounts of this comes not from the Hindus themselves but from Chinese and Western observers. However, a contemporary Indian document, regarded as a military classic of the time, the Siva-Dhanur-veda, offers some insight into the military system of the Guptas. Like Indian kings before them, and centuries afterwards, the Guptas would have utilized war elephants. These thick hided beasts, supplemented by additional armour and the soldiers that they carried, would have provided a powerful offensive and psychological weapon against an unprepared foe. Another advantage was that they could cause the horses of enemy cavalry to panic from their scent, as the Macedonians discovered. However, their use carried the grave risk of the elephants panicking and stampeding, which more clever opponents used to their advantage.

The use of chariots had heavily declined by the time of the Guptas, having already proved their uselessness against the Macedonians, Scythians, and other invaders. In response, the Guptas seemed to have utilized heavy cavalry clad in mail armour and equipped with maces and lances, who would have used shock action to break the enemy line, much like the clibanarii of the Sassanid Persians and Byzantines in the same era. A basic form of the stirrup existed in India at the time, which would have helped cavalry to brace their attack. It is unclear whether they were used to the extent of elephants.

The Guptas seem to have relied heavily on infantry archers, and the bow was one of the dominant weapons of their army. The Hindu version of the longbow was composed of metal, or more typically bamboo, and fired a long bamboo cane arrow with a metal head. Unlike the composite bows of Western and Central Asian foes, bows of this design would be less prone to warping in the damp and moist conditions often prevalent to the region. The Indian longbow was reputedly a powerful weapon capable of great range and penetration and provided an effective counter to invading horse archers. Iron shafts were used against armored elephants, and fire arrows were also part of the bowmen's arsenal. India historically has had a prominent reputation for its steel weapons. One of these was the steel bow. Due to its high tensility, the steel bow was capable of long range and penetration of exceptionally thick armor. These were less common weapons than the bamboo design and found in the hands of noblemen rather than in the ranks. Archers were frequently protected by infantry equipped with shields, javelins, and longswords.

The Guptas also had knowledge of siegecraft, catapults, and other sophisticated war machines.

The Guptas apparently showed little predilection for using horse archers, despite the fact these warriors were a main component in the ranks of their Scythian, Parthian, and Hepthalite (Huna) enemies. However, the Gupta armies were probably better disciplined. Able commanders like Samudragupta and Chandragupta II would have likely understood the need for combined armed tactics and proper logistical organization. Gupta military success likely stemmed from the concerted use elephants, armored cavalry, and foot archers in tandem against both Hindu kingdoms and foreign armies invading from the Northwest. The Guptas also maintained a navy, allowing them to control regional waters.

The collapse of the Gupta Empire in the face of the Huna onslaught was due not directly to the inherent defects of the Gupta army, which after all had initially defeated these barbarians under Skandagupta. More likely, internal dissolution sapped the ability of the Guptas to resist foreign invasion, as was simultenously occurring in Western Europe and China.

HUNA INVASIONS AND THE END OF EMPIRE

Narasimhagupta (467-473) was followed by Kumaragupta II (473-476) and Buddhagupta (476-495). In the 480's the Hephthalite king Toramana broke through the Gupta defenses in the northwest, and much of the empire was overrun by the

Hunas by 500. The empire disintegrated under the attacks of Toramana and his successor, Mihirakula; the Hunas conquered several provinces of the empire, including Malwa, Gujarat, and Thanesar, broke away under the rule of local dynasties.- It appears from inscriptions that the Guptas, although their power was much diminished, continued to resist the Hunas, and allied with the independent kingdoms to drive the Hunas from most of northern India by the 530's. The succession of the sixth-century Guptas is not entirely clear, but the last recognized ruler of the dynasty's main line was Vishnugupta, reigning from 540 to 550.

THE GUPTAS OF MAGADHA

A minor line of the Gupta clan continued to rule Magadha after the disintegration of the empire. These Guptas were ultimately ousted by the Vardhana king Harsha, who established an empire in the first half of the seventh century that, for a brief time, rivalled that of the Guptas in extent. yep. sounds good.

Gupta Arts

Some of India's most magnificient works of art were produced during the Gupta era. The famous cave paintings at Ajanta, the Sarnath Buddha, the Deogarh Dashavatara Temple panels and the Udaygiri Varaha Cave are some marvellous products of the Gupta age. The traditional Buddha iconography from the Gupta empire includes the following: sting-fold style drapery; thicker garments; elongated, idealized bodies; "lotus" eyes; thick, "bee stung" lips; scooped, smooth eyebrows; snail shell curls; and distant, meditative gazes. Also, during the Gupta Empire, metal work and various sculptures were made. The Gupta architecture helped in the consturction of Ajanta and Ellora Caves though this may not be confirmed. The most well-known work from the Ajanta caves is the "Bodhisattva Padmapani." This colorful fresco, made with chaff, white plaster, and pigment, portrays a bodisattva holding a lotus flower.

LEGACY OF THE GUPTA EMPIRE

The Gupta Empire is considered by many scholars to be the "classical age" of Hindu and Buddhist art and literature. The

Rulers of the Gupta Empire were strong supporters of developments in the arts, architecture, science, and literature. The Guptas circulated a large number of gold coins, called dinars, with their inscriptions. This period is also very rich in Sanskrit literature. Several important works were composed by well-known writers, such as The Little Clay Cart and Mrichchakatika by Shudraka, along with ones by Kalidasa and others. Panchatantra, the animal fables by Vishnu Sharma, and 13 plays by Bhasa, were also written in this period. The Gupta Dynasty also left behind an effective administrative system. During times of peace, the Gupta system was decentralized, with only taxation flowing to the capital at Pataliputra. During times of war however, the government realigned and fought its invaders. The system was soon extinguished in fighting off the Hunnic Invasions.

The most significant achievements of this period, however, were in religion, education, mathematics, art, Sanskrit literature and drama, and Kama Sutra, the art of sex. Hinduism witnessed a crystallization of its components: major sectarian deities, image worship, devotionalism, and the importance of the temple. Education included grammar, composition, logic, metaphysics, mathematics, medicine, and astronomy. These subjects became highly specialized and reached an advanced level. The Indian numeral system-sometimes erroneously attributed to the Arabs, who took it from India to Europe where it replaced the Roman system-and the decimal system are Indian inventions of this period. Aryabhatta's expositions on astronomy in 499, moreover, gave calculations of the solar year and the shape and movement of astral bodies with remarkable accuracy.

In medicine, the Guptas were notable for their establishment and patronage of free hospitals. And although progress in physiology and biology was hindered by religious injunctions against contact with dead bodies, which discouraged dissection and anatomy, Indian physicians excelled in pharmacopoeia, caesarean section, bone setting, and skin grafting. Indeed Hindu medical advances were soon adopted in the Arab and Western worlds. The great universities in central and eastern India received an influx of students from many parts of the world. Most notable were the universities of Nalanda and Vikramasila.

CONTRIBUTIONS TO THE WORLD AND ACHIEVEMENTS

Gupta golden age period contributed much to the world. Two of India's earliest mathematicians, Aryabhatta and Varahamihira, also appeared during this period. Their intellectual advances helped to shape many future breakthroughs in technology. The brilliant minds behind the Gupta Empire made major advances in Algebra and also devised the concept of zero and infinity. One of their most important gifts to the world were symbols of the numbers from 1 to 9. These numerals were later adopted by the Arabs through trade and became known as the arabic numerals. And these were eventually adopted by the west.

Gupta astronomers also made advances in astronomy by using their mathematical breakthroughs. It was during this empire that philosophers first proposed that the earth was not flat, but was instead round and rotated on an axis. They also made discoveries about gravity and the planets of the solar system, which they used to tell the horoscopes. Doctors also invented several medical instruments, and even performed operations. These ideas spread throughout the world through trade.

9

Chola Dynasty

The Chola dynasty was a Tamil dynasty that ruled primarily in southern India until the 13th century. The dynasty originated in the fertile valley of the Kaveri River. Karikala Chola was the most famous among the early Chola kings, while Rajaraja Chola, Rajendra Chola and Kulothunga Chola I were famous emperors of the medieval Cholas.

The Cholas were at the height of their power during the tenth, eleventh and twelfth centuries. Under Rajaraja Chola I (Rajaraja the Great) and his son Rajendra Chola, the dynasty became a military, economic and cultural power in Asia. The Chola territories stretched from the islands of the Maldives in the South to as far North as the banks of the Godavari River in Andhra Pradesh. Rajaraja Chola conquered peninsular South India, annexed parts of Sri Lanka and occupied the islands of the Maldives. Rajendra Chola sent a victorious expedition to the North India that touched river Ganga and defeated the Pala ruler of Pataliputra, Mahipala. He also successfully raided kingdoms of the Malay Archipelago. The power of the Cholas declined around the 12th century with the rise of the Pandyas and the Hoysala, eventually coming to an end towards the end of the 13th century.

The Cholas left behind a lasting legacy. Their patronage of Tamil literature and their zeal in building temples have resulted in some great works of Tamil literature and architecture. The Chola kings were avid builders and envisioned the temples in their kingdoms not only as places of worship but also as centres of economic activity. They pioneered a centralised form of government and established a disciplined bureaucracy.

ORIGINS

There is no definite information on the origins of the word Chola. Mentions in the early Sangam literature (c. 150) indicate that the earliest kings of the dynasty antedated 100. Parimelalagar, the annotator of the Tamil classic Tirukkural, mentions that this could be the name of an ancient clan. The most commonly held view is that this is, like Cheras and Pandyas, the name of the ruling family or clan of immemorial antiquity. Attempts have been made to connect the word with the Sanskrit Kala (black) and with Kola, which in the early days designated the dark coloured pre-Aryan population of Southern India in general.

On the history of Cholas there is very little authentic written evidence available. Historians during the past 150 years have gleaned a lot of knowledge on the subject from a variety of sources such as ancient Tamil Sangam literature, oral traditions, religious texts, temple and copperplate inscriptions. The main source for the available information of the early Cholas is the early Tamil literature of the Sangam Period. There are also brief notices on the Chola country and its towns, ports and commerce furnished by the Periplus of the Erythraean Sea (Periplus Maris Erythraei). Periplus is a work by an anonymous Alexandrian merchant, written in the time of Domitian (81-96) and contains very little information of the Chola country. Writing half a century later, the geographer Ptolemy gives more detail about the Chola country, its port and its inland cities. Mahavamsa, a Buddhist text, recounts a number of conflicts between the inhabitants of Ceylon and the Tamil immigrants. Cholas are mentioned in the Pillars of Ashoka (inscribed 273 BC-232 BC) inscriptions, where they are mentioned among the kingdoms which, though not subject to Ashoka, were on friendly terms with him.

HISTORY

The Chola kings

Early Cholas

Ilamcetcenni	Karikala Chola
Nedunkilli	Nalankilli

Killivalavan	Kopperuncholan
Kocengannan	Perunarkilli

Interregnum-c 200-848

Medieval Cholas

Vijayalaya Chola	848-871
Aditya I	871-907
Parantaka Chola I	907-950
Gandaraditya	950-957
Arinjaya Chola	956-957
Sundara Chola	957-970
Uttama Chola	970-985
Rajaraja Chola I	985-1014
Rajendra Chola I	1012-1044
Rajadhiraja Chola	1018-1054
Rajendra Chola II	1051-1063
Virarajendra Chola	1063-1070
Athirajendra Chola	1067-1070

Chalukya Cholas

Kulothunga Chola I	1070-1120
Vikrama Chola	1118-1135
Kulothunga Chola II	1133-1150
Rajaraja Chola II	1146-1163
Rajadhiraja Chola II	1163-1178
Kulothunga Chola III	1178-1218
Rajaraja Chola III	1216-1256
Rajendra Chola III	1246-1279

Chola Society

Chola Government	Chola Military
Chola Art	Chola Literature
Poompuhar	Urayur
Gangaikonda Cholapuram	Thanjavur

Telugu Cholas

The history of the Cholas falls naturally into four periods: the early Cholas of the Sangam literature, the interregnum between the fall of the Sangam Cholas and the rise of the medieval Cholas under Vijayalaya (c. 848), the dynasty of Vijayalaya, and finally the Chalukya Chola dynasty of Kulothunga Chola I from the third quarter of the eleventh century.

EARLY CHOLAS

The earliest Chola kings of whom there is tangible evidence are mentioned in the Sangam literature. Scholars now generally agree that this literature belongs to the first few centuries of the common era. The internal chronology of this literature is still far from settled, and at present a connected account of the history of the period cannot be derived. The Sangam literature is full of names of the kings and the princes, and of the poets who extolled them. Despite a rich literature that depicts the life and work of these people, these cannot be worked into connected history.

The Sangam literature is also full of legends about the mythical Chola kings. The Cholas were looked on as descended from the sun. These myths speak of the Chola king Kantaman, a supposed contemporary of the sage Agastya, whose devotion brought the Kaveri River into existence. Two names stand out prominently from among those Chola kings known from the Sangam literature: Karikala Chola and Kocengannan. There is no sure means of settling the order of succession, of fixing their relations with one another and with many other princelings of about the same period. Urayur (near Thiruchirapalli) was their oldest capital.

INTERREGNUM

Little is known about the transition period of around three centuries from the end of the Sangam age (c. 300) to that in which the Pandyas and Pallavas dominate the Tamil country. An obscure dynasty, the Kalabhras, invaded the Tamil country, displaced the existing kingdoms and ruled for around three centuries. They were displaced by the Pallavas and the Pandyas in the 6th century. Little is known of the fate of the Cholas during the succeeding three centuries until the accession of Vijayalaya in the second quarter of the ninth century.

Epigraphy and literature provide a few faint glimpses of the transformations that came over this ancient line of kings during this long interval. What is certain is that when the power of the Cholas fell to its lowest ebb and that of the Pandyas and Pallavas rose to the north and south of them, this dynasty was compelled to seek refuge and patronage under their more successful rivals. The Pallavas and Pandyas seem to have left the Cholas alone for the most part; however, possibly out of regard for their reputation, they accepted Chola princesses in marriage and employed in their service Chola princes who were willing to accept it. The Chinese pilgrim Xuanzang, who spent several months in Kanchipuram during 639-640 writes about the 'kingdom of Culi-ya'. Numerous inscriptions of Pallavas, Pandyas and Chalukya of this period mention conquering 'the Chola country'. Despite this loss in influence and power, it is unlikely that the Cholas lost total grip of the territory around Urayur, their old capital. Vijayalaya when he rose to prominence hailed from this geographical area.

Around the 7th century, a Chola kingdom flourished in present-day Andhra Pradesh. These Telugu Cholas traced their descent to the early Sangam Cholas. However, nothing definite is known of their connection to the early Cholas. It is possible that a branch of the Tamil Cholas migrated north during the time of the Pallavas to establish a kingdom of their own, away from the dominating influences of the Pandyas and Pallavas.

MEDIEVAL CHOLAS

While there is little reliable information on the Cholas during the period between the early Cholas and Vijayalaya dynasties, there is an abundance of materials from diverse sources on the Vijayalaya and the Chalukya Chola dynasties. A large number of stone inscriptions by the Cholas themselves and by their rival kings, Pandyas and Chalukyas, and copper-plate grants, have been instrumental in constructing the history of Cholas of that period.

Around 850, Vijayalaya rose from obscurity to take an opportunity arising out of a conflict between Pandyas and

Pallavas, captured Thanjavur and eventually established the imperial line of the medieval Cholas.

The Chola dynasty was at the peak of its influence and power during the medieval period. Great kings such as Rajaraja Chola I and Rajendra Chola I occupied the throne, and through their leadership and vision took extended the Chola kingdom beyond the traditional limits of a Tamil kingdom. At its peak, the Chola Empire stretched from the island of Sri Lanka in the south to the Godavari basin in the north. The kingdoms along the east coast of India up to the river Ganges acknowledged Chola suzerainty. Chola navies invaded and conquered Srivijaya in the Malayan archipelago.

Throughout this period, the Cholas were constantly troubled by the ever-resilient Sinhalas, who attempted to overthrow the Chola occupation of Lanka, Pandya princes who tried to win independence for their traditional territories, and by the growing ambitions of the Chalukyas in the western Deccan. This period saw constant warfare between the Cholas and these antagonists. A balance of power existed between the Chalukyas and the Cholas, and there was a tacit acceptance of the Tungabhadra River as the boundary between the two empires. However, the bone of contention between these two powers was the growing Chola influence in the Vengi kingdom.

CHALUKYA CHOLAS

Marital and political alliances between the Eastern Chalukya kings based around Vengi located on the south banks of the River Godavari began during the reign of Rajaraja following his invasion of Vengi. Rajaraja Chola's daughter married prince Vimaladitya. Rajendra Chola's daughter was also married to an Eastern Chalukya prince Rajaraja Narendra.

Virarajendra Chola's son Athirajendra Chola was assassinated in a civil disturbance in 1070 and Kulothunga Chola I ascended the Chola throne starting the Chalukya Chola dynasty. Kulothunga was a son of the Vengi king Rajaraja Narendra.

The Chalukya Chola dynasty saw very capable rulers in Kulothunga Chola I and Vikrama Chola; however, the decline of the Chola power practically started during this period. The Cholas lost control of the island of Lanka and were driven out by the revival of Sinhala power. Around 1118 they lost the control of Vengi to Western Chalukya king Vikramaditya VI and Gangavadi (southern Mysore districts) to the growing power of Hoysala Vishnuvardhana, a Chalukya feudatory. In the Pandya territories, the lack of a controlling central administration prompted a number of claimants to the Pandya throne to cause a civil war in which the Sinhalas and the Cholas were involved by proxy. During the last century of the Cholas, a permanent Hoysala army was stationed in Kanchipuram to protect them from the growing influence of the Pandyas.

The Cholas, under Rajendra Chola III, experienced continuous trouble. At the close of the 12th century, the growing influence of the Hoysalas replaced the declining Chalukyas as the main player in the north. The local feudatories were also becoming sufficiently confident to challenge the central Chola authority. One feudatory, the Kadava chieftain Kopperunchinga I, even held the Chola king as hostage for sometime. The Cholas were exposed to assaults from within and without. The Pandyas in the south had risen to the rank of a great power. The Hoysalas in the west threatened the existence of the Chola empire. Rajendra tried to survive by aligning with the two powers in turn. At the close of Rajendra's reign, the Pandyan Empire was at the height of prosperity and had taken the place of the Chola empire in the eyes of the foreign observers. The last recorded date of Rajendra III is 1279. There is no evidence that Rajendra was followed immediately by another Chola prince. The Chola empire was completely overshadowed by the Pandyan empire, though many small chieftains continued to claim the title "Chola" well into the 15th century.

GOVERNMENT AND SOCIETY

Chola Country

According to Tamil tradition, the old Chola country comprised the region that includes the modern-day Tiruchirapalli District, and the Thanjavur District in Tamil Nadu state. The Kaveri River and its tributaries dominate this landscape of generally flat country that gradually slopes towards the sea, unbroken by major hills or valleys. The river Kaveri, which was also known as Ponni (golden) river, had a special place in the culture of Cholas. The unfailing annual floods in the Kaveri marked an occasion for celebration, Adiperukku, in which the whole nation took part, from the king to the lowliest peasant.

Kaverippattinam on the coast near the Kaveri delta was a major port town. Ptolemy knew of this and the other port town of Nagappattinam as the most important centres of Cholas. These two cosmopolitan towns became hubs of trade and commerce and attracted many religious faiths, including Buddhism. Roman galleys found their way in to these ports. Roman coins dating from the early centuries of the common era have been found near the Kaveri delta.

The other major towns were Thanjavur, Urayur and Kudanthai. After Rajendra Chola moved his kingdom to Gangaikonda Cholapuram, Thanjavur lost prestige. The later Chola kings of the Chalukya Chola dynasty moved around their country frequently and made cities such as Chidambaram, Madurai and Kanchipuram their regional capitals.

Nature of Government

In the age of the Cholas, the whole of South India was, for the first time, brought under a single government, when a serious attempt was made to face and solve the problems of public administration. The Cholas system of government was monarchical, as in the Sangam age. However, there was little in common between the primitive and somewhat tribal chieftaincy of the earlier time, and the almost Byzantine royalty-Rajaraja Chola-and his successors with its numerous palaces, and the pomp and circumstance associated with the royal court.

Between 980, and c. 1150, the Chola Empire comprised the entire south Indian peninsula, extending east to west from coast to coast, and bounded to the north by an irregular line along the Tungabhadra River and the Vengi frontier. Although Vengi had a separate political existence, it was so closely connected to the Chola Empire that, for all practical purposes, the Chola dominion extended up to the banks of the Godavari river. Thanjavur and later Gangaikonda Cholapuram were the imperial capitals. However both Kanchipuram and Madurai were considered to be regional capitals, in which occasional courts were held. The king was the supreme commander and a benevolent dictator. His administrative role consisted of issuing oral commands to responsible officers when representations were made to him. A powerful bureaucracy assisted the king in the tasks of administration and in executing his orders. Due to the lack of a legislature or a legislative system in the modern sense, the fairness of king's orders dependent on the goodness of the man and in his belief in Dharma-a sense of fairness and justice. All Chola kings built temples and endowed great wealth to them. The temples acted not only as places of worship but as centres of economic activity, benefiting their entire community.

Local Government

Every village was a self-governing unit. A number of villages constituted a larger entity known as a Kurram, Nadu or Kottram, depending on the area. A number of Kurrams constituted a valanadu. These structures underwent constant change and refinement throughout the Chola period.

Justice was mostly a local matter in the Chola Empire; minor disputes were settled at the village level. Punishment for minor crimes were in the form of fines or a direction for the offender to donate to some charitable endowment. Even crimes such as manslaughter or murder were punished with fines. Crimes of the state, such as treason, were heard and decided by the king himself; the typical punishment in these cases was either execution or the confiscation of property.

Foreign Trade

Hindu temple complex at Prambanan in Java clearly showing Dravidian architectural influences

The Cholas excelled in foreign trade and maritime activity, extending their influence overseas to China and Southeast Asia. Towards the end of 9th century, the countries of southern India had developed extensive maritime and commercial activity. The Cholas, being in possession of parts of both the west and the east coasts of peninsular India, were at the forefront of these ventures. The Tang dynasty of China, the Srivijaya empire in the Malayan archipelago under the Sailendras, and the Abbasid Kalifat at Bagdad were the main trading partners.

Chinese Song Dynasty reports record that an embassy from Chulian (Chola) reached the Chinese court in the year 1077, and that the king of the Chulien at the time was called Ti-hua-kia-lo. It is possible that these syllables denote "Deva Kulo[tunga]" (Kulothunga Chola I). This embassy was a trading venture and was highly profitable to the visitors, who returned with 81,800 strings of copper coins in exchange for articles of tributes, including glass articles, and spices.

A fragmentary Tamil inscription found in Sumatra cites the name of a merchant guild Nanadesa Tisaiyayiraṭṭu Ainnutruvar (literally, "the five hundred from the four countries and the thousand directions"), a famous merchant guild in the Chola country. The inscription is dated 1088, indicating that there was an active overseas trade during the Chola period.

CHOLA SOCIETY

There is little information on the size and the density of the population during the Chola reign. The overwhelming stability in the core Chola region enabled the people to lead a very productive and contented life. There is only one recorded instance of civil disturbance during the entire period of Chola reign.However, there were reports of widespread famine caused by natural calamities.

The quality of the inscriptions of the regime indicates a presence of high level of literacy and education in the society. The text in these inscriptions was written by court poets and engraved by talented artisans. Education in the contemporary sense was not considered important; there is circumstantial evidence to suggest that some village councils organised schools to teach the basics of reading and writing to children, although there is no evidence of systematic educational system for the masses.

Vocational education was through hereditary training in which the father passed on his skills to his sons. Tamil was the medium of education for the masses; Sanskrit education was restricted to the Brahmins. Religious monasteries (matha or gatika) were centres of learning, which were supported by the government.

CULTURAL CONTRIBUTIONS

Under the Cholas, the Tamil country reached new heights of excellence in art, religion and literature. In all of these spheres, the Chola period marked the culmination of movements that had begun in an earlier age under the Pallavas. Monumental architecture in the form of majestic temples and sculpture in stone and bronze reached a finesse never before achieved in India.

The Cholas excelled in maritime activity in both military and the mercantile fields. Their conquest of Kadaram (Kedah) and the Srivijaya, and their continued commercial contacts with the Chinese Empire, enabled them to influence the local cultures. Many of the surviving examples of the Hindu cultural influence found today throughout the Southeast Asia owe much to the legacy of the Cholas.

ART

The Cholas continued the temple-building traditions of the Pallava dynasty and contributed significantly to the Dravidian temple design. They built numerous temples throughout their kingdom such as the Brihadeshvara Temple. Aditya I built a number of Siva temples along the banks of the river Kaveri. These temples were not on a large scale until the end of the 10th century.

Temple building received great impetus from the conquests and the genius of Rajaraja Chola and his son Rajendra Chola I. The maturity and grandeur to which the Chola architecture had evolved found expression in the two temples of Tanjavur and Gangaikondacholapuram. The magnificent Siva temple of Thanjavur, completed around 1009, is a fitting memorial to the material achievements of the time of Rajaraja. The largest and tallest of all Indian temples of its time, it is at the apex of South Indian architecture.

The temple of Gangaikondcholapuram, the creation of Rajendra Chola, was intended to exceed its predecessor in every way. Completed around 1030, only two decades after the temple at Thanjavur and in much the same style, the greater elaboration in its appearance attests the more affluent state of the Chola Empire under Rajendra.

The Chola period is also remarkable for its sculptures and bronzes. Among the existing specimens in museums around the world and in the temples of South India may be seen many fine figures of Siva in various forms, such as Vishnu and his consort Lakshmi, and the Siva saints. Though conforming generally to the iconographic conventions established by long tradition, the sculptors worked with great freedom in the 11 and the 12 centuries to achieve a classic grace and grandeur. The best example of this can be seen in the form of Nataraja the Divine Dancer.

LITERATURE

The age of the Imperial Cholas (850-1200) was the golden age of Tamil culture, marked by the importance of literature. Chola inscriptions cite many works, and it is a tragedy that most of them have been lost to us.

The revival of Hinduism from its nadir during the Kalabhras spurred the construction of numerous temples and these in turn generated Saiva and Viashnava devotional literature. Jain and Buddhist authors flourished as well, although in fewer numbers than in previous centuries. Jivaka-chintamani by Tirutakkadevar and Sulamani by Tolamoli are among notable by non-Hindu authors. The art of Tirutakkadevar is marked by all the qualities of great poetry. It is considered as the model for Kamban for his masterpiece Ramavatharam.

Kamban flourished during the reign of Kulothunga Chola III. His Ramavatharam is the greatest epic in Tamil Literature, and although the author states that he followed Valmiki, his work is no mere translation or simple adaptation of the Sanskrit epic: Kamban imports into his narration the colour and landscape of his own time; his description of Kosala is an idealised account of the features of the Chola country.

Jayamkondar's masterpiece Kalingattuparani is an example of narrative poetry that draws a clear boundary between history and fictitious conventions. This describes the events during Kulothunga Chola I's war in Kalinga and depicts not only the pomp and circumstance of war, but the gruesome details of the field. The famous Tamil poet Ottakuttan was a contemporary of Kulothunga Chola I. Ottakuttan wrote Kulothunga Solan Ula a poem extolling the virtues of the Chola king. He served at the courts of three of his successors.

The impulse to produce devotional religious literature continued into the Chola period and the arrangement of the Saiva canon into 11 books was the work of Nambi Andar Nambi, who lived close to the end of 10 century. However, relatively few works on Vaishnavite religion were composed during the Chola period, possibly because of the apparent animosity towards the Vaishnavites by the Chaluka Chola monarchs.

RELIGION

In general, Cholas were the adherents of Saivism and Hinduism. Throughout their history, they were not swayed by the rise of Buddhism and Jainism as were the kings, Pallava and Pandya. Even the early Cholas followed a version of the classical Hindu faith. There is evidence in Purananuru for Karikala Chola's faith in the then embryonic Vedic Hinduism in the Tamil country. Kocengannan, another early Chola, was celebrated in both Sangam literature and in the Saiva canon as a saint.

Later Cholas were also staunch Saivites, although there was a sense of toleration towards other sects and religions. Parantaka I and Sundara Chola endowed and built temples for both Siva and Vishnu. Rajaraja Chola I even patronised Buddhists, and built the Chudamani Vihara (a Buddhist monastery) in Nagapattinam at the request of the Srivijaya Sailendra king.

During the period of Chalukya Cholas, there were instances of intolerance towards Vaishnavites-especially towards Ramanuja, the leader of the Vaishnavites. This intolerance led to persecution and Ramanuja went into exile in the Chalukya country. He led a popular upraising that resulted in the assassination of Athirajendra Chola. Kulothunga Chola II is reported to have removed a statue of Vishnu from the Siva temple at Chidambaram. There is ample evidence, from the inscriptions, that Kulothunga II was a religious fanatic who wanted to upset the camaraderie between Hindu faiths in the Chola country.

IN POPULAR CULTURE

The history of the Chola dynasty has inspired many Tamil authors to produce literary and artistic creations during the last several decades. These works of popular literature have helped continue the memory of the great Cholas in the minds of the Tamil people.

The most important work of this genre is the popular Ponniyin Selvan (The son of Ponni), a historical novel in Tamil written by Kalki Krishnamurthy. Written in five volumes, this narrates the story of Rajaraja Chola. Ponniyin Selvan deals with the events leading up to the ascension of Uttama Chola on the Chola throne.

Kalki had cleverly utilised the confusion in the succession to the Chola throne after the demise of Sundara Chola. This book was serialised in the Tamil periodical Kalki during the mid 1950s. The serialisation lasted for nearly five years and every week its publication was awaited with great interest.

Kalki perhaps laid the foundations for this novel in his earlier historical romance Parthiban Kanavu, which deals with the fortunes of an imaginary Chola prince Vikraman who was supposed to have lived as a feudatory of the Pallava king Narasimhavarman I during the 7th century. The period of the story lies within the interregnum during which the Cholas were in eclipse before Vijayalaya Chola revived their fortune. Parthiban Kanavu was also serialised in the Kalki weekly during the early 1950s.

Sandilyan, another popular Tamil novelist, wrote Kadal Pura in the 1960s. It was serialised in the Tamil weekly Kumudam. Kadal Pura is set during the period when Kulothunga Chola I was in exile from the Vengi kingdom, after he was denied the throne that was rightfully his. Kadal Pura speculates the whereabouts of Kulothunga during this period. Sandilyan's earlier work Yavana Rani written in the early 1960s is based on the life of Karikala Chola. More recently, Balakumaran wrote the opus Udaiyar based on the event surrounding Rajaraja Chola's construction of the Brihadisvara Temple in Thanjavur.

There were stage productions based on the life of Rajaraja Chola during the 1950s and in 1973, Shivaji Ganesan acted in a screen adaptation of this play.

The Chola are also featured in the History of the World boardgame, produced by Avalon Hill.

10

Delhi Sultanate

The Delhi Sultanate, or Sultanat-e-Hind / Sultanat-e-Dilli refers to the various Muslim dynasties that ruled in India from 1206 to 1526. Several Turkic and Pashtun dynasties ruled from Delhi: the Slave dynasty (1206-90), the Khilji dynasty (1290-1320), the Tughlaq dynasty (1320-1413), the Sayyid dynasty (1414-51), and the Lodi (1451-1526). In 1526 the Delhi Sultanate was absorbed by the emerging Mughal Empire.

ORIGIN

During the last quarter of the twelfth century, Muhammad of Ghor invaded the Indo-Gangetic plain, conquering in succession Ghazni, Multan, Sindh, Lahore, and Delhi. Qutb-ud-din Aibak, one of his generals, proclaimed himself Sultan of Delhi and established the first dynasty of the Delhi Sultanate, the Slave or Mamluk dynasty (mamluk means "slave") after Muhammad's death in 1206. The territory under control of the Sultans expanded rapidly. By mid-century, northern India from the Khyber Pass to Bengal was under control of the Sultanate, although the northwest was contested with the Mongols. Iltutmish (1210-35), and Balban (1266-87) were among the dynasty's most well-known rulers. Faced with revolts by conquered territories and rival families, the Mamluk dynasty came to an end in 1290.nbn

The Khilji or Khalji dynasty, who had established themselves as rulers of Bengal in the time of Muhammad Ghori, took control of the empire in a coup which eliminated the last of the Mamluks. The Khiljis conquered Gujarat and Malwa, and sent the first expeditions south of the Narmada River, as far south as Tamil Nadu. The Delhi Sultanate rule continued to extend into southern India, first by the Delhi Sultans, then by the breakaway Bahmani Sultanate of Gulbarga, and, after the breakup of the Bahmani state in 1518, by the five independent Deccan Sultanates. The kingdom of Vijayanagar united southern India and arrested the Delhi Sultanate's expansion for a time, until its eventual fall to the Deccan Sultanates in 1565.

In the first half of the 14th century the Sultanate introduced a monetary economy in the provinces (sarkars) and districts (parganas) that had been established and founded a network of market centers through which the traditional village economies were both exploited and stimulated and drawn into the wider culture. State revenues remained based on successful agriculture, which induced Sultan Muhammad bin Tughluq (1325-51) to have village wells dug, offer seed to the peasants and to encourage cash crops like sugar cane (Braudel 1984, pp 96f, 512ff).

The Delhi Sultanate is the only Sultanate to stake a claim to possessing one of the few female rulers in India, Razia Sultan (1236-1240). While her reign was unfortunately short she is regarded well in the eyes of historians. The Princess Raziah Sultanah was very Popular and more Intelligent than her Brothers. She was the very First Queen of the Muslim World in the Early Muslim History of Sub-Continent. She ruled from the east Delhi to the west Peshawar and from the North Kashmir to the South Multan. The Rebels of her Government killed her and her Husband Malik Altuniya.

The Sultans of Delhi enjoyed cordial, if superficial, relations with other Muslim rulers in the Near East but owed them no allegiance. The Sultans based their laws on the Qur'an and the sharia and permitted non-Muslim subjects to practice their religion only if they paid jizya or head tax. The Sultans ruled from urban centers—while military camps and trading posts provided the nuclei for towns that sprang up in the countryside. Perhaps the greatest contribution of the Sultanate was its temporary success in insulating the subcontinent from the potential devastation of the Mongol invasion from Central Asia in the thirteenth century.

The Sultanate ushered in a period of Indian cultural renaissance. The resulting "Indo-Muslim" fusion left lasting monuments in architecture, music, literature, and religion. The Sultanate suffered from the sacking of Delhi in 1398 by Timur (Tamerlane), and soon other independent Sultanates were established in Awadh, Bengal, Jaunpur, Gujarat and Malwa. The Delhi Sultanate revived briefly under the Lodhis before it was conquered by the Mughal emperor Babur in 1526.

SULTANS OF DELHI

Slave Dynasty (1206-1290)

- Qutb-ud-din Aibak (1206-1210)
- Aram Shah (1210-1211)
- Shams ud din Iltutmish (1211-1236)
- Rukn ud din Firuz (1236)
- Raziyyat ud din Sultana (1236-1240)
- Muiz ud din Bahram (1240-1242)
- Ala ud din Masud (1242-1246)
- Nasir ud din Mahmud (1246-1266)
- Ghiyas ud din Balban (1266-1286)
- Muiz ud din Qaiqabad (1286-1290)
- Kayumars (1290)

Khilji (Khalji) Dynasty (1290-1321)

- Jalal ud din Firuz Khilji (1290-1294)
- Ala ud din Khilji (1294-1316)
- Qutb ud din Mubarak Shah (1316-1321)

Tughlaq Dynasty (1321-1398)

- Ghiyas ud din Tughluq Shah I (1321-1325)
- Muhammad Shah II (1325-1351)
- Mahmud Ibn Muhammad (March 1351)
- Firuz Shah Tughluq (1351-1388)
- Ghiyas ud din Tughluq II (1388-1389)

- Abu Baker (1389-1390)
- Nasir ud din Muhammad Shah III (1390-1393)
- Sikander Shah I (March-April 1393)
- Mahmud Nasir ud din (Sultan Mahmud II) at Delhi (1393-1394)
- Nusrat Shah at Firuzabad (1394-1398).

Lodi Dynasty

- Daulat Khan (1413-1414)

Sayyid (Syed) Dynasty (1414-1451)

- Khidr Khan (1414-1421)
- Mubarrak Shah II (1421-1435)
- Muhammad Shah IV (1435-1445)
- Aladdin Alam Shah (1445-1451).

Lodhi (Lodi) Dynasty (1451-1526)

- Bahlul Khan Lodi (1451-1489)
- Sikandar Lodi (1489-1517)
- Ibrahim II (1517-1526).

1526-1540: MUGHAL RULE

Suri Dynasty (1540-1555)

- Sher Shah (1540-1545)
- Islam Shah (1545-1553)
- Muhammad V (1553-1554)
- Firuz (29 April-2 May 1554)
- Ibrahim III (1554-1554/5)
- Sikander Shah (1554/5-1555).

DECCAN SULTANATES

The Deccan sultanates were five Muslim-ruled kingdoms—Bijapur, Golconda, Ahmednagar, Bidar, and Berar of south-central India. The Deccan sultanates were located on the Deccan Plateau, between the Krishna River and the Vindhya Range. They became independent states during the breakup of the Bahmani Sultanate: Bijapur, Ahmednagar and Berar in 1490, Bidar in 1492, and Golconda in 1512. In 1510, Bijapur repulsed an invasion by the Portuguese against the city of Goa, but lost it later that year.

Although generally rivals, they did ally against the Vijayanagara empire in 1565, permanently weakening Vijayanagar in the battle of Talikota. In 1572, after a coup in Berar, Ahmednagar invaded and conquered it. In 1609 Bidar was annexed by Bijapur. The sultanates were later conquered by the Mughal Empire; Berar was stripped from Ahmednagar in 1596, Ahmednagar was completely taken between 1616 and 1633, and Golconda and Bijapur conquered by Aurangzeb's 1686-7 campaign.

11

Hoysala Empire

The Hoysala Empire (Kannada), at their peak throughout the 13th century ruled large parts of southern India. Their were in power from about1000 to 1346 CE, with Belur and later Halebidu, Karnataka as their regal capital. The Hoysala Empire is remembered today primarily for its architecture. Over a hundred surviving temples are scattered across Karnataka, the finest examples of which are found in the cities of Belur, Halebidu and Somnathpura. They came to power at a time when peninsular India saw a four way struggle for hegemony, the other kingdoms being the Pandyas, Kakatiya and Seuna Yadavas of Devagiri. The Hoysala kings were influenced by Jainism and Hinduism. King Vishnuvardhana and his successors were followers of Vaishnavism. Under Vishnuvardhana, the Hoysalas achieved for the first time the dignity of a real kingdom. Kannada was the native language of the Hoysala Kings. They encouraged both Kannada and Sanskrit literature. The Hoysala era is considered a golden age in the development of art, architecture and religion. Literature in Kannada language in the Vaishnava, Shaiva and Jain traditions flourished. Many great Sanskrit works spanning Advaita, Vishishtadvaita and Dvaita philosophies were written. Three of India's great philosophers, Ramanujacharya, Basavanna and Madhvacharya lived during this time and propounded their philosophy. Architecture in the Vesara or Karnata dravida tradition reached its peak of expression.

ORIGIN AND EARLY HISTORY

The origin of the name "Hoysala" is part of popular Kannada folklore. Early in his youth, Sala, a member of what was at that time a tribe, was instructed by his guru Sudatta, a Jain Muni, to strike dead a tiger he encountered in the vicinity of the temple of the goddess Vasantika at Sosevur. Guru Sudatta Muni was teaching his disciples at the temple. The word "strike" literally translates to "hoy" in Hale Kannada (Old Kannada). Hence the name "Hoy-sala". The first written appearance of this legend is the Belur inscription of Vishnuvardhana. However, inconsistencies of facts that are associated with the Sala story, have prevented historians in giving credence to it. However, just about every Hoysala temple has a sculpture showing the fight between Sala and the tiger, either at the doorway leading to the mantapa or on top of the vimana. Some historians speculate that the legend may have gained importance after the victory of Vishnuvardhana over the Cholas at Talakadu, the tiger being the royal emblem of the Cholas.

Some Hoysala inscriptions state that Sala hailed from Shashakapura (Sosevur). Historians have argued that the founders of the dynasty hailed from hill regions of Angadi in Mudigere taluk of Chikmagalur District. Angadi has been identified as Sosevur. The fact that they were originally a family of hill chieftens from Malnad Karnataka (Malepas) is confirmed by their title Maleparolganda or lord of the Male chiefs which is used frequently in their inscriptions. A claim has been made that the Hoysalas find their origins in the coastal areas of Uttara Kannada district and another that they were descendants of the ancient Velir people who were indigenous to the malnad Karnataka and existed since the days of Emperor Ashoka.

Some Historians have identified chieftens earlier to Nripa Kama II, father of Vinayaditya. Their first family record starts from 950 with one Arekalla followed by Maruga as the chief. Munda the chief after Nripa Kama I was possibly the ruler up to 1026. He was followed by the popularly known Nripa kama II who held titles like Permanadi indicating an early Western Ganga Dynasty alliance. From above claims from historians it may be concluded that the Hoysalas were hill people of Malnad Karnataka. Hoysalas began their rule as subordinates of the Chalukyas of Kalyani and gradually established their own empire in Karnataka. Hoysala period is remembered today as one of the brightest periods in the history of Karnataka, next only to the Vijayanagara Empire. Famous kings among the Hoysalas were Vishnuvardhana, Veera Ballala II and Veera Ballala III.

History

Hoysala Kings	(950-1346)
Arekella	(950)
Maruga Nripa Kama I	(978-1006)
Munda	(1006-1026)
Nripa Kama II	(1026-1047)
Hoysala Vinayaditya	(1047-1098)
Ereyanga	(1098-1102)
Veera Ballala I	(1102-1108)
Vishnuvardhana	(1108-1152)
Narasimha I	(1152-1173)
Veera Ballala II	(1173-1220)
Vira Narasimha II	(1220-1235)
Vira Someshwara	(1235-1254)
Narasimha III	(1254-1291)
Ramanatha	(1254-1295)
Visvanatha	(1295-1300)
Veera Ballala III	(1292-1343)
Veera Virupaksha Ballala	(1343-1346)
Harihara Raya (Vijayanagara Empire)	(1342-1355).

During the 11th. century, the Hoysala chiefs distinguished themselves by serving their overlords the Kalyani Chalukyas in their campaingns against the Cholas and the kingdom of Malwa. They also cultivated marital relationships with the Chalukyas in this period. The Hoysalas rose as a prominent feudatory during the long rule of Vinayaditya. During the time of Ereyanga, they moved their capital from Sosevur to Belur. The Hoysalas became an independent power by defeating the Chalukyas during the rule of Veera Ballala II and were the paramount rulers in South India thereafter. The Hoysala dynasty's capital was initially located at Belur where they ruled for about twenty five years. Later they relocated their capital to Halebidu during the rule of Vishnuvardhana. The Hoysalas continued to patron art and literature during the peak of their empire. Vishnuvardhana wrested Gangavadi from the Cholas, and in commemoration of his victory, built the Vijayanarayana (Chennakeshava) Temple at Belur. His commander Ketamalla built the famous Hoysaleshwara Temple in Halebid. Though Vishnuvardhana did not succeed in his efforts to overthrow the Chalukyas, his grandson Veera Ballala II not only freed himself from subordination, but also defeated Seuna Bhillama V at Soraturu in 1190, after defeating Chalukya King Someshwara IV in 1187. Popular Kannada folklore suggests that it was during the time of Veera Ballala II, that the city of Bangalore was founded. Veera Ballala II repulsed the attacks by the Pandyas of Tamil Nadu and later and assumed the title Cholarajyapratishtacharya or "Establisher of the Chola Kingdom". His titles were Dakshina Chakravarthi, Hoysala Chakravarthi. Some historians opine he was the greatest of the Hoysala monarchs.

Later, in the days of his son Vira Narasimha II, the Hoysalas also secured a foothold in Tamil Nadu. The Tamil city of Kannanur Kuppam near Srirangam became the second capital of the Hoysalas. The Hoysalas were regarded as practically the arbiters of South Indian politics. Veera Ballala III, the last Hoysala, was known for his military prowess. He expanded his kingdom to encompass all of South India, south of the Krishna River and faced multiple attacks from the Delhi Sultan whose control over the region had extended south to present day Maharashtra. The rule of Veera Ballala II and Veera Ballala III saw the consolidation and domination of Southern Deccan as a single empire. During the later part of the rule of Veera Ballala III, Tiruvannamalai in Tamil Nadu had been made an alternate capital, from where Ballala III fought the Sultan of Madurai. The Vijayanagara Empire, which was founded during his time at Hosapattana, an alternate capital on the banks of Tungabhadra River, later to be called Vijayanagara by his commanders Harihara (Hakka) and Bukkaraya (Bukka) effectively became the new empire of South India, upon Veera Ballala's death in battle in Madhurai (1343).

ARCHITECTURE

The Hoysala claim to immortality is perhaps more because of their patronship of art and architecture than because of their conquests. Their era saw brisk temple building activity throughout the length and breadth of their kingdom. This they did though constantly under threat from the Pandyas from the south and the Seuna from the north.

The Hoysala style of architecture, an offshoot of the Kalyani Chalukya style, shows distinct Dravidian influences and is considered by many historians to be an independent tradition of architecture. The sculptures are said to be a picture gallery on stone executed with detail and precision.

The Hoysala style of sculpting is an example of art focussed on exhibiting feminine beauty, grace and Physique. Regarding the Vimana, it is said the Hoysala style focussed more on delicate finish rather than soaring ambition and possesses an elastic beauty about it. Temples at Belur, Halebid (both of which are a proposed UNESCO World Heritage Site), Somanathapur, Arasikere and Amrithapura and Belavadi in Karnataka are prime examples of Hoysala art. While most visitors find their temples at Belur and Halebidu awe inspiring because of the sculptural beauty, these temples actually do not convey the full logic and beauty of Hoysala architecture, the way smaller temples built by them do.

The Chennakashava temple at Belur built by Dasoja and Chavana of Balligavi, Shimoga District in 1117, the Hoysaleshwara Temple at Halebidu built by master builder Kedaroja in 1121 and the Keshava temple at Somanathapura built by Ruvari Malithamma 1279 are perhaps the finest examples of the Hoysala architecture. The outer walls of the temple contain an intricate array of stone sculptures.

The great temple of Halebidu, which, had it been completed is one of buildings on which the advocate of Hindu architecture would desire to take his stand. and is considered as a supreme climax of Indian architecture. One of the richest traditions in Indian architecture took shape in the Deccan during this time and is called as Karnata Dravida style as opposed to traditional Dravida style.

RELIGION

While Vedic religion gained popularity from the time of Vishnuvardhana, many backword classes embraced Jainism and Virashaivaism. However, the Hoysala times saw the decline in popularity of Jainsim and the growth of Vedic Hinduism, a practice that continued into the Vijayanagar empire. However, the kings remained tolerant to all religions. Shantala Devi, queen of Vishnuvardhana was a Jaina herself, but commissioned the Kappe Chennigaraya temple in Belur. During the rule of the Hoysalas, three important religious developments took place in present day Karnataka.

Ramanujacharya

Ramanujacharya was born in SriPerumbudur (1017) in Tamil Nadu. While his predecessor Shankaracharya taught the philosophy of strict monism (Advaita), Ramanujacharya propounded the qualified monism or Vishishtadvaita. In his youth, as a student of the great Advaita teacher Yadvaprakasha of Kanchi he learnt the Vedas and Upanishad but later disagreed with his guru (teacher) and took to self study.

The Vaishnava saint Yamuna who headed the Srirangam matha had heard of Ramanujacharya's scholarly attainment, encouraged him to move to Srirangam and initiated him into Srivaishnavism (a sect of Vaishnava faith) and eventually Ramanujacharya succeeded as the head of the monastry after the death of his guru. It was during this time that Ramanujacharya wrote Sribhashya, a critique on the Advaita philosophy of Sankaracharya. He upheld the worship of God with many attributes and provided flexibility in ritual practices to accomodate Shudras (lower caste) in temple worship thus providing emancipation for all.

Ramanujacharya toured the whole of India teaching his philosophy. During this time he came into conflict with the Chola king of Tamil country who was a strict Shaiva (worshipper of Lord Shiva). Ramanujacharya came to Hoysala country and founded a Matha (monastry) at Melkote. He lived here for many years and finally went back to Srirangam. He lived to the age of 120 and died in 1137.

Basavanna

In the early 12th century, a religious leader like none before, Basavanna (or Basava) was born in Bagewadi, Bijapur district in a Brahmin family. He grew up in an age of strict Hindu caste system. This region was then under the control of the Western Chalukyas. They were the overlords of the Hoysalas of South Karnataka region. However by the time Basava began to preach his vision of a casteless society, the political winds had changed. The southern Kalachuri had usurped the throne at Kalyani and Bijjala II was in power. Having refused to accept the Brahmin thread ceremony, Basava who was already very erudite in Sanskrit and Kannada left for Kudala Sangama where he came under the influence of ascetic Ishanyaguru. Basava's stay at Kudala Sangama changed him. He gained a vision, broadened his knowledge and he had glimses of his life's mission. Basava then left for Mangalawada and took service under king Bijjala II and soon rose to a position of authority as a member of the kings council.

It was during this time that he began to teach his beliefs in simple Kannada. Large groups of people seeking emancipation used to gather around him and listen to his discources. When Bijjala II captured Kalyani, the capital of the Western Chalukyas, Basava moved with the king. From the Anubhava Mantapa (a place of religious gatherings), Basava and other great Virashaiva saints like Akka Mahadevi from Shimoga, Allam Prabhu, Madivala Machayya and others spoke of their philosophy and mystic experiences. A new religious order called Virashaivaism with no caste system was being established. A new and unique form of poetry called Vachanas and literature called Vachana sahitya was born. Basava's unorthodox ways gained popularity and people from all over the deccan, hearing of Basava's fame and teachings joined the congregations. They were the Sharanas (devotees) of Lord Shiva. Many famous poets in the Hoysala court like Harihara, Raghavanka were Virashaiva by faith.

Madhvacharya

Another great saint who influenced the growth the Vedic Hinduism during the Hoysala time was Madhvacharya. He was born in Pajaka, Udupi (1238) in present day Karnataka. His teachings had a great influence on the haridasa movement in South India during the 14th-16th century which helped foster strong Hindu sentiment during the rule of the Vijayanagar Empire. Purandaradasa (father of carnatic music) and other great dasas of the time, Kanakadasa, Vyasatirtha and others were followers of Madhvacharya. Many of the Madhwa saints were rajguru to the Vijayanagar kings. Tradition holds that Madhwacharya was an incarnation of Vayu, Hanuman and Bhima. His guru Achyutapreksha, a Advaita saint taught him the vedas and Upanishad. However, when Madhvacharya began to disagree with the philosophy and search for new avenues to answer his questions, his teacher encouraged him. Having defeated his own guru in debates he travelled India twice, trouncing many scholars in debates. He initiated Naraharitirtha, the minister of Kalinga into his order.

The images of Lord Krishna and Balarama at Udupi were brought by him from Dwaraka. He wrote 37 works on Dvaita philosophy (Dulaism) in Sanskrit and founded eight mathas in Udupi. He was critical of the philosophy of the teachings of Shankaracharya and argued that the world is real and not an illusion. Though a devotee of Lord Vishnu, Madhvacharya did not oppose the worship of Shiva. The teachings of Madhvacharya enriched Kannada literature through the creation of devotional songs by the Kannada haridasas. This unique and original poetic literature, a sum contribution from all sects of Hindu society is called Dasa Sahitya (Haridasa literature).

LITERATURE

Kannada

Kannada literature saw the ascent of great poets Famous among them were Rudrabhatta the first Brahmin poet who wrote Jagannatha Vijaya, Janna who wrote Yashodharacharite, Ananthanathapurana, and Nemichandra who wrote Lilavati and Neminathapurana. They were patronised by Veera Ballala II. Haridasa Naraharitirtha composed many early devaranama of Lord Vishnu. Harihara whose greatest contributions are Girijakalyana in Champu style, Basavarajadevararagale in Ragale style, Pampasatakaand Sivaganadaragalegalu was patronised by Narasimha I. Raghavanka of Hampi who established the Shatpadi style in Kannada wrote Harishchandrakavya, Siddaramapurana, Somanathacharite, Hariharamahatva, Viresvaracharita and Sarabhacharitra. Nagachandra who wrote Ramachandra Charitapuranam and Mallinathapurana was patronised by Veera Ballala I, Rajaditya who was patronised by Vishnuvardhana wrote Vyavaharaganita, Kshetraganita and Lilavati on mathematics.

Padmarasa who was patronised by Narasimha I wrote Dikshabodhe and would later become the hero of another work Padmarajapurana. Mallikarjuna wrote Suktisudharnava, Keshiraja wrote Shabdamanidarpana, Bhanduvarma wrote Harivamsabhyudaya and Jivasambhdana. Sisumayana introduced a new form of composition called Sangatya wrote Anjanacharita and Tripuradhahana, Andayya wrote Madana Vijaya, Kumudendu wrote a Jaina version of Ramayana, Ratta Kavi wrote Rattasutra a work on treatment of natural phenomenon like rain, earthquakes and lightening, Nagaraja wrote Punyasrava. Palkuriki Somanatha from Godavari district wrote Silasampadane, Sahasragananama and Pancaratna. Devakavi wrote Kusumavali and Somaraja wrote Sringarasara. Sumanobana were also famous.

Sanskrit

The Hoysala period was an age of great Sanskrit works Madhwacharya, propounder of the dvaita philosophy wrote Rigbhshya on Brahmasutras, Anuvyakhya, a commentary on Upanishads and Bhagavadgita, an epitome on Mahabharatha called Bharatatatparyanirnaya, a commentary on hymns of Rig Veda called Rigvedavyakhya and a number of polemical works rebutting the doctrines of other schools of Vedas. Ramanujacharya expounded his Vishisadwaita from his Matha in Melkote Vidyatirtha wrote Rudraprshnabhashya. These works were later absorbed and assimilated by Sayanacharya, brother of Vidyaranya. Bharatasvamin who was patronised by Ramanatha wrote a commentary on Samaveda, Shadgurusishya wrote commentary on Aitareya Brahmana and Aranyaka, Katyayana wrote Sarvanukramani. A family of hereditary poets called the Vidyacharkravarti (whose names have not been preserved) wrote Gadyakarnamrita describing a war between

Vira Narasimha II and the Pandyas, Rukminikalyana (poems), Alankarasarvasva and Kavyaprakasa. Kalyani Devi, Trivikarma and Naryana Pandita were other famous Sanskrit scholars of this time. Sanskrit literature were mostly of the devotional kind.

ADMINISTRATION

Governance

The Hoysalas followed the Western Chalukya and Western Ganga Dynasty method of governance. Some historians opine that in the Hoysala empire which was highly centralised, the king sought the advice of five ministers (Pancha Pradhanas) while others claim a higher number.. Under any circumstance, by the 13th century, with the empire having grown to its largest extent, the number of ministers had grown considerably with each having limited authority.

Inscriptions mention many names with responsibilities tied to foreign affairs (Sandhivigrahi), treasurer (Mahabhandari or Hiranyabhandari), personal secretary (Paramavishvasi), chief master of robes (Mahapasayita), justice (Dharmadhikari), central register or Kaditha, head of the State Secretariat (Srikaranadhikari) etc. Some ministers also oversaw clusters of departments (Sarvadhikari). The military affairs were handled by Dandanayaka also called Senadhipati, commanders who were transferable.

The Garudas were the elite bodyguards of kings and queens who committed suicide upon the demise of their master. They were known as lenkas (heroes) or jolavalis (indebted to the king for food) and velavalis (those who stood by the king at all times). They served the king the way the mythical eagle Garuda served Lord Vishnu. Virgal (Hero stone) erected in memory of such heroes are called Garuda pillar. The Garuda pillar at the Hoysaleshwara temple in Halebidu depicts heroes brandishing knives and others cutting their own heads. Kuvara Lakshma, a minister and body guard of Veera Ballala II took his own life and that of his wife and other body guards upon the death of his master. The details of his loyalty is etched on this shasana (inscription).

LAND MANAGEMENT

The kingdom was divided into Nadu and Vishayas. Further division of land was into Kampanas and Deshas. Under the caretaker Dandanayaka were Mahapradhana (minister), Bhandari (treasurer), Senabove (clerk) and Heggades (junior officers). Feudatory families like Alupas, Santharas, Chengalvas, Kongalvas, Sindas were allowed to continue to govern their respective territories. The Hoysalas minted gold coins with Kannada and Devanagari legends such as Nolambavadigonda, Talakadugonda. Their gold coin was called Honnu or Gadyana and weighed 62 grains of gold. Pana or Hana was 1/10 of the Honnu. Haga was ¼ of the Pana. Visa was ¼th of Haga. There were coins called Bele and Kani as well. It must be noted that some of these terms Hana, Bele are still used in Kannada language and mean "money" and "cost" respectively.

AGRICULTURE AND TRADE

Irrigation

The administration sustained itself through agriculture Land grants were made by the kings to religious beneficieries and persons rewarded for services rendered to the king. The main land owners were the Brahmins and Jains. The type of land grant was generally wetland which was already under cultivation. This was popular in the fertile river valleys of the Tungabhadra and Kaveri. In addition, clearing of forests for cultivation was viewed favourably as it not ony brought new sources of revenue but also created job opportunities for the landless and introduced forest dwellers to a more agrarian life style. Sometimes wasteland was also given as gift. Whenever land was cleared for cultivation, it was on a large scale. Knowledge of agriculture included assessing irrigation systems like tanks, reservoirs with sluices, canals and wells which were built and maintained at the expense of local villagers. The more impressive irrigation tanks such as Vishnusagara, Shantisagara, Ballalarayasagara were created at the expense of the state. Irrespective of whether the expense and control came from local or state bodies, organizing labour to till the land was taken up at the village and across village levels and the job of cultivation was largely that of the landless. Cattle farming was attractive in the highlands (malnad regions) from where diary products, fruits and spices came. Paddy and corn were popular in the plains (Bailnad). In Kannada country, key figures in rural areas were the rich land owners called gavunda or gauda and heggade. They are mentioned in inscriptions relating to land transactions, maintenence of irrigation, collection of taxes and works of village council. The praja gavunda (gavunda of people) was lower in status than the wealthy prabhu gavunda (lord of gavundas). The gavundas sometimes had a dual role as village representatives and appointees of the state. Some judicial responsibilities were also included like raising a militia if required.

IMPORTS AND EXPORTS

Import of horses on the western seaboard was a flourishing business and inscriptions speak of many Brahmin merchants who were active. Arabs made immense wealth from the unending need for horses from Indian kingdoms. Rich forest produce like Teak was exported through ports of present day Kerela. Merchants from this region settled down in Arasikere, Halebidu in addition to Jain traders. Many virgal (hero stone) in the coastal areas depict ships indicating active sea trade and also a technologically developed shipping fleets. Piracy was common and virgals made for fallen heros have been found. Many inscriptions mention a flourishing textle industry. Trade with overseas kingdoms reached unprecedented levels. Sung dynasty records from China mention Indian merchants in ports of South China. Chinese interest in Indian astrology and Alchemy is well known. South India exported Elephants, textiles, spices, medicinal plants, precious stones, pottery, salt made from salt pans, jewels, gold, ivory, Rhino horn, ebony and camphor to China. The same products and others like aloe wood, perfumes, Sandalwood and condiments reached western ports like Dhofar, Aden, Siraf on the Persian gulf. Cairo and Alexandria were in active trade across the Arabian sea.

TAX SYSTEM

Tax assessment was done by the village assembly who were responsible for collecting for the government. Land revenue was called Siddhaya and included Kula or original assessment and various cesses. Cesses were collected in proportion to Kula. Taxes were levied on professions, marraige, goods in transit on chariots, carraiges, domesticated animals. Taxes on commodities like gold, precious stones, perfumes, Sandalwood, ropes, yarn, residence, hearth, shops, cattle pans, sugarcane presses and produce like black pepper, betel leaves, ghee, paddy, spices, palm leaves, coconuts and sugar are mentioned in records. Cattle tax was called balavana and looms tax was called maggadere. Fines for violating laws were also collected. In addition to collecting taxes, the village assembly could levy tax for a specific purpose like construction of a water tanks.

SOCIETY

Women

The Hoysala society was comparatively liberal. Woman enjoyed administrative powers like queen Umadevi who administered Halebidu in the absence of Veera Ballala II. Women made progress in the realms of music, dance, literature, poetry, politics and administration. Queen Shantaladevi was a noted dancer. Akka Mahadevi, a great Vachana poet who renounced the temporal world in favour of one of devotion became an example for woman of the day. The practice of sati was prevalent and prostitution enjoyed social acceptance. devadasis (temple dancers) were common in temples and some were well educated. They came to be treated with deference. Because of their accomplishments they had more freedom of movement in that they could distance themselves from social conventions to a greater degree. Like in most of India, the Indian caste system was conspicuiously present. Architects (Vishwakarmas), sculptors, quarry workers, goldsmiths and others whose trade directly or indirectly related to construction of temples were also prosperous due to the vigorous temple building activities undertaken. Some 1500 monuments built during these times helped spur business in transportation of raw materials for construction.

Town and Market

Trade on the west coast brought many foreigners to India including Arabs, Jews, Persians, Chinese and from the Malay peninsula. Large scale migration of people from Kannada country to present day Tamil Nadu happened during this time. With the expansion of Hoysala territory in Tamil country, these immigrants went as officers and soldiers of the empire having been given land concessions. Migration of Tamil sculptors to Belur and Halebidu is also apparent from the presence of some Chola style sculptures in a few Hoysala temples. The marketplace was the nuclei of urban centers. This is where materials and produce was brought and exchanged hands. These were the locals of recurring festivals and fairs. In South India, towns were called Pattana or Pattanam and the market place Naraga or Nagaram. Important market places gradually grew into townships and so did famous pilgrim places. Shravanabelagola in Hassan district, the seat of the Hoysala empire developed from a place of religion in the 7th century to an important settlement by the 12th century. Many rich Jains were established here. The market place was also closely tied with temple administration.

Role of Temples

Temple construction, which was prolific was not entirely for religious reasons. Temples acted as local courts or as surrogate courts, especially when built from royal endowments. They were visualised as palaces and the rituals marking daily routine of the deity imitated those of the king. Temples also received local patronage, especially from rich landlords. Temples built from royal patronage took on a auro of leading ceremonial centers. When Vishnuvardhana built the Vaishnava Chennakeshava temple at Belur, the town was transformed into a great city. Competition from the Shaiva merchants of Halebidu resulted in the construction of the famous Hoysaleshvara temple, which brought the town into prominence. Temples not built from royal patronage evolved into complex institutions related not only to religious requirements but also to fiscal, political and cultural needs. These temples were normally built in rural areas. Irrespective of source patronage, temples were also establishments that provided employment to hundreds of people. Temple funds maintained families of priests, record keepers, administrators, guards, service providers, garland makers, dancers, devadasis, sculptors, carpenters and craftsmen. Temples were also source of loans. Inscriptions mention 12%-15% interest on loans. In short, Hindu temples began to take on the shape of wealthy Buddhist monasteries.

LANGUAGE

Usage of Kannada and Sanskrit were extensive. Temples served as local schools where learned Brahmins imparted education in Sanskrit. Schools of higher learning were called Ghatikas. Jain and Buddhist monasteries educated novice monks. Kannada the local language found extensive use in multiple areas. The rise of devotional movements saw the usage of Kannada as a means to express ecstatic experience of closeness to the deity (Vachanas). At another level, Kannada was used in local and state archives to record locations and rights related to land grants. Many literary works were written in the local language on palm leaves which were tied together. Where as in the previous centuries, Jain works had dominated Kannada literature, Shaiva, early Brahminical works also became popular. Works in Sanskrit included, poetry, grammar, lexicon, manuals, rhetoric, commentaries on older works, prose fiction and drama. Inscriptions were of three kinds. They were in Kannada, Sanskrit and also bilingual. Those sections of bilingual inscriptions that stated the title, genealogy, origin myths of the king and benedictions tended to be in Sanskrit but the actual terms of the grants which included information on the land, its boundaries, participation of local authorities, rights and obligations of the grantee, taxes and dues, witnesses etc. would be in Kannada to ensure the content was well understood by the locals without ambiguity.

12

Vijayanagara Empire

The Vijayanagara empire (Kannada, Telugu) was based in the Deccan, in peninsular and southern India, from 1336 CE onwards. It was founded by Harihara, also known as Hakka, and his brother Bukka Raya with the support of saint Vidyaranya. It is named after its capital city Vijayanagara, whose impressive ruins surround Hampi in modern Karnataka, India.

It lasted from about 1336 CE to perhaps about 1660 CE, though throughout its last century it was in a slow decline due to a catastrophic defeat at the hands of an alliance of the Sultanates. Its founding, and even great part of its history are only now being discovered, but its power and wealth are attested by the writings of many European travellers, such as the Portuguese travelers Domingo Paes and Nuniz, and the Venetian Niccolò Da Conti in 1420. Several works of literature in local vernaculars also provide critical information needed to piece together the history of the empire.

The empire left behind a legacy of great monuments spread all over South India, the finest of which are at the regal capital Vijayanagara (Hampi), a UNESCO World Heritage Site. Literature and poetry reached a new peak in Kannada, Telugu, Tamil and Sanskrit with works spanning Advaita, Dvaita, Virashaiva and Jaina faith. Efficient administration and overseas trade brought many new technologies to South India, especially in the field of irrigation and water management. Mingling of the people of South India, irrespective of faith and vernacular brought new inspiration in architecture resulting in the construction of Hindu temples in the Deccan style and later in the dravidian idiom using locally available granite. The traditions that had been acquired in temple building during the rule of previous great empires of South India seemed to all come together into one style, ealled the Vijayanagar Architecture. Many royal structures were also built in secular style showing influences from the Sultanates of Northern Deccan. This era saw the birth of Carnatic music in its current form. Above all, the empire created an epoch in the history of South India which rose above the politics of narrow regionalism espousing the cause of the ancient and indegenous Hindu dharma.

THE EMPIRE

Vijayanagara Empire

Sangama Dynasty	
Harihara Raya I	1336-1356
Bukka Raya I	1356-1377
Harihara Raya II	1377-1404
Virupaksha Raya	1404-1405
Bukka Raya II	1405-1406
Deva Raya I	1406-1422
Ramachandra Raya	1422
Vira Vijaya Bukka Raya	1422-1424
Deva Raya II	1424-1446
Mallikarjuna Raya	1446-1465
Virupaksha Raya II	1465-1485
Praudha Raya	1485
Saluva Dynasty	
Saluva Narasimha Deva Raya	1485-1491
Thimma Bhupala	1491
Narasimha Raya II	1491-1505
Tuluva Dynasty	
Tuluva Narasa Nayaka	1491-1503
Viranarasimha Raya	1503-1509

Krishna Deva Raya	1509-1529
Achyuta Deva Raya	1529-1542
Sadashiva Raya	1542-1570
Aravidu Dynasty	
Aliya Rama Raya	1542-1565
Tirumala Deva Raya	1565-1572
Sriranga Deva Raya	1572-1586
Venkatapati Deva Raya	1586-1614
Sriranga Raya	1614
Ramadevaraya	1617-1632
Venkatapati Raya	1632-1642
Sriranga Raya II	1642-1646
Venkatapati Raya II	

FOUNDING

The founding of the original kingdom was based on the principality of Anegondi, based on a fortified town on the Tungabhadra river in the Deccan. In the century preceding the founding of the empire, the old kingdoms of the Deccan had been overrun by Muslim invaders from the north. From 1309, Malik Kafur reached and captured Warangal, later on reaching the Malabar kingdoms. Mubarak of Delhi reached Warangal again in 1323. Between 1334 and 1336, Muhammad Tughlaq of Delhi again overran the region, capturing Anegondi.

Many theories have been propounded about the origin of Vijayanagar empire. Well known historians from Archeological Survey of India hold their own opinions about the origin of the empire. Prof. K.A. Nilakanta Sastry, Dr. N. Ventakaramanayya and B. Surya Narayana Rao claim a Telugu origin of Harihara and Bukka Raya. The Telugu origin theory is based on works by Robert Sewell and records written by Muslim writers of those times. Historians such as Dr. P.B. Desai, Fr. Henry Heras, Prof. Dr. B.A. Saletore, G.S. Gai, Prof. William Coelho Dr. Suryanath U. Kamat attest to the empire's Kannada origin. The Kannada origin theory is based on epigraphy (study of inscriptions, numismatics etc.) and Kannada literary works of

Vijayanagar times like Kumara Rama charita, Chikkadevaraya Vamshavali and Keladinripa Vijayam.

To sum up, unless new evidence is discovered the exact origin and ancestry of Vijayanagar founders will remain a controversial matter.

CONSOLIDATION

Within the first two decades of coming to power Harihara I came to rule much of the area south of Tungabhadra river. He gained titles like Purvapaschima Samudradhishavara or master of the eastern and western oceans. His patronage of Sringeri Peetha started from his 1346 grant to build the Vidyasharnaka temple there. His four brothers became governers of various regions of the kingdom. By 1371 Bukka Raya who succeeded Harihara I defeated the chiefdom of Arcot (1360), Reddis of Kodavidu and Sultan of Madurai and annexed it into the kingdom. By 1374, the regions of Goa, Tungabhadra-Krishna River doab came under their control. The island of Lanka paid tributes and ambassadors were exchanged with the Ming dynasty of China.

Vijayanagar Kingdom was now beginning to look like an imperial empire. His second son Harihara II defeated the Bahmani Sulthan Mujahid and captured ports of Goa, Chaul and Dabhol in North Konkan, Udayagiri in north eastern Andhra and defeated the Velamas of Rachakonda north of the Krishna river. The whole of South India now was under the Vijayanagar umbrella. Deva Raya I was the next capable ruler who fought the Gajapatis of Orissa successfully. Great works of fortification and irrigation were under taken during his time. Deva Raya II, possibly the most capable of the Sangama dynasty rulers took control in 1424. He was called Gajabetekara or hunter of elephants. His rule saw success against the Gajapatis of Orissa and Reddys' of Kondavidu, Zamorin of Calicut who though may not have been in direct control may have paid tributes, Quilon, and even an invasion of Lanka brought rich tributes. Even the kings of Burma at Pegu and Tanasserim paid tributes. Persian traveller Abdur Razzak who travelled in Vijayanagar in 1443 C.E. paid rich tributes to the king and his empire. His rule also saw the patronage of many scholars in Kannada, Telugu and Sanskrit. The next forty years saw the decline of the empire due to weak rulers and a lot of territory was lost. They were followed by an able commander Saluva Narasimha in 1485 under whose rule a serious attempt was made to reconsolidate the empire. Sripadaraya, the Madhwa Haridasa was his able Rajguru. He was followed by his able general Narasa Nayaka, son of Tuluva Isvara in 1491 who took proxy control of the empire and fought many wars to prevent disintegration of the empire. After nearly two decades of trying to bring rebellious chieftens under control, The empire eventually came under the rule of the able son of Tuluva Narasa Nayaka, Krishnadevaraya.

THE EMPIRE AT ITS PEAK

In the following decades, the Vijayanagar empire dominated all of southern India having grown into a powerful empire. The empire during that period served as a bulwark against invasion from the Turkic Sultanates of the Indo-Gangetic Plain and remained in constant competition and conflict with the five Deccan Sultanates that established themselves in the Deccan to the north of it.

In about 1510, Goa, which had been under the rule of the Sultan of Bijapur, was captured by the Portuguese, possibly with the approval or connivance of Vijayanagara. Commerce between the Portuguese and Vijayanagara became very important to both sides.

The empire is generally considered to have reached its peak during the rule of Krishna Deva Raya. During this time, Vijayanagar armies were successful and victorous everywhere. The annexation of Bijapur, Raichur and Bidar, conquer of territories on the east of the Deccan that belonged previously to Orissa including Kalinga, the acceptance of Vijayanagar supremacy by the rebellious feudatories of Kondavidu, Rachakonda, Ummatur and chiefs of Tamil country all brought the whole of South India under one umbrella. Many of the great monuments of the empire either were completed or commissioned during his time. Among these are the Hazara Rama temple, the Krishna temple and the Ugra Narasimha idol, all at Vijayanagara.

Krishna Deva Raya was followed by Achyuta Raya in 1530. In 1542, Achyuta was succeeded by Sada Siva Raya. But the real power lay with Aliya Rama Raya, son-in-law of Krishnadevaraya (of the fourth dynasty, who followed him), who seems to have made a point of unnecessarily provoking the Deccan sultanates, so that eventually they allied against him. However some historians disagree with this. They believe Rama Raya's involvement in Sultanate affairs was with the best interests of Vijayanagar itself.

DEFEAT

In 1565, at the battle of Talikota, after what seemed like an easy victory for Vijayanagar, the sudden capture and killing of Rama Raya created havoc and confusion in the Vijayanagar army.

The army of Vijayanagara was routed by an alliance of the Deccan sultanates who attacked and plundered Hampi reducing it to ruins as it stands today. With this, the last significant Hindu state in the Deccan came to an end. Tirumala Raya, the sole survivor left Vijayanagar with treasure on back of 550 elephants to Penukonda. Though the battle is called "Battle of Talikota", some scholars say the war was actually fought in between two towns Rakkasagi and Tangadigi in modern Bijapur district close to Talikota and is also called "Battle of Rakkasa-Tangadi", while another scholar claims Bannihatti was the actual battle ground.

Many theories have been proposed for the sudden defeat but the most prominent cause seems to be betrayal by two commanders called Gilani brothers who were employed by Rama Raya. Regarding the pillage of Vijayanagara, though some scholars say this was in revenge for similar atrocities committed by Rama Raya in the Sultanate kingdoms earlier, this theory has not found too much support because it is well known that Rama Raya was a secular man and that many Muslims had been promoted to very high cadre in his government.

Vijayanagara is considered by many today, especially in the states of Karnataka and Andhra Pradesh, to have been a golden age of culture and learning.

DECLINE

While the empire still continued to have some power, and commanded respect, it went into a steady decline, with the capital being changed on three occassions. It is known however that they continued to trade with the Portuguese, and that they gave the British the land grant that enabled the establishment of Madras. The Telugu work Vasucharitamu refers to Tirumala (Aliya Tirumala, another son-in-law of Krishnadevaraya), the first of the Aravidu line of coronated rulers as the reviver of the Karnata Empire. He is said to have crowned himself as king in 1570 at Penukonda. His brother Aliya Rama Raya was the first from the Aravidu family to rule in Vijayanagara but without official coronation. After the defeat at Talikota, Tirumala fled to Penukonda in present day Andhra Pradesh and ruled a highly reduced empire. He was succeeded by his son Sriranga I during whose rule the empire shrank further. Next came his brother Venkata II who made Chandragiri his capital. He was an able ruler and repulsed the invasion of the Bahamani Sultans and saved Penukonda from being captured. His death brought internal revolt for succession and finally Ramadeva took power and ruled till 1632. After his death, the grandson of Aliya Rama Raya, Venkata III became king and ruled for about ten years. During the rule of Sriranga III, Vellore had become the capital and the empire came to an end with a successful invasion of Vijayanagar territory by the Sultan of Bijapur and Golkonda. Following this, the largest feudatories of the erstwhile empire, the Nayakas of Karnataka, Tamil Nadu and the kingdom of Mysore became the main powers in South India.

RELIGION

The empire was born with the intention of protecting Hindu dharma from the onslaughts of the Mugal invasion of South India. However, like true Hindus, the kings of the empire were tolerant to all religions and sects. They did not discriminate against Muslims and Christians. The travelogues of many foreign visitors to the empire attests to this. The Vijayanagar kings used titles like Gobrahamana Pratipalanacharya, Hindurayasuratrana, Vaidikamarga Samsthapanacharya which gives an idea of their intention to protect Hinduism. The founders of the empire Harihara I and Bukka Raya I were Shaiva

Hindus but were patronised Vaishnava Sringeri Peetha with Vidyaranya as their patron saint. They made Varaha (boar, an avatar of Vishnu) their emblem. The later Saluva and Tuluva kings including Krishnadevaraya were Sri- Vaishnava but worshipped at the feet of Lord Virupaksha (Shiva) at Hampi and Lord Venkateshwara at Tirupati. A Sanskrit work Jambavati Kalyanam by king Krishnadevaraya calls Lord Virupaksha Karnata Rajya Raksha Mani (Protective jewel of Karnata Empire). They patronised the saints of the dvaita Madhvacharya peetha at Udupi.

The Haridasa movement presented, like the Virashaiva movement, another strong current of bhakthi, pervading the lives of millions. Thus the haridasas presented two groups, the Vyasakuta and Dasakuta. The former were required to be proficient in the Vedas, Upanishads and other Darshanas, while the Dasakuta merely conveyed the message of Madhwacharya through Kannada language to the people in the form of Devaranamas and Kirthanas.

The philosophy of Madhvacharya was preserved and perpetuated by his eminent disciples like Vyasatirtha, Naraharitirtha, Padmanabha Tirtha, Akshobhya Tirtha, Jayatirtha, Sripadaraya, Vadirajatirtha and others. In the 15th. century, the haridasa movement took shape under Sripadaraya of Mulbagal but his disciple Vyasatirtha provided it a strong organizational base. He was intimately associated with the Vijayanagar Empire, where he became a great moral and spiritual force. His eminent disciples were Sri Vadirajatirtha, Purandaradasa (Father of Carnatic music) and Kanakadasa. Vyasathirtha was the guru of Krishnadevaraya who considered the saint his Kuladevata and highly honoured him. During this time, another great composer of early carnatic music, Tallapakam Annamacharya composed hundreds of Kirthanas in Tirupati. Together, Vyasatirtha, Sripadaraya and Vadirajatirtha are called the Yathi Trayaru or the holy Trinity.

LITERATURE

The Vijayanagar era is considered a golden age of arts and cultural developments. Great works in Sanskrit, Kannada, Telugu and Tamil were written. A magnificent epoch in the history of South India, the period saw the rise of Telugu language as a popular literary medium, reaching its peak under the patronship of Krishnadevaraya.

Kannada

The Vijayanagar era continued the ancient tradition of Kannada literature. In Kannada, famous Jain poets were Madhura (patronised by Harihara II and Deva Raya I), Ratnakaravarni and others. Virashaiva literature saw a renaissance with many famous works by Singiraja, Mallanarya (who was patronised by Krishnadevaraya). Deva Raya II patronised several Virashaivas like Lakkana Dandesa, Chamarasa, Jakkanarya. Tontada Siddesvara was the guru of Virupaksha Raya II. Famous among Vaishnava scholars were, Kumara Vyasa (patronised by Deva Raya II), Timmanna Kavi and Chatu Vittalanatha patronised by Krishnadevaraya and Achyuta Raya, Narahari and Kanakadasa. Purandaradasa (who was patronised by Achyuta Raya) and Kanakadasa wrote Dasa Sahithya and Keerthanas sowing the seeds of carnatic music. Nanjunda, Kereya Padmarasa, Mangaraja and Linganna were other famous poets.

Telugu

The Vijayanagar period was the golden age of Telugu literature. Famous among Telugu scholars were Srinatha (who was patronised by the Kondavidu Reddy Kings and Sangama brothers), Mallayya, Singayya, Vishvanatha Nayani and Nachanna Soma (who was patronised by Bukka Raya I). During the reign of Krishnadevaraya Telugu culture and literature flourished and reached their heyday. The great emperor was himself a celebrated poet having composed Amuktamalyada. In his court, eight Telugu poets were regarded as the eight pillars of the literary assembly. These poets were Allasani Peddana, Nandi Thimmana, Madayyagari Mallana, Dhurjati, Ayyalaraju Ramambhadrudu, Pingali Surana, Ramarajabhushanudu, and Tenali Ramakrishna.

Sanskrit

Sanskrit literature was given state patronage by the Vijayanagar kings. Some important scholars were Sayana,

Madhva Vidyaranya, the spiritual force behind the founding empire, Devanna Bhatta, Gangadevi and Tirumalamba Devi, Rajanatha Dindima, Rajanatha Dindima II, Vedanta Desika, Gunda Dindima and Gangambika. Some Vijayanagar kings were also scholars. Deva Raya I, Saluva Narasimha Deva Raya, Krishnadevaraya were accomplished scholars in Sanskrit. Krishnadevaraya also patronised Tamil poets Haridasa, Arunagirinatha, Svarupananda Deshika, Tattuvaraya, Pugalendi, Jnanprakashar, Andari, Kacchiyappa Shivacharya and Ilanjuriyar.

ARCHITECTURE

The architecture of Vijayanagar Empire is considered by many historians as a vibrant combination of Chalukya, Hoysala, Pandya and Chola styles. They left behind a legacy of sculpture, architecture and painting that influenced the development of arts long after the empire came to an end.

The hallmark of their style was the ornate pillared Kalyanamantapa, Vasanthamantapa and the towering Rayagopura. The use of locally available granite was popularised and favoured over the previously popular soapstone or other materials. This was infact due to an imperative need for durability rather than sculptability, the kingdom being under constant threat of invasions. While their monuments are spread over the whole of Southern India, nothing surpasses the vast open air mueseum of monuments at their regal capital at Vijayanagar, a UNESCO World Heritage Site. During the 14th century the kings continued to build Vesara or deccan style monuments but during the 15th. century a slow transition occurred when they incorporated dravida style gopurams to meet their ritualistic needs. The Prasanna Virupaksha temple (underground temple) of Bukka I, Hazare Rama temple of Deva Raya I are examples of Deccan style temples. The varied and intricate treatment given to various style of pillars was their special feature. At Hampi, though the Vitthala temple is the epitome of their pillared Kalyanamantapa style, the Hazara Ramaswamy temple is a more modest but perfectly finished example of this style. The conspicuous feature of their style was the return of simplistic and serene art of the Badami Chalukya.

The grandest specimen of Vijayanagar art, the Vitthala temple shows patronage given to it during the entire reign of the Tuluva kings.

Other important features of Vijayanagar style was the creation of large monolithics like the Sasivekalu Ganesha, Kadalekalu Ganesha at Hampi, Gomoteshwara statues in Karkala and Venur in coastal Karnataka, the Nandi bull in Lepakshi (the largest in India), Andhra Pradesh. Vijayanagar temples of Bhatkal, and other towns of coastal Karnataka, Kanakagiri, Sringeri in malnad Karnataka, Tadpatri and Lepakshi in Andhra Pradesh, Vellore, Kumbakonam, Kanchi and Srirangam in Tamil Nadu are also great examples of their style.

The Vijayanagar style also includes paintings. Paintings of Dasavathara and Girijakalyana in the Virupaksha temple at Hampi, Shivapurana paintings at Virabhadra temple at Lepakshi and paintings at the Jains basadi, Kamaskshi and Varadaraja temples at Kanchi are some examples.

Historians feel that keeping in pitch with the task at hand of protecting Hindu dharma, South Indian architecture attained richness and fulfilment. In the Vijayanagar architecture, the art of decoration perhaps surpassed anything else similar in Hindu India, the Vitthala temple reaching the extreme zenith of artistic ferver. A certain freshness seemed to have evolved to break a static spell in Hindu rock architecture.

Some structures in Hampi also exhibit secular architecture with mixing of Hindu and Islamic styles. A dimension of the Vijayanagar architecture that brings out the cosmopolitian lifestyle of the great city is the presence of many secular structures bearing Islamic influence. While political history concentrates on the ongoing conflict between the Vijayanagar empire and the Deccan Sultanates, the architectural record reflects a more creative interaction. There are many arches, domes and vaults that betray this influence. The concentration of structures like pavilions, stables and towers indicates they were for use by royalty. The decorative details of these secular structures seem to have migrated into Vijayanagara during the rule of Firuz Shah and Ahamad Shah of the Bahamani kingdoms. This period coincides with the rule of Deva Raya I and Deva

Raya II who are known to have employed many Muslims in their army and court, some of whom may have been architects. This harmanious exchange of architectural ideas must have happened during rare periods of harmony between the Hindu and Muslim kingdoms. Even the great platform called Mahanavmi dibba has relief carvings which appear to depict figures of central Asian Turks. It is well known that these Turks were employed as royal attendents.

BACKGROUND

Land

The principality of Vijayanagar from its outermost fortification consists of Anegondi in the north to the town of Hospet in the south covering in total about 650sq. kms. The core area of Vijayanagar covers around 25sq Kms. The sorroundings of the city are magnificent. The Tungabhadra flows through a rocky terrain with massive boulders piled up in fantastic formations. This landscape is a naturally inaccessible fortification. In addition, man made fortifications sorrounded the regal city in several layers. The rocky hilloks made excellent sentinel points or watch towers. The boulders provided raw material for temple construction activities. Going south from the river, the rocky landscape disappears replaced by flat cultivable land. Here is where the massive temple complexes are situated. The largest populations were located to the south of the irrigated lands, fed by clever ducts and anecut channeling water to the capital from the river. At its peak, Vijayanagara may have had upto a million residents.

Legend

There are two important legends associated with Hampi, the core area of Vijayanagar. One legend has it that a local goddess called Pampa married Virupaksha (Lord Shiva) on the Hemakuta Hill and hence came to be considered an incarnation of Parvati. From Pampa came the name Pampe or in Kannada Hampe. The other legend draws from the Hindu epic Ramayana. Lord Rama and Lakshmana came looking for Sita to the area, the location of the ancient capital of Kishkindha and met Hanuman on the Rishyamuka Hill. Then followed a covenant between Sugreeva, the monkey king in exile and Lord Rama to mutually help each other in finding Sita and getting rid of evil king Vali. The agreement is celebrated by the presence of the only temple in India with idols of Lord Rama, Lakshmana and Sugreeva. Hanuman himself is said to have been born on Anjenadri Hill, near Tungabhadra river facing Hampi. Archaeologically, Hampi traces back to neolithic settlements. There is sufficient inscriptional evidence that in more recent times the area came under the rule of the Chalukyas, Rashtrakutas, Hoysalas and finally the tiny kingdom of Kampili.

Choice of Capital

The legendary associations of the area with Lord Virupaksha (Harihara and Bukka Raya being of Shaiva faith) and Lord Rama, the personification of the perfect king was not lost to the founders of the empire. Its natural ruggedness and inaccessability must have all been reasons to choose this area as the capital of the new empire. During the rule of the empire, Vijayanagara came to known as one of the most beautiful cities in India. An copper plate inscription (Tamarashasana) of Marappa, one of the Sangama brothers dated 1346 gives the Sangama genealogy and identifies family deity (gotradhidaivam) of the Sangama family as Lord Virupaksha Many inscriptions attesting the elevation of Lord Virupaksha to Rashtra devata (God of the Kingdom) have been found. By the time of Bukka I, the capital had already grown into a great capital. An inscription calls it great Nagari named Vijaya situated in Hemakuta..

Coins and Inscriptions

The Empire minted coins with Devanagari, Kannada and Telugu legends, usually giving the name of the ruler. The empire had its mints in Hampi, Penugonda and Tirupati. Gold, silver and copper were used to make coins. Gadyana, Varaha, Pon, Pagoda, Pratapa, Pana, Kasu and Jital were the various coins issued in the Vijayanagar period. The most beautiful Vijayanagar coins were those with the images of various gods and goddesses and animals and birds. The earliest coins feature Hanuman and the Garuda (divine eagle), the mount of Lord Vishnu. The Vijayanagar rulers also issued gold coins featuring divine couples. Venkatapatiraya III, one of the last Vijayanagar rulers, minted coins showing Vishnu with Sridevi and Bhudevi. Krishnadevaraya issued many coins featuring Balakrishna. He issued these coins after he built a Krishna Temple at Hampi and installed in it an image of Krishna that he had brought from Udayagiri after conquering it from the Gajapati ruler of Orissa. On these coins, the playful Krishna is seen seated. Lord Venkateshwara, the presiding deity of the temple at Tirumala (Tirupati), also figures on Vijayanagar coins. A rare copper coin of the Vijayanagar ruler Sriranga I shows a standing figure of the emperor with a sword in his hand. Another rare copper coin issued by Sadasivaraya shows a fully caparisoned galloping horse. The elephant and the bull too appear on many Vijayanagar coins. Kannada and Telugu inscriptions have been deciphered and recorded by historians.

SUCCESSORS OF VIJAYANAGAR EMPIRE

After the decline of the empire, The Nayaka feudatories gained independence. They were the Nayakas in Karnataka and TamilNadu. They made a major impact in the later political scene. Among them the Madurai Nayaks ruled till 1734, The kingdom of Mysore lasted until Indian independence in 1947, although during the later part of their rule, from 1799 CE., they came under the British Raj. The Keladi and Chitradurga Nayakas also ruled till the end of 18th. century.

- Nayaks of Madurai
- Nayaks of Tanjore
- Keladi Nayakas of Shimoga
- Nayakas of Chitradurga
- Mysore Kingdom
- Nayakas of Gingee

13

Mughal Era

THE MUGHAL EMPIRE

India in the 16th century presented a fragmented picture of rulers, both Muslim and Hindu, who lacked concern for their subjects and who failed to create a common body of laws or institutions. Outside developments also played a role in shaping events. The circumnavigation of Africa by the Portuguese explorer Vasco da Gama in 1498 allowed Europeans to challenge Arab control of the trading routes between Europe and Asia. In Central Asia and Afghanistan, shifts in power pushed Babur of Ferghana (in present-day Uzbekistan) southward, first to Kabul and then to India. The dynasty he founded endured for more than three centuries. Claiming descent from both Genghis Khan and Timur, Babur combined strength and courage with a love of beauty,and military ability with cultivation. Babur concentrated on gaining control of northwestern India. He did so in 1526 by defeating the last Lodhi sultan at the First battle of Panipat, a town north of Delhi. Babur then turned to the tasks of persuading his Central Asian followers to stay on in India and of overcoming other contenders for power, mainly the Rajputs and the Afghans. He succeeded in both tasks but died shortly thereafter in 1530. The Mughal Empire was one of the largest centralized states in premodern history and was the precursor to the British Indian Empire.

ESTABLISHMENT AND REIGN OF BABUR

In the early 16th century, Muslim armies consisting of Mongol, Turkic, Persian, and Afghan warriors invaded India under the leadership of the Timurid prince Zahir-ud-Din-

Muhammad Babur. Babur was the great-grandson of Central Asian conqueror Timur-e Lang (Timur the Lame, from which the Western name Tamerlane is derived), who had invaded India in 1398 before retiring to Samarkand who himself claimed descent from the Mongol ruler, Genghis Khan. Babur was driven from Samarkand by the Uzbeks and initially established his rule in Kabul in 1504. Later, taking advantage of internal discontent in the Delhi sultanate under Ibrahim Lodi, and following an invitation from Daulat Khan Lodhi (governor of Punjab) and Alam Khan (uncle of the Sultan), Babur invaded India in 1526.

Babur, a seasoned military commander, entered India in 1526 with his well-trained veteran army of 12,000 to meet the sultan's huge but unwieldy and disunited force of more than 100,000 men. Babur defeated the Lodhi sultan decisively at the first Battle of Panipat. Employing gun carts, moveable artillery, superior cavalry tactics, and the highly regarded Mughal composite bow, a weapon even more powerful than the English longbow of the same period. Babur achieved a resounding victory and the Sultan was killed. A year later (1527) he decisively defeated, at the Battle of Khanwa, a Rajput confederacy led by Rana Pratap Singh of Chittor. A third major battle was fought in 1529 when, at the battle of Gogra, Babur routed the joint forces of Afghans and the sultan of Bengal. Babur died in 1530 at Agra before he could consolidate his military gains. During his short five-year reign, Babur took considerable interest in erecting buildings, though few have survived. He left behind as his chief legacy a set of descendants who would fulfill his dream of establishing an empire in the Indian subcontinent.

Babur's will to Humayun

According to the document available in the State Library of Bhopal, Babur left the following will to Humayun:

"My son take note of the following: Do not harbour religious prejudice in your heart. You should dispense justice while taking note of the people's religious sensitivities, and rites. Avoid slaughtering cows in order that you could gain a place in the heart of natives. This will take you nearer to the people.

Do not demolish or damage places of worship of any faith and dispense full justice to all to ensure peace in the country. Islam can better be preached by the sword of love and affection, rather than the sword of tyranny and persecution. Avoid the differences between the shias and sunnis. Look at the various characteristics of your people just as characteristics of various seasons."

The perennial question of who was the greatest of the six "Great Mughals" receives varying answers in present-day Pakistan and India. Some favour Babur the pioneer and others his great-grandson, Shah Jahan (r. 1628-58), builder of the Taj Mahal and other magnificent buildings. The other two towering figures of the era by general consensus were Akbar (r. 1556-1605) and Aurangzeb (r. 1658-1707). Both rulers expanded the empire greatly and were able administrators. However, Akbar was known for his religious tolerance and administrative genius, whereas Aurangzeb was a zealous ruler and fierce proselytizer of orthodox Islam across the heterodox Indian landscape.

HUMAYUN (1508-1556)

Babur's favorite son Humayun took the reins of the empire after his father succumbed to disease at the young age of forty-seven. However, he lacked his father's craftiness and athleticism. Though he could be a formidable warrior when he chose to be, he was more laid back and indolent. He also was addicted to opium and depended on it for solace much more than a king with insecure borders should indulge in. He also made the mistake of trusting his three brothers, which served as a lesson to future Mughal rulers, who would not repeat this folly. Humayun made his brother Prince Kamran the regent in Kabul, who quickly added Panjab under his control. Humayun, appearing to be weak, did not object and this emboldened his two other brothers, Askari and Hindal to seek more independence.

Humayun's first campaign was to confront a Sher Khan Sur, an Afghan, who was quietly expanding his territory in the east. Half way through the counter offensive Humayun had to abandon it and concentrate on Gujarat, where a threat from Ahmed Shah had to be squelched. In this he succeeded and annexed Gujarat and Malwa. Champaner and the great fort of Mandu followed next. Following this great triumph, Humayun made another tactical error in installing his brother Prince Askari in Ahmadabad instead of the defeated Ahmed Shah as a feudatory. To savor his victory, Humayun celebrated in Mandu fort for many months, binging on opium and spending too much time in the company of his favourites. When he finally headed home to Agra, he found his brother Askari at his doorstep making a serious bid for the throne. Though his older brother thwarted this effort, Askari was pardoned, which only exhibited royal weakness to his loyal subjects.

Humayun again fell into one of his many periods of laziness and lassitude and resorted to his pipe and playmates. All this time he also neglected to confront Sher Khan Sur, who was gathering land and feudatories in the east. As an administrator Sher Khan was far superior to Humayun. In 1539, Humayun and Sher Khan met in battle in Chausa, between Varanasi and Patna. Humayun barely escaped with his own life and in the next year, in 1540, his army of 40,000 lost to the Afghan army of 15,000 of Sher Khan. Humayun's brothers refused to help him and he found himself a fugitive in Rajastan and Sindh.

Finally, the Shah of Iran, Shah Tamasp, gave him refuge in Persia. Of course, Humayun put his famous diamond to full diplomatic use because Shah Tamasp was a lover of diamonds. Koh-I-Noor, would serve as the bribe that the Shah Tamasp needed to support Humayun with a large Persian military offensive on Sher Khan Sur in 1544. Humayun found fraternal opposition again in Kandahar, where he was stalled for eight years but eventually won back Afghanistan.

Sher Khan had now become the monarch in Delhi under the name Sher Shah Sur and ruled from 1540 to 1545. He consolidated his kingdom form Panjab to Bengal (first one to enter Bengal after Ala-ud-din Khilji did more than two centuries earlier). But Sher Shah tragically died in an accidental explosion of gunpowder during an offensive in Kalinjar. A superb administrator, he was credited to have organized the government and military in such a way that future Mughal kings used it as their own models. He also added to the fort in Delhi (supposed site of Indraprastha), first started by Humayun, and now called the Purana Qila or the old fort. He built the mosque Qila-I-Kuhna there that was a masterpiece of the period, though only parts of it have survived.

The charred remains of Sher Shah were taken to a tomb in Sahasaram, midway between Varanasi and Gaya. Although rarely visited, it is another glorious triumph in architecture that the future great Mughal builders like Akbar, Jahangir and Shah Jahan tried to emulate. Massive in scale, three stories and fifty meters high, it appears as much a palace as a mausoleum. Sher Shah's son Islam Shah held on to power until 1553 and following his death the Sur dynasty lost most of its clout due factious strife and severe famine.

In 1554, Humayun attacked the confused and divided state of Sur rulers and in 1555 claimed Delhi again. But in 1556 tragedy struck the Mughals when Humayun tripped and fell to his death while descending the steps after gazing at the stars (he was a keen astronomer) from the rooftop of Sher Shah's Delhi palace. Thus Humayun ruled in India barley for ten years and died at the age of forty-eight, leaving behind a thirteen-year-old boy, Akbar as his heir. As a tribute to his father, Akbar later built the Humayun's tomb in Delhi (completed in 1571), from red sandstone, of majestic outline that would become the precursor of future Mughal architecture. Akbar's mother and Humayun's wife Hamida Begum personally supervised the building of the tomb.

AKBAR THE GREAT (1543-1605)

Akbar succeeded his father, Humayun (r. 1530-40 and 1555-56), whose rule was interrupted by the Afghan Sur Dynasty, which rebelled against him. It was only just before his death that Humayun was able to regain the empire and leave it to his son. In restoring and expanding Mughal rule, Akbar based his authority on the ability and loyalty of his followers, irrespective of their religion. In 1564 the jizya on non-Muslims was abolished, and bans on temple building and Hindu pilgrimages were lifted.

Akbar's methods of administration reinforced his power against two possible sources of challenge—the Afghan-Turkish aristocracy and the traditional interpreters of Islamic law, the ulama. He created a ranked imperial service based on ability rather than birth, whose members were obliged to serve wherever required. They were remunerated with cash rather than land and were kept away from their inherited estates, thus centralizing the imperial power base and assuring its supremacy. The military and political functions of the imperial service were separate from those of revenue collection, which was supervised by the imperial treasury. This system of administration, known as the mansabdari, was based on loyal service and cash payments and was the backbone of the Mughal Empire; its effectiveness depended on personal loyalty to the emperor and his ability and willingness to choose, remunerate, and supervise.

Akbar declared himself the final arbiter in all disputes of law derived from the Qur'an and the sharia. He backed his religious authority primarily with his authority in the state. In 1580 he also initiated a syncretic court religion called the Din-i-Ilahi (Divine Faith). In theory, the new faith was compatible with any other, provided that the devotee was loyal to the emperor. In practice, however, its ritual and content profoundly offended orthodox Muslims. The ulama found their influence undermined. The concept of Islam as a superior religion with a historic mission in the world appeared to be compromised. The syncretism of the court and its tolerance of both Hindus and unorthodox Shia sects among Muslims triggered a reaction among Sunni Muslims. In the fratricidal war of succession that closed the reign of Akbar's grandson Shah Jahan in 1658.

JAHANGIR (1569-1627)

Prince Salim (b. 1569 of Hindu Rajput princess from Amber), who would later be known as Emperor Jahangir showed signs of restlessness at the end of a long reign by his father Akbar. During the absence of his father from Agra he pronounced himself as the king and turned rebellious. Akbar was able to wrestle the throne back but the prince was showing no signs of remorse. There was also an unconfirmed story of strained relationship between father and son due to Salim's amorous advances to an ordinary dancing girl. Deeply in love and enchanted by the dancing girl, Anarkali, who was of common birth, Salim was ready to make her his queen. This union, surprisingly, was said to have been unacceptable to Akbar and the girl was abducted and executed. Though the historians do not mention the existence of such a girl called Anarkali, the folklore certainly has survived. This also might have exacerbated the strain between the monarch and the prince.

Salim did not have to worry about his sibling's aspirations to the throne. His two brothers, Murad and Daniyal, had both died early from alcoholism. Ironically a similar fate would await Salim at the end of his reign when he also succumbed to the ill effects of excessive drinking. But his challenge came from a surprising member of his family. His son Khusrau was favoured by the nobles and made an attempt to unseat Salim, who by 1602 had proclaimed himself as the emperor and renamed himself Jahangir (World Conqueror). Khusrau laid siege to Lahore but was captured by Jahangir and blinded. The cruelty of the previous Sultans of Delhi had now pervaded into the Mughal emperors. Hitherto unknown fraternal and filial murder and torture at the time of succession was to become the norm and almost expected in the kingdom. Jahangir explained that a king should consider no man his relation and sovereignty did not regard the relation between father and son. Treacherous perfidy during succession would not shock any future Mughal heirs.

Jahangir began his era as a Mughal emperor after the death of Akbar in the year 1605. He considered his third son Prince Khurram (future Shah Jahan-born 1592 of Hindu Rajput princess Manmati), his favourite. Rana of Mewar and Prince Khurram had a standoff that resulted in a treaty acceptable to both parties. Khurram was kept busy with several campaigns in Bengal and Kashmir. Jahangir claimed the victories of Khurram-Shah Jahan as his own. However, Kandahar, which had been won by Akbar, was lost to Persia's Shah Abbas. Further defeats were handed in Northern Afghanistan. Some success was at hand in the Deccan when an African slave, Malik Ambar, brought from Baghdad, serving under the sultante of Ahmadnagar, helped Khurram-Shah Jahan.

The monarch meanwhile was basking in the glory of his son's victories. He also had unlimited sources of revenue largely due to a systematic organization of the administration by his father, Akbar. The opulence of the Mughals had reached its pinnacle during Jahangir and Shah Jahan's rule, thanks to Akbar's foresight. Jahangir built his famous gardens in Kashmir and spent much time relaxing and delegating his work to others. One such person was Jahangir's wife, Nur Jahan, whom he married in 1611. She was the thirty-year-old widow of one of his Afghan nobles. Her father, Persian born Itimad-ud-Daula became a minister and closest advisor to the emperor. Very able Nur Jahan along with her father and brother Asaf Khan, who was a successful general, ran the kingdom. Jahangir was the monarch in absentia. Addicted to alcohol, he was content to let his wife govern.

After the fiasco in Kandahar, the relationship between Khurram and Jahangir soured. Khurram suspected that Nur Jahan favoured her son-in-law Prince Shariyar (son of Jahangir from a slave), who was married to her daughter Ladli Begum, from her first marriage. Khurram was in rebellion with his father and in this the African slave Malik Ambar and Nur Jahan's brother Asaf Khan aided him. Khurram-Shah Jahan was married to Asaf Khan's daughter Mumtaz Mahal. Prince Shariyar was murdered and Nur Jahan spent her last years building a tomb for her father Itimad-ud-Daula in Agra. She could have little influence over the willful Shah Jahan or her niece Mumtaz Mahal.

Jahangir had kept a diary that can pass marginally as memoirs. He describes inane and insignificant details of his garden and daily happenings around the palace. It only serves to give a glimpse of the emperor's life in a superficial way. Though not a soldier, Jahangir was an ardent patron of Mughal art and an avid builder. He built Akbar's five-tiered tomb in Sikandra. The emperor kept busy building in Lahore, Allahabad and Agra. While the de facto emperor, Nur Jahan was attending to administrative details, Jahangir found solace in loitering in his gardens and appreciating art and nature.

The darkest incident of his rule perhaps was the disposition of a peaceful leader of newly formed religion called Sikhism. Akbar had watched the blossoming of the new religion founded by Guru Nanak, with fascination. Jahangir, in a controversy with its leader, was responsible for the death of Sikh Guru Arjan Singh (who died in Mughal prison) and this would have lasting consequences for future Mughal emperors. The peaceful religion of Sikhism would turn militant later when Jahangir's grandson Aurangzeb murdered the ninth Sikh Guru Tegh Bahadur. Jahangir, the laid back emperor died in 1627 from alcohol abuse and Prince Khurram-Shah Jahan's reign as the emperor began.

SHAH JAHAN

Prince Khurram, who would later be known as Emperor Shah Jahan, ascended to the throne after a tumultuous succession battle worthy of a Mughal Prince. His own father,Jahangir, had already handicapped Khusrau, when the son aspired to unseat the father. Younger brother Prince Khurram promptly had him killed, as fraternal ambitions were not to be encouraged, even though the wretched Prince Khusrau was blind. Prince Shariyar, Nur Jahan's son-in-law had lost his bid to the throne and murdered by Khurram's father-in-law, Asaf Khan (also Nur Jahan's brother). Another brother Parwiz was of no consequence.

With the wealth created by Akbar, the Mughal kingdom was probably the richest in the world. Prince Khurram gave himself the title of Shah Jahan, the 'King of the World' and this was the name that was immortalized by history. With his imagination and aspiration, Shah Jahan gained a reputation as an aesthete par excellence. He built the black marble pavilion at the Shalimar Gardens in Srinagar and a white marble palace in Ajmer. He also built a tomb for his father, Jahangir in Lahore and built a massive city Shahajanabad in Delhi but his imagination surpassed all Mughal glory in his most famous building Taj Mahal. It was in Shahajanabad that his daughter Roshanara built the marketplace called Chandni Chowk. His beloved wife Arjuman Banu (daughter of Asaf Khan and niece of Nur Jahan) passed away while delivering their fourteenth child in the year 1631. The distraught emperor started building a memorial for her the following year. The Taj Mahal, named for Arjuman Banu, who was called Mumtaz Mahal, became one of the Seven Wonders of the World. The beauty of the white marble structure is unsurpassed. Almost four hundred years later it still is the awe inspiring place where lovers hold hands and swoon over each other. The thrill one feels at the first sight of Taj Mahal through its main archway is beyond description.

The great Juma Masjid built by him was the largest in India at the time. Shah Jahan also built or renovated forts in Delhi and in Agra. White marble chambers that served as living quarters and other halls for public audiences are examples of classic Mughal architecture. Here in Agra fort, Shah Jahan would spend eight of his last years as a prisoner of his son, Aurangzeb shuffling between the hallways of the palace, squinting at the distant silhouette of his famous Taj Mahal on the banks of River Jamuna.

Shah Jahan's earlier years were spent in doing his father's bidding in various campaigns and territorial expansion. However, the territories gained were significant only in a symbolic way. In fact, land and prestige was lost in Kandahar and Northern Afghanistan. The dream of Babur to extend the empire into and beyond Afghanistan into the homeland of the Timurs in Samarkhand was permanently shelved by his progeny, after the humiliating defeats in Kandahar in the hands of Persian king. Never again would a Mughal venture into the northwest. In Deccan, Shah Jahan had initial failures in the hands of an African habshi (Negro) slave from Baghdad, a Malik Ambar, who was under the Bijapur sultan. Later, however, he joined Shah Jahan and helped him quell the threat from his brothers who had aspirations to conquer the throne. Golconda (Hyderabad) and Bijapur (Karnataka), two powerful states of the south were forced to become vassal states but were left alone to govern as they pleased. At least on paper Shah Jahan's empire had extended deep into the south in Deccan and beyond. The cover of Mughal suzerainty only helped the southern sultanates to extend their borders well into Chola heartland of Tamil Nadu and Mysore. Muslim rule, now effectively extended to the mouth of Kaveri River.

Though Khurram was the favoured son of Jahangir in his earlier days, the influence of Nur Jahan on the emperor had a deleterious effect on his relationship with his father. She was trying to prop up her own son-in-law, a brother of Shah Jahan as the legal heir. This alarmed Shah Jahan and with the help of his father-in-law and Malik Ambar he was able to muscle his way into Delhi and pronounce himself the emperor. In September of 1657, Shah Jahan, in his waning years, suffered from acute constipation and rumours of his imminent death spread rapidly through the land.

The potential successors to the throne, four brothers, were alarmed and moved with haste to claim the throne. His third son Aurangzeb eventually claimed the empire, in the year 1658. Shah Jahan would recover from his illness only to spend his last days as an old and decrepit man, imprisoned by his son Aurangzeb, in the fort in Agra. There he was to remain in house arrest for eight years watching the magnificent monument he had built for his beloved wife Mumtaz. Shah Jahan died in the year 1666, at age seventy-four, eight years after losing his throne to his son. He was interned in the Taj Mahal, next to his beloved wife Mumtaz Mahal.The aristocracy supported the austere military commander Aurangzeb against his learned and eclectic brother Dara Shikoh, whom Aurangzeb defeated in battle and later had decapitated in 1662.

AURANGZEB

Aurangzeb's reign ushered in the decline of the Mughal Empire. Aurangzeb, who in the latter half of his long rule assumed the title "Alamgir" or "world-seizer," was known for aggressively expanding the empire's frontiers and for his militant enforcement of orthodox Sunni Islam. He hated non-believers and destroyed many Hindu and Buddhist temples throughout India. During his reign, the Mughal empire reached its greatest extent, although it is likely that his policies also led to its dissolution. Still, there is some belief that his policies may have slowed the decline of the Empire rather than precipitated it.

Although he was an outstanding general and a rigorous administrator, Mughal fiscal and military standards declined as security and luxury increased. Land rather than cash became the usual means of remunerating high-ranking officials, and divisive tendencies in his large empire further undermined central authority.

In 1679 Aurangzeb reimposed the hated jizyah on Hindus. Coming after a series of other taxes and also discriminatory measures favouring Sunni Muslims this action by the emperor, incited rebellion among Hindus and others in many parts of the empire—Jat, Sikh, and Rajput forces in the north and Maratha forces in the Deccan. The emperor managed to crush the rebellions in the north, but at a high cost to agricultural productivity and to the legitimacy of Mughal rule. Aurangzeb was compelled to move his headquarters to Daulatabad in the Deccan to mount a costly campaign against Maratha guerrilla fighters led by Shivaji, which lasted twenty-six-years until he died in 1707 at the age of ninety. Aurangzeb, oppressed by a sense of failure, isolation, and impending doom, lamented that in life he "came alone" and would "go as a stranger."

In the century-and one-half that followed, effective control by Aurangzeb's successors weakened. Succession to imperial and even provincial power, which had often become hereditary, was subject to intrigue and force. The mansabdari system gave way to the zamindari system, in which high-ranking officials took on the appearance of hereditary landed aristocracy with powers of collecting rents. As Delhi's control waned, other contenders for power emerged and clashed, thus preparing the way for the eventual British takeover.

LATER MUGHALS

When Aurangzeb died close to the age of ninety, there were seventeen legitimate claimants to the throne that included not only his sons but also his grandsons and great grandsons. After the death of the emperor two brothers fought near Agra (in the same battle site that Aurangzeb had fought his brother Dara Shikoh. Prince Muazzam prevailed and killed his brother Prince Azam Shah and assumed the title Bahadur Shah I (or Shah Alam I). Another brother entered the fight a year later and was killed. Bahadur Shah was well in his sixties when he took control of the empire and soon died in 1712. During those five years he was busy fighting the insurgents in Rajastan and Panjab. Then in 1708 the last Sikh guru, Gobind Singh disappred by his spiritul power. Sikhs under Guru Gobind Singh had already transformed into a radical group after the execution of Guru Teg Bahadur by Aurangzeb. A year later a Banda Bahadur relentlessly stormed Muslim towns and became a thorn on the Mughal emperor's side.

Bahadur Shah's son Jahandar Shah succeeded after his death. However, during his tenure he gained a reputation as a womanizing drunk whose outrageous mistress Lal Kunwar took full advantage of the emperor's condition and enriched herself as well as her brood. Jahandar Shah was killed in 1713 and then Bahadur's grandson Farrukhsiyar acceded to the throne. With the help of two brothers called Saiyids, Farrukhsiyar restored some sanity to the Mughal rule. Later the Saiyids became intolerable to the emperor and one of them was sent away from Delhi to Deccan and the other was kept in constant watch in Delhi. In Deccan Saiyid Husain Ali Khan colluded with the Marathas and attacked Delhi and using trickery and intrigue seized Farrukhsiyar in the Red Fort. The emperor was blinded and caged and later poisoned as well as stabbed to death. However, prior to his death, Farrukhsiyar had the dubious distinction of aiding the British to have a firm foothold in India, by signing the much-coveted farman (an imperial directive) that would seal the future of British takeover of India.

A wretched youth, Shah Jahan II was made to occupy the throne after the murder of Farrukhsiyar but his rule lasted only three months. The Saiyids enthroned another pawn, Muhammad Shah as the Mughal emperor. He had an unexpected reign of close to thirty years. The Saiyids were disposed off but the emperor had little penchant for ruling. It was during his rule the notorious raids of Delhi by Nadir shah of Persia and the Afghan Ahmad Shah Abdali took place.

Marathas were now constantly attacking Delhi. Of more consequence and humiliating was the plunder of Delhi by Nadir Shah. A Timur descendent, Nadir Shah usurped the throne in Persia and seized Kandahar and Kabul. He marched through Panjab and was invited by Muhammad Shah as a guest to Delhi (only because he had neither the will nor the resources to fight him). Within forty-eight hours, using a lame excuse, Nadir Shah ordered a general massacre of Delhi citizens and looted every bit of wealth they could extort out of the royalty as well as Delhi's citizenry. Nadir Shah remained in Delhi for forty eighty days and departed with millions worth of gold, jewelry and coins. Even the emperor's throne, the bejeweled peacock throne of Shah Jahan was packed on elephants and carried away to Persia. Another prize, the Koh-I-nur diamond (Humayun's diamond now passed back into Persian hands). To add insult to injury, the Shah humiliated the emperor by re-crowning him as the Mughal emperor in an ignoble celebration. Later an Afghani, Ahmad Shah Abdali started his incursions into Delhi just for the purpose of looting the capital. In a series of attacks starting in 1748 until 1761, Abdali would not only pillage and loot Delhi, he also cleaned out Mathura, Kashmir and cities in Panjab. From the east the British defeated the Nawab of Bengal and occupied the state of Bengal. The vast Mughal Empire was coming undone at its seams. The fortunes of the British in India were intertwined with the misfortunes of the Mughals.

The raids by Nadir Shah and repeated incursions of Abdali resulted in quick disposal of the next two emperors Ahmad Shah and Alamgir II until in 1759 Shah Alam II ascended the throne. His reign would last several decades. However, he would preside over more loss of territory to the British. When the Nawab of Bengal lost to Robert Clive, Shah Alam II was forced to recognize Clive as a diwan (chancellor) and Bengal slipped to the British hands permanently. Shah Alam II ruled well until his eighties and died as sightless wretch dressed in rags when an army from Bengal led by General Gerald Lake stormed Delhi and Agra. The Marathas like Scindias, Holkars and the Nagpur Bhonsles also had to relinquish power to the British and the British would now boast that they were complete masters of the whole of India.

In 1806 Shah Alam's son Akbar Shah II acceded to the much diminished empire of the Mughals and ruled until 1837. His son Bahadur Shah Zafar II would be the last emperor of Mughals before the British deposed him in 1858 and the Mughal dynasty would officially come to a dishonourable end. During the Indian Rebellion of 1857, Bahadur Shah II was forced to take the side of the mutineers though he had no power to affect the outcome of the events. The mutineers had outwitted his

British sponsors and now the emperor neither had the troops nor the competence. He had no choice but to join the winning side. However, the success of the mutineers was soon reversed and the octogenarian (he was eighty-two years old) was relieved of his empire and deposed in 1858. The British also unleashed a flurry of revenge attacks on Delhi as well as luckless Bahadur Shah. Two of his sons and a grandson were shot while in custody. The emperor was then exiled to Rangoon in Burma where he died in obscurity in 1862.

The glory of the Mughal kingdom established in 1526 by the tiger from Kabul, Babur would end in 1858 and India's fate was in the hands another expansionist foreign force, the imperial British.

ARRIVAL OF THE EUROPEANS

Vasco da Gama led the first documented European expedition to India, sailing into Calicut on the southwest coast in 1498. In 1510 the Portuguese captured Goa, which became the seat of their activity. Under Admiral Alfonso de Albuquerque, Portugal successfully challenged Arab power in the Indian Ocean and dominated the sea routes for a century. Jesuits came to convert, to converse, and to record observations of India. The Protestant countries of the Netherlands and England, upset by the Portuguese monopoly, formed private trading companies at the turn of the seventeenth century to challenge the Portuguese.

Mughal officials permitted the new carriers of India's considerable export trade to establish trading posts (factories) in India. The Dutch East India Company concentrated mainly on the spice trade from present-day Indonesia. Britain's East India Company carried on trade with India. The French East India Company also set up factories.

An engraving titled "Sepoy Indian troops dividing the spoils after their mutiny against British rule" gives a contemporary view of events from the British perspective.

During the wars of the 18th century, the factories served not only as collection and transshipment points for trade but also increasingly as fortified centres of refuge for both foreigners and Indians. British factories gradually began to apply British law to disputes arising within their jurisdiction. The posts also began to grow in area and population. Armed company servants were effective protectors of trade. As rival contenders for power called for armed assistance and as individual European adventurers found permanent homes in India, British and French companies found themselves more and more involved in local politics in the south and in Bengal. Plots and counterplots climaxed when British East India Company forces, led by Robert Clive, decisively defeated the larger but divided forces of Nawab Siraj-ud-Dawlah at Plassey (Pilasi) in Bengal in 1757.

THE NIZAMS OF HYDERABAD

Maratha raids into Berar, Kandesh, Gujarat and Malwa resumed after the death of Aurangzeb, and loosened Mughal control in the Deccan. In 1724 Asaf Jah, the Mughal Nizam ul Mulk, or viceroy, of the Deccan, defeated several contenders for control of the Mughal southern provinces, and established himself of ruler of an independent state with its capital at Hyderabad. He and his successors ruled as hereditary Nizams, and their state, known as Hyderabad after the capital, outlasted the Mughal empire, persisting until it was incorporated into newly-independent India in 1948.The state of Hyderabad was formed by Nizam-ul-Mulk Asaf Jahi in 1724.He was a strong ruler & established an orderly system of administration.He also attempted to reform the revenue system.The dynasty founded by him came to be known as the Asaf Jahi dynasty.His successors were known as Nizams.

ECONOMIC COMPETITION

Economic competition among the European nations led to the founding of commercial companies in England (the East India Company, founded in 1600) and in the Netherlands (Verenigde Oost-Indische Compagnie—the United East India Company, founded in 1602), whose primary aim was to capture the spice trade by breaking the Portuguese monopoly in Asia. Although the Dutch, with a large supply of capital and support from their government, preempted and ultimately excluded the British from the heartland of spices in the East Indies (modern-day Indonesia), both companies managed to establish trading "factories" (actually warehouses) along the Indian coast. The Dutch, for example, used various ports on the Coromandel Coast in South India, especially Pulicat (about twenty kilometers north of Madras), as major sources for slaves for their plantations in the East Indies and for cotton cloth as early as 1609. (The English, however, established their first factory at what today is known as Madras only in 1639.) Indian rulers enthusiastically accommodated the newcomers in hopes of pitting them against the Portuguese. In 1619 Jahangir granted them permission to trade in his territories at Surat (in Gujarat) on the west coast and Hughli (in West Bengal) in the east. These and other locations on the peninsula became centers of international trade in spices, cotton, sugar, raw silk, saltpeter, calico, and indigo.

The Great Mughal Emperors

Emperor	Name	Reign start	Reign end
Babur	Zahiruddin Mohammed	1526	1530
Humayun	Nasiruddin Mohammed	1530	1540
Interregnum *		**1540**	**1555**
Humayun	Nasiruddin Mohammed	1555	1556
Akbar	Jalaluddin Mohammed	1556	1605
Jahangir	Nuruddin Mohammed	1605	1627
Shah Jahan	Shahabuddin Mohammed	1627	1658
Aurangzeb	Moinuddin Mohammed	1658	1707

* Afghan Rule (Sher Shah Suri and his descendants)

Successors-"The Lesser Mughals"

- Bahadur Shah I (Shah Alam I), b. October 14, 1643 at Burhanpur, ruler from 1707-1712, d. February 1712 in Lahore.
- Jahandar Shah, b. 1664, ruler from 1712-1713, d. February 11, 1713 in Delhi.
- Furrukhsiyar (b.1683, r.1713-1719, d.1719 at Delhi).
- Rafi Ul-Darjat, ruler 1719, d. 1719 in Delhi.

- Rafi Ud-Daulat (Shah Jahan II), ruler 1719, d. 1719 in Delhi.
- Nikusiyar, ruler 1719, d. 1719 in Delhi.
- Mohammed Ibrahim, ruler 1720, d. 1720 in Delhi.
- Mohammed Shah, b. 1702, ruler from 1719-1720, 1720-1748, d. April 26, 1748 in Delhi.
- Ahmad Shah Bahadur, b. 1725, ruler from 1748-1754, d. January 1775 in Delhi.
- Alamgir II, b. 1699, ruler from 1754-1759, d. 1759.
- Shah Jahan III, ruler 1760
- Shah Alam II, b. 1728, ruler from 1759-1806, d. 1806.
- Akbar Shah II, b. 1760, ruler from 1806-1837, d. 1837.
- Bahadur Shah II aka Bahadur Shah Zafar, b. 1775 in Delhi, ruler from 1837-1857, d. 1862 in exile in Rangoon, Burma.

14

Colonial India

In 1498, the Portuguese set foot in India, landing near the city of Calicut in the present-day state of Kerala in South India. The pursuit of trade and competition between European powers saw the entry of the British and French, among others, into India. The fractured kingdoms of India were eventually taken over by the Europeans, who indirectly assumed control by subjugating rulers. In 1757, Mir Qasim, a minister to the Nawab of Bengal secretly connived with the British, asking logistic support to overthrow the Nawab in return for trade grants.

The British forces, whose sole duty until then was guarding their East India Company property, were far superior to the Bengali armed forces. At the battle of Plassey on 23 June 1757 fought between the British under the command of Robert Clive and the Nawab, Mir Qasim's forces betrayed the Nawab and defeated him. Qasim was installed on the throne as a British subservient ruler. The battle transformed British perspective as they realized their strength and potential to conquer petty Indian kingdoms, and marked the beginning of the imperial or colonial era.

By the early 19 century, the British had assumed direct or indirect control over all of present-day India. In 1857, a local rebellion by an army of sepoys snowballed into the Rebellion of 1857. This resistance, although short-lived, was triggered by widespread resentment against certain discriminatory policies of the British. As a result of this, the British East India Company was abolished and India formally became a crown colony. The slow but momentous reform movement, perhaps influenced in India by contact with European ideas and institutions, developed gradually into the Indian Non-Native Expulsion Movement. During the years of the First World War, the hitherto bourgeoise "home-rule" movement was transformed into a popular mass movement by Mohandas Karamchand Gandhi-a pacifist. Also aided by revolutionaries such as Saheed Bhagat Singh, Chandrashekar Azad, Subhash Chandra Bose who were feared by the British in the later stages. This independence movement attained its objective with the Independence of India on August 15, 1947.

EUROPEAN COLONIES IN INDIA

European colonies in India were set up by several European nations beginning at the end of the 15th century. In 1498, the Portuguese set foot in Goa. Rivalry between reigning European powers saw the entry of the Dutch, British and French among others. The fractured debilitated kingdoms of India were gradually taken over by the Europeans and indirectly controlled by puppet rulers. By the 19th century, the British had assumed direct and indirect control over most of India.

PORTUGUESE INDIA

Portuguese India (Portuguese: Índia Portuguesa or Estado da Índia) was the aggregate of Portugal's colonial holdings in India. At the time of India's independence in 1947, Portuguese India included a number of enclaves on India's western coast, including Goa proper, as well as the coastal enclaves of Daman (Port: Damão) and Diu, and the enclaves of Dadra and Nagar Haveli, which lie inland from Daman. The territories of Portuguese India were sometimes referred to collectively as Goa.

Early History

The first Portuguese encounter with India was on May 20, 1498 when Vasco da Gama landed in Calicut (present-day Kozhikode). Over the objections of Arab merchants, da Gama secured an ambiguous letter of concession for trading rights from Zamorin, Calicut's local ruler, but had to sail off without warning after the Zamorin insisted on his leaving behind all his goods as collateral. Gama kept his goods, but left behind a few Portuguese with orders to start a trading post.

In 1510, Portuguese admiral Afonso de Albuquerque defeated the Bijapur sultans on behalf of a local sovereign, Timayya, leading to the establishment of a permanent settlement in Velha Goa (or Old Goa). The Southern Province, also known simply as Goa, was the headquarters of Portuguese India, and seat of the Portuguese viceroy who governed the Portuguese possessions in Asia.

The Portuguese acquired several territories from the Sultans of Gujarat: Daman (occupied 1531, formally ceded 1539); Salsette, Bombay, and Baçaim (occupied 1534); and Diu (ceded 1535). These possessions became the Northern Province of Portuguese India, which extended almost 100 km along the coast from Daman to Chaul, and in places 30-50 km inland. The province was ruled from the fortress-town of Baçaim. Bombay (present day Mumbai) was given to Britain in 1661 as part of the Portuguese Princess Catherine of Braganza's dowry to Charles II of England. Most of the Northern Province was lost to the Marathas in 1739, and Portugal acquired Dadra and Nagar Haveli in 1779.

After India's Independence

After India's independence from the British in 1947, Portugal refused to accede to India's request to relinquish control of its Indian possessions. The decision given by the International Court of Justice at The Hague, with respect to the invasion of Dadra and Nagar Haveli by a group of armed civilians and un-uniformed members of the Maratha police, in the 1950's, was an impase: the Portuguese had rights to move across the Indian airspace to the inland territories of Dadra and Nagar Haveli, and India had rights to prevent the Portuguese from doing so. This decision, however, did not give India the rights to demand that the territories of Estado da Índia Portuguesa be given to the Indian Republic.

From 1954, peaceful Satyagrahis attempts at forcing the Portugese to leave Goa failed. In December 1961, India militarly invaded Goa, Daman, and Diu. Portugese offered insignificant resistance and surrendered quickly. This was the first and only post-independence military conflict India faced with a European nation and had prevailed..

The Salazar regime in Portugal refused to recognise Indian sovereignty over Goa, Daman and Diu, which continued to be represented in Portugal's National Assembly until 1974. Following the Carnation Revolution that year, the new government in Lisbon restored diplomatic relations with India, and recognised Indian sovereignty over Portuguese India. However, the people of its former Indian territories continued to have the right to Portuguese citizenship. In the year 2006, this has been restricted to those who were born during Portuguese rule.

BRITISH REIGN

The British Empire at its zenith in 1919. India and other countries of the subcontinent under British dominion are highlighted in purple.

The British Raj refers to the British rule of the Indian subcontinent, or present-day India, Bangladesh, Pakistan, and Myanmar, during which period these lands were under the colonial control of Britain as part of the British Empire. Since the independence of these countries their pre-independent existence has been loosely termed British India, although prior to Independence that term referred only to those portions of the subcontinent under direct rule by the British administration in Delhi and previously Calcutta. Much of the territory under British sway during this time was not directly ruled by the British, but were nominally independent Princely States which were directly under the rule of the Maharajas, Rajas, Thakurs and Nawabs who entered into treaties as sovereigns with the British monarch as their feudal superior. Aden was part of "British India" from 1839, as was Burma from 1886; both became separate crown colonies of the British Empire in 1937. It lasted from 1858, when the rule of the British East India Company was transferred to the Crown, until 1947, when pre-independence India was partitioned into two sovereign states, India and Pakistan. Although Sri Lanka (then Ceylon) is peripheral to the Indian subcontinent, it is not counted part of the Raj, as it was ruled as a Crown Colony from London rather than by the Viceroy of India as a part of the Indian Empire. French India and Portuguese India consisted of small coastal enclaves governed by France and Portugal, respectively; they were integrated into India after Indian independence.

History

On December 31, 1600, Queen Elizabeth I of England granted a royal charter to the British East India Company to carry out trade with the East. Company ships first arrived in India in 1608, docking at Surat in modern-day Gujarat. Four years later, British traders defeated the Portuguese at the Battle of Swally, gaining the favour of the Mughal emperor Jahangir in the process. In 1615, King James I sent Sir Thomas Roe as his ambassador to Jahangir's court, and a commercial treaty was concluded in which the Mughals allowed the Company to build trading posts in India in return for goods from Europe. The Company traded in such commodities as cotton, silk, saltpetre, indigo, and tea.

By the mid-1600s, the Company had established trading posts or "factories" in major Indian cities, such as Bombay, Calcutta, and Madras in addition to their first factory at Surat (built in 1612). In 1670, King Charles II granted the company the right to acquire territory, raise an army, mint its own money, and exercise legal jurisdiction in areas under its control.

By the last decade of the 17th century, the Company was arguably its own "nation" on the Indian subcontinent, possessing considerable military might and ruling three presidencies.

The British first established a territorial foothold in the Indian subcontinent when Company-funded soldiers commanded by Robert Clive defeated the Bengali Nawab Siraj Ud Daulah at the Battle of Plassey in 1757. Bengal's riches were expropriated, the East India Company monopolised Bengali trade and Bengal became a British protectorate directly under its rule. Bengali farmers and craftsmen were obliged to render their labour for minimal remuneration while their collective tax burden increased greatly. As a consequence, the famine of 1769 to 1773 cost the lives of 10 million Bengalis. A similar catastrophe occurred almost a century later, after Britain had extended its rule across the Indian subcontinent, when 40 million Indians perished from famine amidst the collapse of India's indigenous industries.

Building the Raj: British Expansion Across India

The Regulating Act of 1773 that was passed by the British Parliament asserted Whitehall's ultimate control of the company. It also established the post of Governor-General of India, the first occupant of which was Warren Hastings. Further acts, such as the Charter Acts of 1813 and 1833, further defined the relationship of the Company and the British government.

At the turn of the 19th century, Governor-General Lord Wellesley began expanding the Company's domain on a large scale, defeating Tippoo Sultan (also spelled Tipu Sultan), annexing Mysore in southern India, and removing all French influence from the subcontinent. In the mid-19th century, Governor-General Lord Dalhousie launched perhaps the Company's most ambitious expansion, defeating the Sikhs in the Anglo-Sikh Wars (and annexing Punjab with the exception of the Phulkian States) and subduing Burma in the Second Burmese War. He also justified the takeover of small princely states such as Satara, Sambalpur, Jhansi, and Nagpur by way of the doctrine of lapse, which permitted the Company to annex any princely state whose ruler had died without a male heir. The annexation of Oudh in 1856 proved to be the Company's final territorial acquisition, as the following year saw the boiling over of Indian grievances toward the so-called "Company Raj".

INDIAN REBELLION OF 1857

An engraving titled Sepoy Indian troops dividing the spoils after their mutiny against British rule gives a contemporary view of events from a strictly British perspective.

The Indian Rebellion of 1857, also known as the First War of Indian Independence, the Sepoy Rebellion and the Indian Mutiny, was a prolonged period of armed uprisings in Northern and Central India against British occupation of that part of the subcontinent. Small precursors of brewing discontent involving incidences of arson in cantonment areas began to manifest themselves in January. Later, a large-scale rebellion broke out in May and turned into what may be called a full-fledged war in the affected regions. This war brought about the end of the British East India Company's rule in India, and led to direct rule by the British government (British Raj) of much of the

Indian subcontinent for the next 90 years, although some states retained nominal independence under their respective Rajas, or kings.

BRITISH EXPANSION IN INDIA

The British East India Company won the power of Diwani in Bengal after winning the Battle of Plassey in 1757, under Robert Clive. Their victory in the Battle of Buxar in 1764 won them the Nizamat of Bengal as well. Following the Permanent Settlement of Bengal shortly thereafter, the Company began to vigorously expand its area of control in India.

In 1845 the Company managed to extend its control over Sindh province after a gruelling and bloody campaign (of Napier's 'Peccavi' fame). In 1848 the Second Anglo-Sikh War took place and the Company gained control of the Punjab as well in 1849, after the British India Army won a hard-fought victory against the Khalsa Army, who were betrayed by the Kashmiri Dogra Ministers Lal Singh and Gulab Singh (who were not Sikhs). To show their appreciation the British made Gulab Singh the Maharaja of Kashmir which was part of Punjab. In 1853 the leader of the Marathas, Nana Sahib was denied his titles and his pension was stopped. In 1854 Berar was annexed into the Company's domains. In 1856 the state of Awadh/Oudh was also annexed by the Company.

Causes

The rebellion had diverse political, economic, military, religious and social causes.

The sepoys (from sipahi, Hindi for soldier, used for native Indian soldiers) of the Bengal Army had their own list of grievances against the Company Raj, mainly caused by the ethnic gulf between the British officers and their Indian troops. It was also rumoured that the British had started to issue new bullets that had cow and pig fat on them, which insulted both Hindus and Muslims. Other than Indian units of the British East India Company's army, much of the resistance came from the old aristocracy, who were seeing their power steadily eroded under the British.

Frictions

Some Indians came to believe that the British intended to convert them either by force or by deception (e.g. causing them to lose caste) to Christianity. This view which was perhaps not entirely unfounded, as the British religious fashion of the time was Evangelism, and many Honourable East India Company officers took it upon themselves to try to convert their Sepoys. This was strongly discouraged by the Company, which was aware of the potential for religion to become a flashpoint.

Under the Doctrine of lapse policy of Lord Dalhousie many kingdoms like Jhansi,Awadh or Oudh,Satara,Nagpur and Sambalpur were annexed turning the heirs of these kingdoms into 'pensioners' overnight. Nobility, feudal landholders, and royal armies found themselves unemployed and humiliated. These people were ready to avenge the injustice at the hands of the British. In addition the Bengal army of the East India Company drew many recruits from Awadh. They could not remain disaffected by the discontent back home. The jewels of the royal family of Nagpur were publicly auctioned in Calcutta, a move that was seen as a sign of abject disrespect by the remnants of the Indian aristocracy.

Indians were unhappy with the heavy-handed rule of the Company which had embarked on a project of rather rapid expansion and westernisation. This included the outlawing of many religious customs, both Muslim and Hindu, which were viewed as uncivilized by the British. This included a ban on sati(widow burning)though it should be noted that the Sikhs had long ago abolished sati and the Bengali reformer Ram Mohan Roy was campaigning against it. These laws caused outrage in some quarters, particularly amongst the population of Bengal The British abolished child marriage, and claimed to have ended female infanticide, but this claim is doubtful without accompanying demographic data. The suppression of Thuggee was a less controversial reform, although the true nature of Thuggee (whether it was truly a widespread religious cult, or simply dacoity) is still disputed.

The justice system was considered inherently unfair to the Indians. In 1853, the British Prime Minister Lord Aberdeen opened the Indian Civil Service to native Indians; however, this was viewed by some of educated India as an insufficient reform. The official Blue Books-entitled "East India (Torture) 1855-1857"-that were laid before the House of Commons during the sessions of 1856 and 1857, revealed that Company officers were allowed an extended series of appeals if convicted or accused of brutality or crimes against Indians. The Company also practised financial extortion through heavy taxation. Failure to pay these taxes almost invariably resulted in appropriation of property.

The British policy of expansionism (the Doctrine of Lapse) was also greatly resented by the rulers who were displaced, and outraged many if not most of their subjects, particularly in Oudh. In eight years Lord Dalhousie, the then Governor-General of India, had annexed a quarter of a million square miles (650,000 km^2) of land to the Company's territory.

Many of the Company's modernising efforts were viewed with automatic distrust; for example, it was feared that the railway, the first of which began running out of Bombay in the 1850s, was a demon.

However, some historians have suggested that the impact of these reforms has been greatly exaggerated, as the British did not have the resources to enforce them, meaning that away from Calcutta their effect was negligible. This was not the view taken by the British themselves after 1857: instead they scaled down their programme of reform, increased the racial distance between Europeans and native Indians, and also sought to appease the gentry and princely families, especially Muslim, who had been major instigators of the 1857 revolt. After 1857, Zamindari (regional feudal officials) became more oppressive, the Caste System became more pronounced, and the communal divide between Hindus and Muslims became marked and visible, which some historians argue was due in great part to British efforts to keep Indian society divided. This tactic has become known as Divide and rule.

Economics

The British East India Company was a massive export company that was the force behind much of the colonization of India. The power of the Company took nearly 150 years to build. As early as 1693, the annual expenditure in political "gifts" to men in power reached nearly 90,000 pounds. In bribing the Government, the Company was allowed to operate in overseas markets despite the fact that the cheap imports of South Asian silk, cotton, and other products hurt domestic business. By 1767, the Company was forced into an agreement to pay 400,000 pounds into the National Exchequer annually.

By 1848, however, the Company's financial difficulties had reached a point where expanding revenue required expanding British territories in South Asia massively. The Company began to set aside adoption rights of native princes and began the process of annexation of more than a dozen independent Rajas between 1848 and 1854. In an article published in The New York Daily Tribune on July 28, 1857, Karl Marx notes that "... in 1854 the Raj of Berar, which comprise 80,000 square miles of land, a population from four to five million, and enormous treasures, was forcibly seized".

In order to consolidate and control these new holdings, a well-established army of 200,000 Indians officered by 40,000 British soldiers dominated India by 1857. The last vestiges of independent Indian states had disappeared and the Company exported untold quantities of gold, jewels, silver, silk, cotton, and a host of other precious materials back to England every year. This extraordinary quantity of wealth, much of it collected as 'taxes', was absolutely critical in expanding public and private infrastructure in Britain and in financing British expansionism elsewhere in Asia and Africa. In no uncertain terms, this very wealth funded, in large part, the Industrial Revolution.

The land was reorganised under the comparatively harsh Zamindari system to facilitate the collection of taxes. In certain areas farmers were forced to switch from subsistence farming to commercial crops such as indigo, jute, coffee and tea. This resulted in hardship to the farmers and increases in food prices.

Local industry, specifically the famous weavers of Bengal and elsewhere, also suffered under British rule. Tariffs were kept low, according to traditional British free-market sentiments, and thus the Indian market was flooded with cheap clothing from Britain. Indigenous industry simply could not compete, and where once India had produced much of England's luxury cloth, the country was now reduced to growing cotton which was shipped to Britain to be manufactured into clothing, which was subsequently shipped back to India to be purchased by Indians.

The Indians felt that the British were levying very heavy taxation on the locals. This included an increase in the taxation on land.

Political Interference

If a landowner did not leave a male heir through natural process i.e. own child, not the adopted one, the land became the property of the British East India Company via the doctrine of lapse carried out by Dalhousie and his successor, Lord Canning. Dalhousie used this doctrine to possess a number of Indian kingdoms, most notably those of Pune, Nagpur and Jhansi, causing the disenfranchised yet still popular rulers of these kingdoms to join sides with the rebellious Indian troops. This was applied to feudal lands as well as to the states.

Sepoys

Sepoys were native Indian soldiers serving in the Bengal army of the British East India Company under British officers trained in the East India Company College, the company's own military school in England. The presidencies of Bombay, Madras and Bengal maintained their own army each with its own commander-in-chief. They fielded more troops than the official army of the British Empire. In 1857 there were 257,000 sepoys.

Unlike the Bombay and Madras Armies, which were far more heterogeneous, the Bengal Army recruited almost exclusively amongst the landowning Bhumihar Brahmins and Rajputs of the Ganges Valley. Partly owing to this, Bengal Sepoys were not subject to the penalty of flogging as were the British soldiers. Caste privileges and customs within the Bengal Army were not merely tolerated but encouraged in the early years of the Company's Rule. This meant that when they came to be threatened by modernising regimes in Calcutta from the 1840s onwards, the sepoys had become accustomed to very high ritual status, and were extremely sensitive to suggestions that their caste might be polluted. In 1851-2 sepoys were required to serve overseas during a war in Burma. Hindu tradition states that those who 'travel the black waters' (Kala Pani) will lose their caste and be outside the Hindu community. The Sepoys were thus very displeased with their deployment to Burma.

The sepoys gradually became dissatisfied with various aspects of army life. Their pay was relatively low and after the British troops conquered Awadh and the Punjab, the soldiers no longer received extra pay (batta) for service there, because they were no longer considered "foreign missions". Finally, officers of an evangelical persuasion in the Company's Army (such as Herbert Edwardes and Colonel S.G. Wheler) had taken to preaching to their Sepoys in the hope of converting them to Christianity. The controversy over the new Enfield Rifle, in the eyes of many Sepoys, added substance to the alarming rumours circulating about their imminent forced conversion to Christianity.

The Enfield Rifle

The mutiny was, literally, triggered by a gun. Sepoys throughout India were issued with a new rifle, the Pattern of 1853 Enfield Percussion cap rifled musket-a more powerful and accurate weapon than the old smoothbore Brown Bess they had been using for the last several decades. Brown Bess was the standard issue long gun throughout the British army for over a century before finally being phased out in 1838, so that the sepoys were being moved from an obsolete, inaccurate weapon to a modern rifle.

The innovations were that the firing mechanism switched from the old, unreliable Flintlock to Percussion caps, and rifling inside the musket barrel ensured accuracy at much greater distances than was possible with old smoothbore muskets. One thing did not change in this new musket-the loading process, which did not change significantly till the introduction of metallic cartridges a few decades later.

To load the new Enfield, just like the previous muskets they were issued with, soldiers had to bite the cartridge open and pour the gunpowder it contained into the rifle's muzzle, then stuff the cartridge case, which was typically paper coated with some kind of grease to make it waterproof, into the musket as wadding, before loading it with a ball.

A rumour spread that the cartridges that were standard issue with this rifle were greased with lard (pork fat) or tallow (beef fat)-this was offensive to Hindu and Muslim soldiers alike, who were forbidden by their religions to eat beef or pork respectively.

The sepoys' British officers dismissed these claims as rumours, and suggested that the Sepoys make a batch of fresh cartridges, and grease these with beeswax or mutton fat. This, not too surprisingly, reinforced the rumour that the original issue cartridges were indeed greased with lard and tallow. Another suggestion they put forward was to introduce a new drill, in which the cartridge was not bitten with the teeth but torn open with the hand.

The sepoys rejected this concept of a new drill, pointing out that they might very well forget and bite the cartridge, not surprising given the extensive drilling that 19th century soldiers received in loading and firing their muskets. This intensive drilling allowed British troops to fire up to 4 rounds a minute, although most units were able to achieve 3 rounds a minute with consistency. However, an integral part of the loading procedure involved biting off the bullet from the cartridge so that one hand can hold the musket steady whilst the other hand pours the charge of powder into the barrel. Of course, this meant that biting a musket cartridge was second nature, and instinctive, to the Sepoys, some of whom had decades of service in the Company's army, and who had been doing Musket drill for every day of their service.

The Commander in Chief in India, General George Anson reacted to this crisis by saying, "I'll never give in to their beastly prejudices", and despite the pleas of his junior officers he did not compromise.

Prophecies, Omens and Signs

Another rumour that spread was an old prophecy that the Company's rule would end after a hundred years. Their rule in India had begun with the Battle of Plassey in 1757.

Chapaties and Lotus Flowers began to circulate around large parts of India, quoting the famous line "Sab laal hoga." (Everything will turn Red.), passed around by people from town to town and village to village, as a symbol of the prophecy and a sign of the coming revolt.

Start of the War

On 9 May, 85 troopers of the 3rd Light Cavalry at Meerut refused to use their cartridges. They were imprisoned, sentenced to ten years of hard labour, and stripped of their uniforms in public. It has been said that the town prostitutes made fun of the manhood of the sepoys during the night and this is what goaded them. This claim is however not substantiated by historical accounts. Malleson records that the troops were constantly berated by their imprisoned comrades while processing on a long and humiliating march to the jail. It was this insult by their own comrades which provoked the mutiny. The sepoys knew it was very likely that they would also be asked to use the new cartridges and they too would have to refuse in order to save their caste, religion and social status. Since their comrades had acted only in deference to their religious beliefs the punishment meted out by the British colonial rulers was perceived as unjust by many.

When the 11th and 20th native cavalry of the Bengal Army assembled in Meerut on 10 May, they broke rank and turned on their commanding officers. They then liberated the 3rd Regiment and attacked the European cantonment where they are reported to have killed all the Europeans they could find, including women and children, and burned their houses. There are however some contemporary British accounts that suggest that some sepoys escorted their officers to safety and then rejoined their mutinous comrades. In Malleson's words: "It is due to some of them [sepoys] to state that they did not quit Meerut before they had seen to a place of safety those officers whom they most respected. This remark applies specially to the men of the 11th N.I., who had gone most reluctantly into the movement. Before they left, two sipáhís of that regiment had escorted two ladies with their children to the carabineer barracks. They had then rejoined their comrades". Some officers and their families escaped to Rampur, where they found refuge with the Nawab. Despite this, at the time wild rumours circulated about the complete massacre of all Europeans and native Christians at Meerut, the first of many such stories which would lead British forces to extremely violent reprisals against innocent civilians and mutinous sepoys alike during the later suppression of the Revolt.

The rebellious forces were then engaged by the remaining British forces in Meerut. Meerut had the largest percentage of British troops of any station in India: 2,038 European troops with twelve field guns versus 2,357 sepoys lacking artillery. Some commentators believe that the British forces could have stopped the sepoys from marching on Delhi, but the British commanders of the Meerut garrison were extraordinarily slow in reacting to the crisis. They did not even send immediate word to other British cantonments that a rebellion was in process. It seems likely that they believed they would be able to contain the Indians by themselves. This misjudgment would cost them dearly.

Support and Opposition

The rebellion now spread beyond the armed forces, but it did not result in a complete popular uprising as its leaders hoped. The Indian side was not completely unified. While Bahadur Shah Zafar was restored to the imperial throne there was a faction that wanted the Maratha rulers to be enthroned as well, and the Awadhis wanted to retain the powers that their Nawab used to have. The war was mainly centred in northern and central areas of India. Delhi, Lucknow, Cawnpore, Jhansi, Bareilly, Arrah and Jagdishpur were the main centres of conflict. The Bhojpurias of Arrah and Jagdishpur supported the Marathas. The Marathas, Rohillas and the Awadhis supported Bahadur Shah Zafar and were against the British.

There were calls for jihad by some leaders including the millenarian Ahmedullah Shah, taken up by the Muslims, particularly Muslim artisans, which caused the British to think that the Muslims were the main force behind this event. In Awadh, Sunni Muslims did not want to see a return to Shiite rule, so they often refused to join what they perceived to be a Shia rebellion.

In Thana Bhawan, the Sunnis declared Haji Imdadullah their Ameer. In May 1857 the famous Battle of Shamli took place between the forces of Haji Imdadullah and the British.

Many Indians supported the British, partly due to their dislike at the idea of return of Mughal rule and partly because of the lack of a notion of Indianness. The Sikhs and Pathans of the Punjab and North-West Frontier Province supported the British and helped in the capture of Delhi. The Sikhs wanted to avenge the annexation of Punjab 8 years ago by the British with the help of Purbhais (Bengali's and Marathi's-Easterner) who helped the British. The Gurkhas of Nepal continued to support the British as well, although Nepal remained an independent country throughout the rebellion. Most of southern India remained passive with only sporadic and haphazard outbreaks of violence. Most of the states did not take part in the war as many parts of the region were ruled by the Nizams or the Mysore royalty and were thus not directly under British rule.

Initial Stages

Bahadur Shah Zafar proclaimed himself the Emperor of the whole of India. Most contemporary and modern accounts however suggest that he was coerced by the sepoys and his courtiers-against his own will-to sign the proclamation. The civilians, nobility and other dignitaries took the oath of allegiance to the Emperor. The Emperor issued coins in his name, one of the oldest ways of asserting Imperial status, and his name was added to the Khutbah, the acceptance by Muslims that he is their King.

Initially, the Indian soldiers were able to significantly push back Company forces. The sepoys captured several important towns in Haryana, Bihar, Central Provinces and the United Provinces. The British forces at Meerut and Ambala held out resolutely and withstood the sepoy attacks for several months.

The British proved to be formidable foes, largely due to their superior weapons, training, and strategy. The sepoys who mutinied were especially handicapped by their lack of a centralized command and control system.

Rao Tularam of Haryana went to collect arms from Russia which had just been in a war with the British in the Crimea, but he died on the way. When a tribal leader from Peshawar sent a letter offering help, the king replied that he should not come to Delhi because the treasury was empty and the army had become uncontrollable.

Delhi

The British were slow to strike back at first but eventually two columns left Meerut and Simla. They proceeded slowly towards Delhi and fought, killed, and hanged numerous Indians along the way. At the same time, the British moved regiments from the Crimean War, and diverted European regiments headed for China to India.

After a march lasting two months, the British fought the main army of the rebels near Delhi in Badl-ke-Serai and drove them back to Delhi. The British established a base on the Delhi ridge to the north of the city and the siege began. The siege of Delhi lasted roughly from the 1st of July to the 31st of August. However, the encirclement was hardly complete-the rebels could easily receive resources and reinforcements. Later the British were joined by the Punjab Movable Column of Sikh and Pathan soldiers under John Nicholson and elements of the Gurkha Brigade.

Eagerly-awaited heavy siege guns did not guarantee an easy victory against the numerical superiority of the sepoys. Eventually the British broke through the Kashmiri gate and began a week of street fighting. When the British reached the Red Fort, Bahadur Shah had already fled to Humayun's tomb. The British had retaken the city.

The troops of the besieging force proceeded to loot and pillage the city. A large number of the citizens were slaughtered in retaliation for the Europeans and Indian 'collaborators' that had been killed by the rebel sepoys. Artillery was set up in the main mosque in the city and the neighbourhoods within the range of artillery were bombarded. These included the homes of the Muslim nobility from all over India, and contained innumerable cultural, artistic, literary and monetary riches. An example would be the loss of most of the works of Mirza

Asadullah Khan Ghalib, thought of as the greatest Indian poet of that era.

The British soon arrested Bahadur Shah, and the next day British officer William Hodson shot his sons Mirza Mughal, Mirza Khizr Sultan, and Mirza Abu Bakr under his own authority at the Khooni Darwaza (the bloody gate) near Delhi Gate. Their heads were reportedly presented to their father the next day.

RETALIATION-"THE DEVIL'S WIND"

From the end of 1857, the British had begun to gain ground again. Lucknow was retaken in March 1858. On 8 July 1858, a peace treaty was signed and the war ended. The last rebels were defeated in Gwalior on 20 June 1858. By 1859, rebel leaders Bakht Khan and Nana Sahib had either been slain or had fled. The British adopted the old Mughal punishment for mutiny and sentenced rebels were lashed to the mouth of cannons and blown to pieces. It was a crude and brutal war, with both sides resorting to what would now be described as war crimes. In the end, however, in terms of sheer numbers, the casualties were significantly higher on the Indian side. A letter published after the fall of Delhi in the "Bombay Telegraph" and subsequently reproduced in the British press testified to the scale of the retaliation:

".... All the city people found within the walls (of the city of Delhi) when our troops entered were bayoneted on the spot, and the number was considerable, as you may suppose, when I tell you that in some houses forty and fifty people were hiding. These were not mutineers but residents of the city, who trusted to our well-known mild rule for pardon. I am glad to say they were disappointed".

Another brief letter from General Montgomery to Captain Hodson, the conqueror of Delhi exposes how the British military high command approved of the cold blooded massacre of Delhites: "All honour to you for catching the king and slaying his sons. I hope you will bag many more!"

Another comment to the conduct of the British soldiers after the fall of Delhi is of Captain Hodson himself in his book,

"Twelve years in India": "With all my love for the army, I must confess, the conduct of professed Christians, on this occasion, was one of the most humiliating facts connected with the siege."

As a result, the end of the war was followed by the execution of a vast majority of combatants from the Indian side as well as large numbers of civilians perceived to be sympathetic to the rebel cause. The British press and British government did not advocate clemency of any kind, though Governor General Canning tried to be sympathetic to native sensibilities, earning the scornful sobriquet "Clemency Canning". Soldiers took very few prisoners and often executed them later. Whole villages were wiped out for apparent pro-rebel sympathies. The Indians called this retaliation "the Devil's Wind."

REORGANISATION

Bahadur Shah Zafar exiled in Rangoon. Photograph by Robert Tytler and Charles Shepherd, May 1858. The rebellion also saw the end of the British East India Company's rule in India. In August, by the Queen's Proclamation of 1858, power was transferred to the British Crown. A secretary of state was entrusted with the authority of Indian affairs and the Crown's viceroy in India was to be the chief executive. The British embarked on a program of reform, trying to integrate Indian higher castes and rulers into the government and abolishing the East India Company.

Militarily, the rebellion transformed both the 'native' and European armies of British India. The British also increased the number of British soldiers in relation to native ones. Regiments which had remained loyal to the British were retained, and Gurkha units, which had been crucial in the Delhi campaign, were increased. The inefficiencies of the old organisation, which had estranged sepoys from their British officers, were addressed, and the post-1857 units were mainly organised on the 'irregular' system. Sepoy artillery was abolished also, leaving all artillery in British hands. The post-rebellion changes formed the basis of the military organisation of British India until the early twentieth century.

The East India Company's European forces in the three presidency armies (of Bengal, Madras and Bombay) were transferred to the Queen's army. This move precipitated the 'white mutiny' of 1859. European troops, who had enlisted for the Company's army and hoped to secure a bounty for re-engagement with the British army or simply to go home, reacted strongly to the change. European troops in Bengal mounted the largest collective protest the British army has ever seen, forcing the Government of India to offer men their discharge, which over 10,000 accepted. The protest left European military force in India in the hands of the Queen's army.

The viceroy stopped land grabs, decreed religious tolerance and admitted Indians into civil service, albeit mainly as subordinates. Bahadur Shah was tried for treason by a military commission assembled at Delhi, and exiled to Rangoon where he died in 1862, finally bringing the Mughal dynasty to an end. In 1877 Queen Victoria took the title of Empress of India on the advice of her Prime Minister, Benjamin Disraeli.

POST-REBELLION DEVELOPMENTS

The rebellion was a major turning point in the history of modern India. In May 1858, the British exiled Emperor Bahadur Shah Zafar II (r. 1837-57) to Rangoon, Burma (now Yangon, Myanmar), after executing most of his family, thus formally liquidating the Mughal Empire.

Bahadur Shah Zafar, known as the Poet King, contributed some of Urdu's most beautiful poetry, with the underlying theme of the freedom struggle. The Emperor was not allowed to return and died in solitary confinement in 1862. The Emperor's three sons, also involved in the War of Independence, were arrested and shot in Delhi by Major Hodson William Stephen Raikes Hodson of the British Indian Army.

Cultural and religious centres were closed down, properties and estates were confiscated. At the same time, the British abolished the British East India Company and replaced it with direct rule under the British Crown.

In proclaiming the new direct-rule policy to "the Princes, Chiefs, and Peoples of India", Queen Victoria (who was given the title Empress of India in 1877) promised equal treatment under British law, but Indian mistrust of British rule had become a legacy of the 1857 rebellion. Many existing economic and revenue policies remained virtually unchanged in the post-1857 period, but several administrative modifications were introduced, beginning with the creation in London of a cabinet post, the Secretary of State for India. The governor-general (called viceroy when acting as representative to the nominally sovereign "princely states" or "native states"), headquartered in Calcutta, ran the administration in India, assisted by executive and legislative councils. Beneath the governor-general were the governors of Provinces of India, who held power over the division and district officials, who formed the lower rungs of the Indian Civil Service. For decades the Indian Civil Service was the exclusive preserve of the British-born, as were the superior ranks in such other professions as law and medicine. The British administrators were imbued with a sense of duty in ruling India and were rewarded with good salaries, high status, and opportunities for promotion. Not until the 1910s did the British reluctantly permit a few Indians into their cadre as the number of English-educated Indians rose steadily.

The Viceroy of India announced in 1858 that the government would honour former treaties with princely states and renounced the "Doctrine of Lapse", whereby the East India Company had annexed territories of rulers who died without male heirs. About 40 percent of Indian territory and 20-25 percent of the population remained under the control of 562 princes notable for their religious (Islamic, Hindu, Sikh and other) and ethnic diversity. Their propensity for pomp and ceremony became proverbial, while their domains, varying in size and wealth, lagged behind socio-political transformations that took place elsewhere in British-controlled India.

A more thorough re-organisation was effected in the constitution of army and government finances. Shocked by the extent of solidarity among Indian soldiers during the rebellion, the government separated the army into the three presidencies.

The Indian Councils Act of 1861 restored legislative powers to the presidencies, which had been given exclusively to the governor-general by the Charter Act of 1833. British attitudes toward Indians shifted from relative openness to insularity and xenophobia, even against those with comparable background and achievement as well as loyalty. British families and their servants lived in cantonments at a distance from Indian settlements. Private clubs where the British gathered for social interaction became symbols of exclusivity and snobbery that refused to disappear decades after the British had left India. In 1883 the government of India attempted to remove race barriers in criminal jurisdictions by introducing a bill empowering Indian judges to adjudicate offences committed by Europeans. Public protests and editorials in the British press, however, forced the viceroy George Robinson, First Marquess of Ripon, (who served from 1880 to 1884), to capitulate and modify the bill drastically. The Bengali "Hindu intelligentsia" learned a valuable political lesson from this "white mutiny": the effectiveness of well-orchestrated agitation through demonstrations in the streets and publicity in the media when seeking redress for real and imagined grievances.

Post-1857 India also experienced a period of unprecedented calamity when the region was swept by a series of frequent and devastating famines, among the most catastrophic on record. Approximately 25 major famines spread through states such as Tamil Nadu in South India, Bihar in the north, and Bengal in the east in the latter half of the 19th century, killing between 30-40 million Indians. The famines were a product both of uneven rainfall and British economic and administrative policies, which since 1857 had led to the seizure and conversion of local farmland to foreign-owned plantations, restrictions on internal trade, heavy taxation of Indian citizens to support unsuccessful British expeditions in Afghanistan, inflationary measures that increased the price of food, and substantial exports of staple crops from India to the United Kingdom (Dutt, 1900 and 1902; Srivastava, 1968; Sen, 1982; Bhatia, 1985). Some British citizens such as William Digby agitated for policy reforms and better famine relief, but Lord Lytton, son of the poet Edward Bulwer-Lytton and the governing British viceroy in India, opposed such changes in the belief that they would stimulate shirking by Indian workers. Most famine relief projects involved putting famine victims to work on public employment schemes-even though the work was too demanding for malnourished people. Less doctrinaire approaches to famine relief were adopted during the famine of 1907-1908; this ensure that this famine did not become a catastrophe. Native industries in India were also decimated in the aftermath of the 1857 rebellion, particularly during the three decades from 1870 to 1900 (with the notable exception of the jute industry, which benefited from the global industrial revolution). The famines continued until independence in 1947, with the Bengal Famine of 1943-44-among the most devastating-killing 3-4 million Indians during World War II.

BEGINNINGS OF SELF-GOVERNMENT

The first steps were taken toward self-government in British India in the late 19th century with the appointment of Indian counsellors to advise the British viceroy and the establishment of provincial councils with Indian members; the British subsequently widened participation in legislative councils with the Indian Councils Act of 1892.

The Government of India Act of 1909-also known as the Morley-Minto Reforms (John Morley was the secretary of state for India, and Gilbert Elliot, fourth earl of Minto, was viceroy)-gave Indians limited roles in the central and provincial legislatures, known as legislative councils. Indians had previously been appointed to legislative councils, but after the reforms some were elected to them. At the centre, the majority of council members continued to be government-appointed officials, and the viceroy was in no way responsible to the legislature. At the provincial level, the elected members, together with unofficial appointees, outnumbered the appointed officials, but responsibility of the governor to the legislature was not contemplated. Morley made it clear in introducing the legislation to the British Parliament that parliamentary self-government was not the goal of the British government.

The Morley-Minto Reforms were a milestone. Step by step, the elective principle was introduced for membership in Indian legislative councils. The "electorate" was limited, however, to a small group of upper-class Indians. These elected members increasingly became an "opposition" to the "official government". Communal electorates were later extended to other communities and made a political factor of the Indian tendency toward group identification through religion. The practice created certain vital questions for all concerned. The intentions of the British were questioned. How humanitarian was their concern for the minorities? Were separate electorates a manifestation of "divide and rule"?

For Muslims it was important both to gain a place in all-India politics and to retain their Muslim identity, objectives that required varying responses according to circumstances, as the example of Muhammed Ali Jinnah illustrates. Jinnah, who was born in 1876, studied law in England and began his career as an enthusiastic liberal in Congress on returning to India. In 1913 he joined the Muslim League, which had been shocked by the 1911 annulment of the partition of Bengal into cooperating with Congress to make demands on the British. Jinnah continued his membership in Congress until 1919. During this dual membership period, he was described by a leading Congress spokesperson, Mrs. Sarojini Naidu, as the "ambassador of Hindu-Muslim unity".

AFTER FIRST WORLD WAR

India's important contributions to the efforts of the British Empire in World War I stimulated further demands by Indians and further response from the British. The Congress Party and the Muslim League met in joint session in December 1916. Under the leadership of Jinnah and Pandit Motilal Nehru (father of Jawaharlal Nehru), unity was preached and a proposal for constitutional reform was made that included the concept of separate electorates. The resulting Congress-Muslim League Pact (often referred to as the Lucknow Pact) was a sincere effort to compromise. Congress accepted the separate electorates demanded by the Muslim League, and the Muslim League joined with Congress in demanding self-government. The pact was expected to lead to permanent and constitutional united action.

In August 1917 the British government formally announced a policy of "increasing association of Indians in every branch of the administration and the gradual development of self-governing institutions with a view to the progressive realization of responsible government in India as an integral part of the British Empire." Constitutional reforms were embodied in the

Government of India Act 1919, also known as the Montagu-Chelmsford Reforms (Edwin Samuel Montagu was the United Kingdom's Secretary of State for India; the Viscount Chelmsford was viceroy). These reforms represented the maximum concessions the British were prepared to make at that time. The franchise was extended, and increased authority was given to central and provincial legislative councils, but the viceroy remained responsible only to London.

The changes at the provincial level were significant, as the provincial legislative councils contained a considerable majority of elected members. In a system called "dyarchy", based on an approach developed by Lionel Curtis, the nation-building departments of government-agriculture, education, public works, and the like-were placed under ministers who were individually responsible to the legislature. The departments that made up the "steel frame" of British rule-finance, revenue, and home affairs-were retained by executive councillors who were often (but not always) British, and who were responsible to the governor.

The 1919 reforms did not satisfy political demands in India. The British repressed opposition and restrictions on the press and on movement were re-enacted. An apparently unwitting example of violation of rules against the gathering of people led to the massacre at Jalianwala Bagh in Amritsar in April 1919. This tragedy galvanized such political leaders as Jawaharlal Nehru (1889-1964) and Mohandas Karamchand "Mahatma" Gandhi (1869-1948) and the masses who followed them to press for further action.

The Allies' post-World War I peace settlement with Turkey provided an additional stimulus to the grievances of the Muslims, who feared that one goal of the Allies was to end the caliphate of the Ottoman sultan. After the end of the Mughal Empire, the Ottoman caliph had become the symbol of Islamic authority and unity to Indian Sunni Muslims. A pan-Islamic movement, known as the Khilafat Movement, spread in India. It was a mass repudiation of Muslim loyalty to British rule and thus legitimated Muslim participation in the Indian nationalist movement. The leaders of the Khilafat Movement used Islamic symbols to unite the diverse but assertive Muslim community on an all-India basis and bargain with both Congress leaders and the British for recognition of minority rights and political concessions.

Muslim leaders from the Deoband and Aligarh movements joined Gandhi in mobilising the masses for the 1920 and 1921 demonstrations of civil disobedience and non-cooperation in response to the massacre at Amritsar. At the same time, Gandhi endorsed the Khilafat Movement, thereby placing many Hindus behind what had been solely a Muslim demand.

Despite impressive achievements, however, the Khilafat Movement failed. Turkey rejected the caliphate and became a secular state. Furthermore, the religious, mass-based aspects of the movement alienated such Western-oriented constitutional politicians as Jinnah, who resigned from Congress. Other Muslims also were uncomfortable with Gandhi's leadership. The British historian Sir Percival Spear wrote that "a mass appeal in his Gandhi's hands could not be other than a Hindu one. He could transcend caste but not community. The Hindu devices he used went sour in the mouths of Muslims". In the final analysis, the movement failed to lay a lasting foundation of Indian unity and served only to aggravate Hindu-Muslim differences among masses that were being politicised. Indeed, as India moved closer to the self-government implied in the Montagu-Chelmsford Reforms, rivalry over what might be called the spoils of independence sharpened the differences between the communities.

FURTHER REFORM

The political picture in India was not at all clear when the mandated decennial review of the Government of India Act of 1919 became due in 1929. Prospects of further constitutional reforms spurred greater agitation and a frenzy of demands from different groups. The Simon Commission headed by Sir John Simon, who recommended further constitutional change, but it was not until 1935 that a new Government of India Act was passed. The Indian Round Table Conferences 1931-1933 were held in London, at which a wide variety of interests from India were represented. The major disagreement concerned the continuation of separate electorates, which Gandhi and

Congress strongly opposed. As a result, the decision was forced on the British government. Prime Minister Ramsay MacDonald issued his "communal award," which continued the system of separate electorates at both the central and the provincial level.

The principal result of the act was provincial autonomy. The dyarchical system was discontinued, and all subjects were placed under ministers who were individually and collectively responsible to the former legislative councils, which were renamed legislative assemblies (In a few provinces, including Bengal, a bicameral system was established; the upper house continued to be called a legislative council). Almost all assembly members were elected, with the exception of some special and otherwise unrepresented groups. After the elections, provincial chief ministers and cabinets took office, although the governors had limited emergency powers. Sindh was separated from Bombay and became a province. The 1919 reforms had earlier been introduced in the North-West Frontier Province. Balochistan, however, retained special status; it had no legislature and was governed by an "agent general to the governor general." At the centre, the act essentially provided for the establishment of dyarchy, but it also provided for a federal system that included the princes. The princes refused to join a system that might force them to accept decisions made by elected politicians. Thus, the full provisions of the 1935 act did not come into force at the centre.

WORLD WAR II AND THE END OF BRITISH REIGN

By 1942, Indians were divided over World War II, as the British had unilaterally and without consultation entered India into the war. Some wanted to support the British during the Battle of Britain, hoping for eventual independence through this support. Others were enraged by the British disregard for Indian intelligence and civil rights, and were unsympathetic to the travails of the British people, which they saw as rightful revenge for the enslavement of Indians. The British Indian army came to be the largest all-volunteer army in the history of the world. However, even during the war, in July, 1942, the Indian National Congress had passed a resolution demanding complete independence from Britain. The draft proposed that if the British did not accede to the demands, massive civil disobedience would be launched. In August 1942 the Quit India Resolution was passed at the Bombay session of the All-India Congress Committee (AICC) marking the start of what was the Quit India Movement. The movement was to see massive, and initially peaceful demonstrations and denial of authority, undermining the British War effort. Large-scale protests and demonstrations were held all over the country. Workers remained absent en masse and strikes were called. The movement also saw widespread acts of sabotage, Indian underground organization carried out bomb attacks on allied supply convoys, government buildings were set on fire, electricity lines were disconnected and transport and communication lines were severed. The movement soon became a leaderless act of defiance, with a number of acts that deviated from Gandhi's principle of non-violence. In large parts of the country, the local underground organizations took over the movement. However, by 1943, Quit India had petered out.

However, at the time the war was at its bloodiest in Europe and Asia, the Indian revolutionary leader Netaji Subhas Chandra Bose escaped from house arrest in Calcutta and ultimately made his way to Germany, and then to Japanese south asia to seek Axis help to raise an army to fight the shackles of the Raj. Bose formed what came to be known as the Azad Hind Government as the Provisional Free Indian Government in exile, and organized the Indian National Army with Indian POWs and Indian expatriates south-east asia with the help of the Japanese. Its aim was to reach India as a fighting force that would inspire public resentment and revolts within the Indian soldiers to defeat the Raj. The INA fought hard in the forests of Assam, Bengal and Burma, laying siege to Imphal and Kohima with the Japanese 15th Army. It would ultimately fail, owing to disrupted logistics, poor arms and supplies from the Japanese, and lack of support and training. However, Bose's audacious actions and radical initiative energized a new generation of Indians. Many historians have argued that it was the INA and the mutinies it inspired among the British Indian Armed forces that was the true driving force for India's independence. The stories of the Azad Hind movement and its army that came to public attention during the trials of soldiers of the INA in 1945, were seen as so inflammatory that, fearing mass revolts and uprisings-not just in India, but across its empire-the British Government forbade the BBC to broadcast their story. Newspapers reported at the time a summary execution of INA soldiers held at Red Fort. During and after the trial, mutinies broke out in the British Indian Armed forces, most notably in the Royal Indian Navy which found public support throughout India, from Karachi to Bombay and from Vizag to Calcutta...

These revolts, faced by the weakened post-war Raj, coupled with the fact that the faith in the British Indian Armed forces had been lost, ultimately shaped the decision to end the Raj. By early 1946, all political prisoners had been released. British openly adopted a political dialogue with the Indian National Congress for the eventual independence of India. On August 15, 1947, the transfer of Power took place. At midnight on August 14, 1947 Pakistan (including modern Bangladesh) was granted independence. India was granted independence the following day.

Most people would give these dates as the end of the British Raj. However, some people argue that it continued until 1950 in India when it adopted a republican constitution.

Bibliography

Ahmad, Imtiaz: *State and Foreign Policy: India's Role in South Asia*, New Delhi, Vikas, 1993.

Ali, Tariq: *An Indian Dynasty: The Story of the Nehru-Gandhi Family*, New York, Putnam, 1985.

Asher, Catherine Ella Blanshard: *The New Cambridge History of India, I.4: Architecture in Mughal India*, Cambridge, Cambridge University Press, 1992.

Ashton, S.R.: *British Policy Towards the Indian States, 1905-1939*, London, Curzon, 1982.

Baker, Christopher J.: *The Politics of South India, 1920-1937*, Cambridge, Cambridge University Press, 1976.

Barker, A.J.: *Bastard War: The Mesopotamian Campaign of 1914-1918*, New York, Dial, 1967.

Basham, A.L.: *A Cultural History of India*, Oxford, Clarendon Press, 1975.

Beach, Milo Cleveland: *Mughal and Rajput Painting*, Cambridge, Cambridge University Press, 1992.

Bhattacharjee, Arun: *Rajiv Gandhi: Life and Message*, New Delhi, Ashish, 1992.

Bose, Sugata: *Peasant Labour and Colonial Capital: Rural Bengal since 1770*, Cambridge, Cambridge University Press, 1993.

Brown, Judith M.: *Modern India: The Origins of an Asian Democracy*, New Delhi, Oxford University Press, 1985.

Cunningham, Joseph Davey: *History of the Sikhs, From the Origins of the Nation to the Battles of the Sutlej*, Delhi, Sultan Chand, 1955.

Das, Kamal Kishore: *Economic History of Mughal India: An Annotated Bibliography, 1526-1875*, Calcutta, Santiniketan, 1991.

Dhanagare, D.N.: *Peasant Movements in India, 1920-1950*, New Delhi, Oxford University Press, 1983.

Dikshit, D.P.: *Political History of the Chalukyas of Badami*, New Delhi, Abhinav, 1980.

Ellinwood, DeWitt C., and S.P. Pradhan: *India and World War I*, New Delhi, Manohar, 1978.

Embree, Ainslie T.: *1857 in India: Mutiny or War of Independence*, Lexington, Massachusetts, 1963.

Erickson, Erik H.: *Gandhi's Truth: On the Origins of Militant Nonviolence*, New York, Norton, 1970.

Fischer, Louis: *The Life of Mahatma Gandhi*, New York, Harper, 1950.

Fisher, Michael: *A Clash of Cultures: Awadh, the British, and the Mughals*, New Delhi, Manohar, 1987.

Ganguly, D.K.: *Ancient India: History and Archaeology*, New Delhi, Abhinav, 1994.

Gascoigne, Bamber: *The Great Mughals*, London, Cape, 1971.

Goalen, Paul: *India: From Mughal Empire to British Raj*, Cambridge, Cambridge University Press, 1993.

Goradia, Nayana: *Lord Curzon: The Last of the British Mughals*, New Delhi, Oxford University Press, 1993.

Habib, Irfan: *An Atlas of the Mughal Empire*, Delhi, Oxford University Press, 1982.

Hamilton, J.R.: *Alexander the Great*, Oxford, Clarendon Press, 1965.

Haynes, Douglas E.: *Rhetoric and Ritual in Colonial India: The Shaping of a Public Culture in Surat City, 1852-1928*, Berkeley, University of California Press, 1991.

Humbers, Philippe: *The Rajiv Gandhi Years: Sunshine and Shadows*, New Delhi, Vimot, 1992.

Hutchins, Francis: *Spontaneous Revolution: The Quit India Movement*, New Delhi, Manohar, 1971.

Jeffrey, Robin: *People, Princes, and Paramount Power: Society and Politics in Indian Princely States*, New Delhi, Oxford University Press, 1978.

Kapur, Rajiv: *Sikh Separatism: The Politics of Faith*, New Delhi, Vikas, 1987.

Keay, John: *The Honourable Company: A History of the English East India Company*, London, Harper Collins, 1991.

Kopf, David: *The Brahmo Samaj and the Shaping of the Modern Indian Mind*, Princeton, Princeton University Press, 1979.

Krishna Murari: *The Calukyas of Kalyani, from circa 973 A.D. to 1200 A.D.*, Delhi, Concept, 1977.

Kulke, Hermann: *The State in India, 1000-1700*, Delhi, Oxford University Press, 1995.

Mahalingam, T.V.: *Administration and Social Life under Vijayanagar*, Madras, University of Madras, 1969-75.

Marshall, P.J.: *Problems of Empire: Britain and India, 1757-1813*, New York, Barnes and Noble, 1968.

McLane, John R.: *Indian Nationalism and the Early Congress*, Princeton, Princeton University Press, 1977.

Mehra, Parshotam: *A Dictionary of Modern Indian History, 1707-1947*, New Delhi, Oxford University Press, 1985.

Metcalf, Thomas R.: *The Aftermath of the Revolt: India, 1857-1870*, Princeton, Princeton University, 1964.

Minakshi, C.: *Administration and Social Life under the Pallavas*, Madras, University of Madras, 1977.

Misra, Satya Swarup: *The Aryan Problem: A Linguistic Approach*, New Delhi, Munshiram Manoharlal, 1992.

Moon, Penderel: *The British Conquest and Dominion of India*, London, Duckworth, 1989.

Mukhia, Harbans: *Perspectives on Medieval History*, New Delhi, Vikas, 1993.

Patnaik, Naveen: *A Second Paradise: Indian Courtly Life, 1590-1947*, Garden City, New Jersey: Doubleday, 1985.

Pearson, M.N.: *Before Colonialism: Theories of Asian-European Relations, 1500-1750*, New Delhi, Oxford University Press, 1988.

Possehl, Gregory L.: *The Harappan Civilization*, London, Aris and Phillips, 1982.

Rangarajan, L.N.: *Kautilya: The Arthasastra*, New York, Penguin, 1992.

Robb, Peter G.: *The Evolution of British Policy Towards Indian Politics, 1880-1920*, Westwood, Riverdale, 1992.

Sangwan, Satpal: *Science, Technology, and Colonisation: An Indian Experience, 1757-1857*, New Delhi, Anmika Prakashan, 1991.

SarDesai, D.R., and Anand Mohan: *The Legacy of Nehru: A Centennial Assessment*, New Delhi, Promilla, 1992.

Sarkar, Jadhunath: *Fall of the Mughal Empire*, Bombay, Orient Longman, 1964.

Sarkar, Sumit: *Modern India, 1885-1947*, Delhi, MacMillan, 1983.

Sewell, Robert: *A Forgotten Empire: Vijayanagar*, London, Sonnenschein, 1900.

Sharma, Kususm: *Ambedkar and Indian Constitution*, New Delhi, Ashish, 1992.

Sharma, Ram Sharman: *Land Revenue in Ancient India: Historical Studies*, Delhi, Motilal Banarsidass, 1971.

Singh, Birendra Kumar: *Early Chalukyas of Vatapi, circa A.D. 500 to 757*, Delhi, Eastern Book Linkers, 1991.

Singh, Gopal: *A History of the Sikh People, 1469-1978*, New Delhi, World Sikh University Press, 1979.

Sitaramayya, B. Pattabhi: *History of the Indian National Congress*, Bombay, Padma, 1947.

Smith, Bardwell L.: *Essays on Gupta Culture*, Delhi, Motilal Banarsidass, 1983.

Venkataramanayya, N.: *The Eastern Calukyas of Vengi*, Madras, Vedam Venkataray Sastry, 1950.

Washbrook, David A.: *The Emergence of Provincial Politics: The Madras Presidency, 1870-1920*, Cambridge, Cambridge University Press, 1976.

Wheeler, Robert Eric Mortimer: *Civilization of the Indus Valley and Beyond*, New York, McGraw-Hill, 1966.

Wolpert, Stanley: *Jinnah of Pakistan*, New York, Oxford University Press, 1984.

Zimmer, Heinrich: *The Art of Indian Asia*, New York, Pantheon, 1955.

Index

S

T

U

V

W

Y

Z

□□□